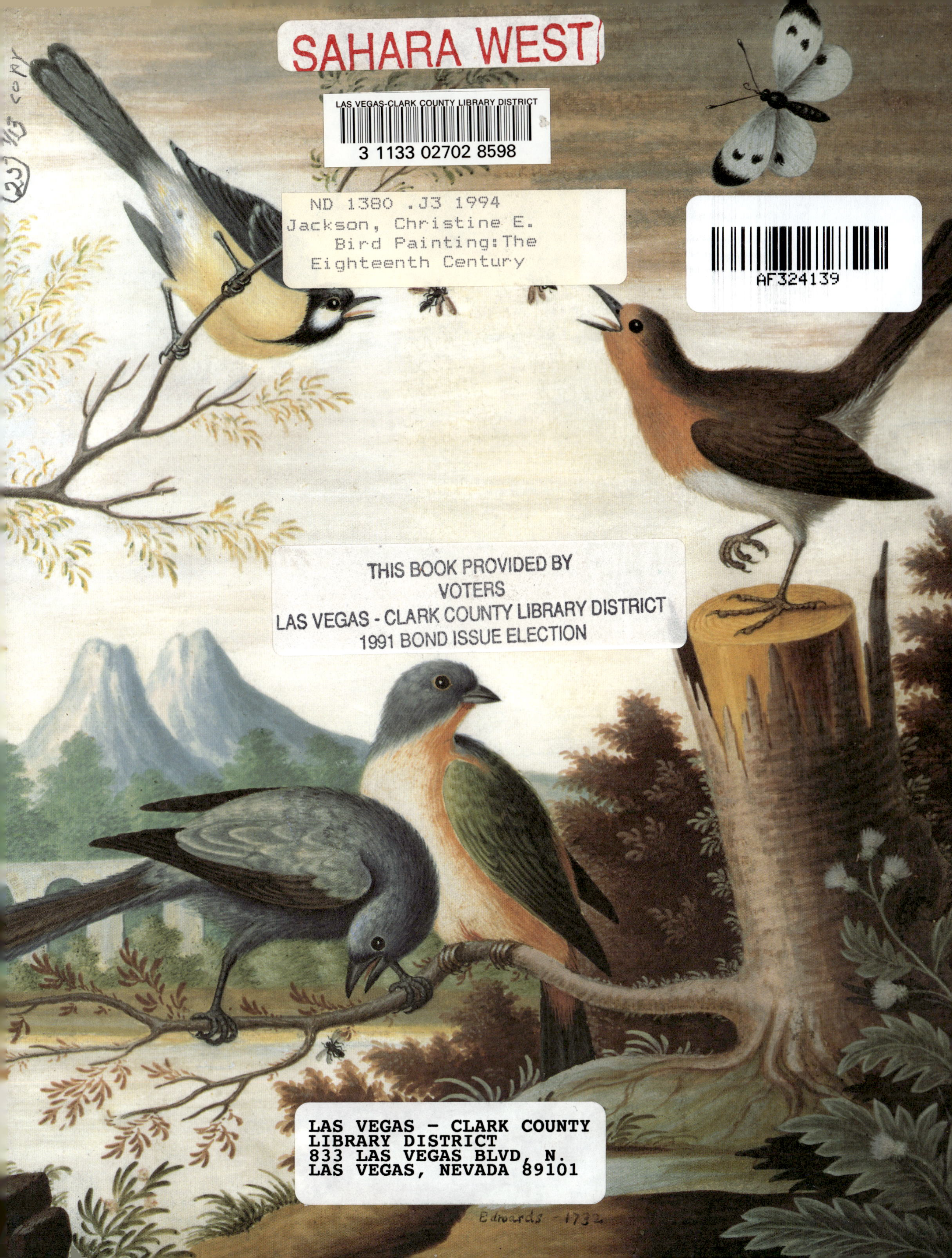

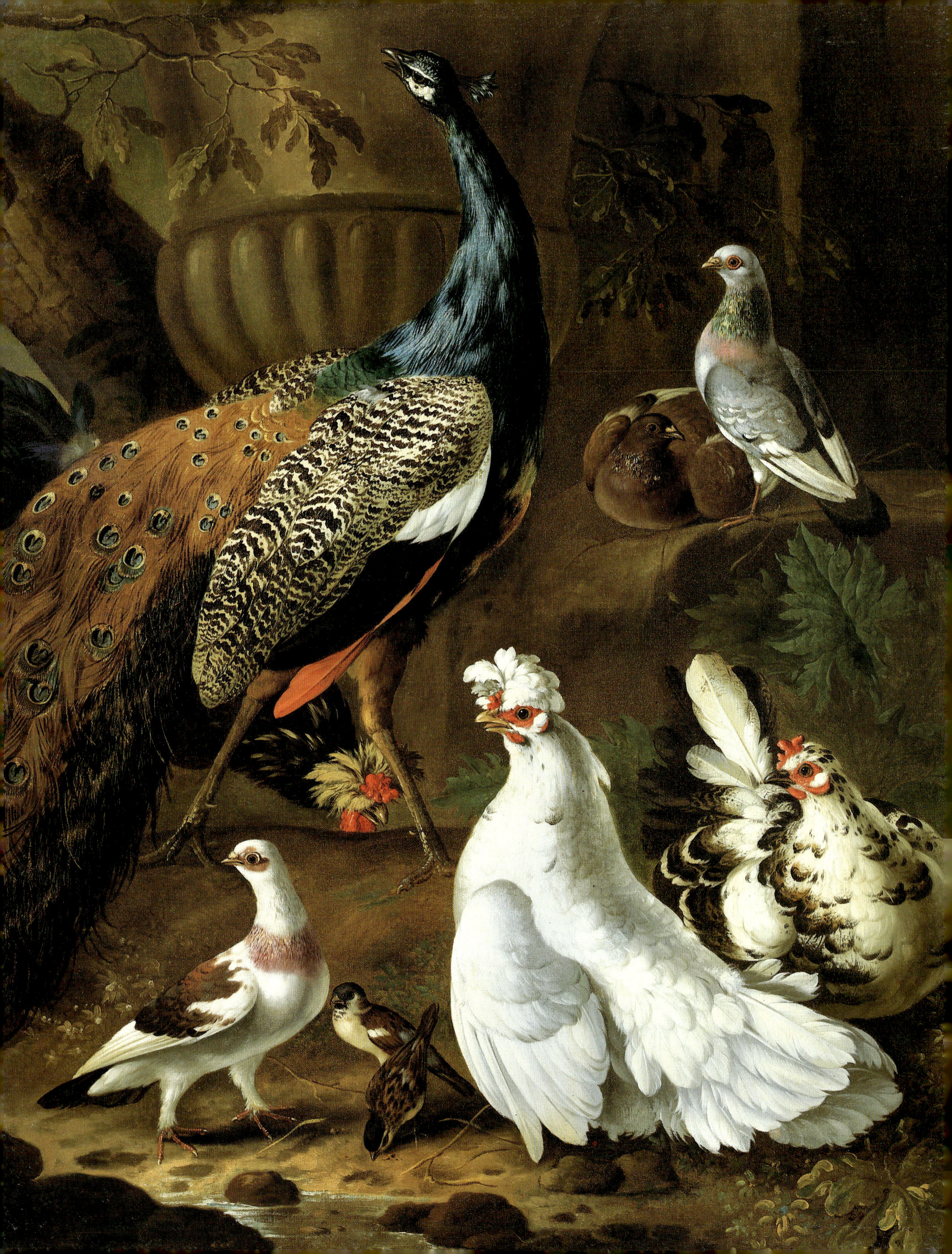

BIRD PAINTING

The Eighteenth Century

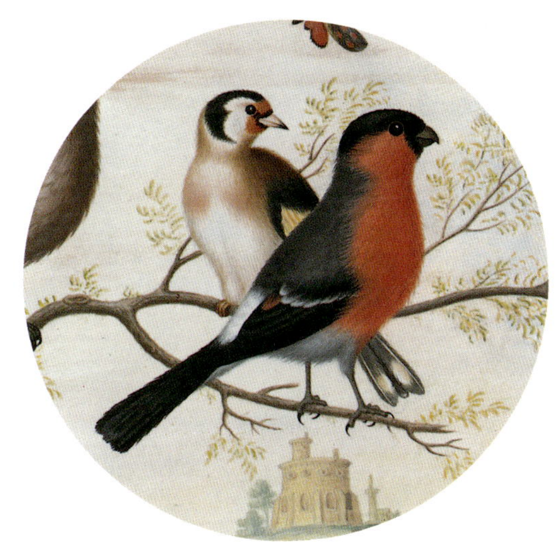

CHRISTINE E. JACKSON

Antique Collectors' Club

ISBN 1 85149 199 6

British Library Cataloguing-in-Publication Data
A catalogue record for this book is available from the British Library

Other books by Christine E. Jackson
British Names of Birds, 1968
Bird Illustrators: some artists in early lithography, 1975
Collecting Bird Stamps, 1977
Wood Engravings of Birds, 1978
Bird etchings: the illustrators and their books 1655-1855, 1985
Prideaux John Selby: a gentleman naturalist, 1992
Great Bird Paintings of the World: Volume I: The Old Masters, 1993

Frontispiece: Ornamental Fowl in a Garden *by Pieter Casteels (see page 56)*

Printed in England
by the Antique Collectors' Club Ltd., Woodbridge, Suffolk
on Consort Royal Satin paper
supplied by the Donside Paper Company, Aberdeen, Scotland

CONTENTS

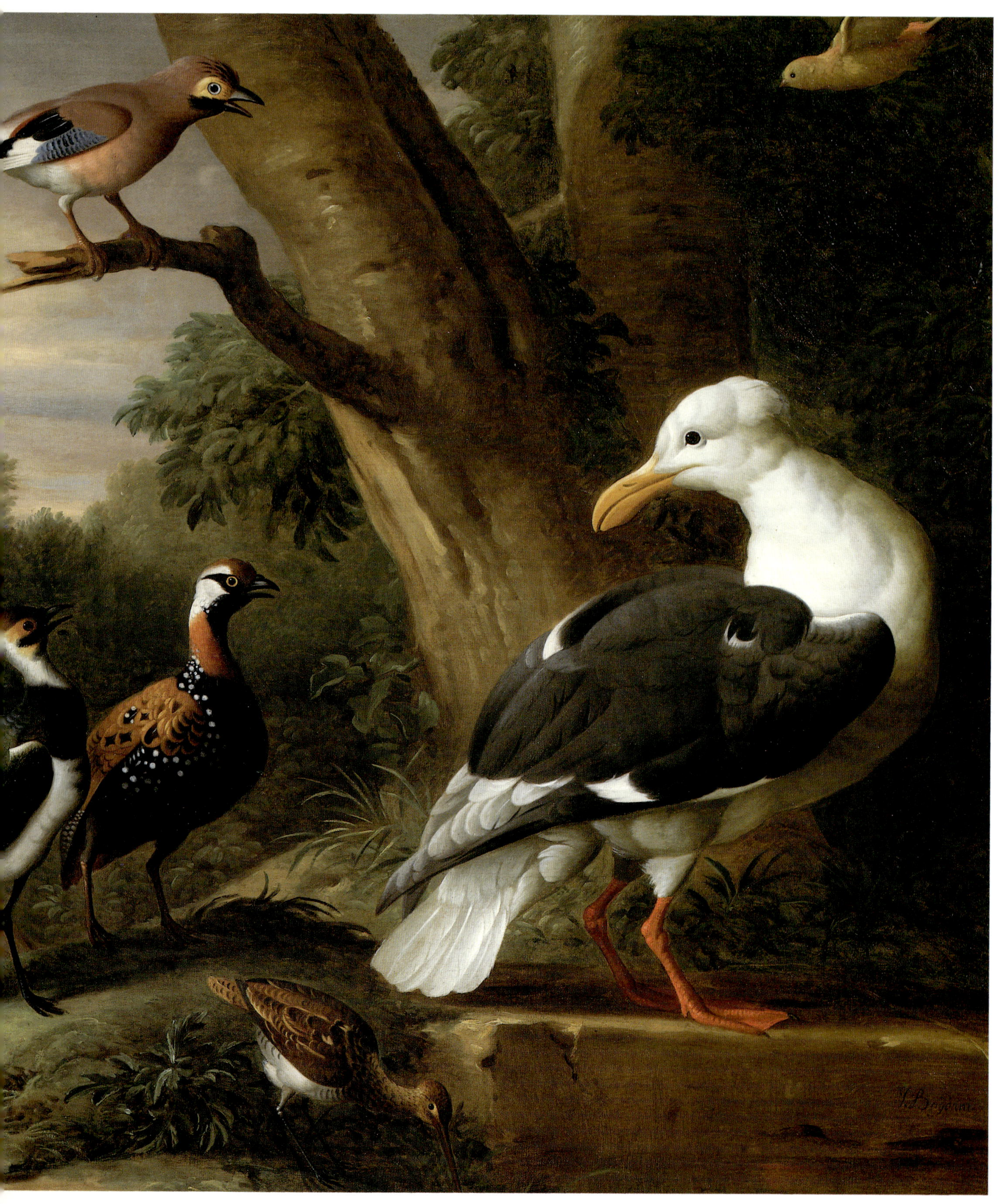

FOREWORD

I am delighted that the Antique Collectors' Club have decided to publish a second volume in this splendid series on bird painting. This volume, devoted to eighteenth century painters of the European schools, includes illustrations from the work of the major artists of that period, including examples by Pieter Casteels, Marmaduke Cradock, Willem Frederick van Royen, Tobias Stranover, Jakob Bogdani and Abraham Bisschop.

The eighteenth century was a golden age for decorative paintings of all kinds, whether the subject matter be flowers, architectural designs or animals and bird pictures.

Houses were grander and large fortunes had been made, especially in the Dutch East Indies and in the English West Indies, and the demand for grand exotic pictures for the new wealthy classes was much stronger than it had been in the seventeenth century. The architecture of the time afforded larger rooms and more generous lighting and this inspired clients to commission bright, colourful paintings for their walls. This demand was taken up by an exceptionally able generation of painters from England, Holland, France and Italy and a number of other artists from Hungary, like Jakob Bogdani.

The late seventeenth century had inspired a great interest, particularly in Holland and England, for menageries – the precursor of today's zoos – and owners of collections of such exotic animals and birds were keen to have them portrayed in oil, intricate marquetry work and tapestry. Artists like Aert Schouman were commissioned to produce major works for the Dutch royal family which depicted magnificent arrays of exotically plumed wild birds.

This was indeed the golden age of bird painting and on a personal note I have always enjoyed the acquisition and selling of these pictures. I am, therefore, delighted that such a wonderful book as this, together with the first volume published in 1993 and subsequent volumes which are to follow, will be available to an ever more interested public.

Rafael Valls
July 1994

INTRODUCTION

The art of any period in history is one indicator of the prevailing attitudes and influences current at that time. Even though bird art is but a very small portion of the whole corpus of paintings, the prevailing fashions in taste are in evidence.

In the first volume of this series, *Great Bird Paintings: the Old Masters* the powerful influence exerted by the Roman Catholic church on both the subjects and elaborate symbolism of pictures, was described. During that period, the golden age of Dutch and Flemish painting reached its peak and exerted an influence far beyond the borders of the Low Countries. In other European countries, following the Renaissance, there was a growing curiosity about the natural world that was reflected in the care and minuteness with which each element in still life pictures was painted. Birds formed part of this intense scrutiny of nature.

By the end of the seventeenth century the church's influence on artists had waned, and the predominance of Dutch and Flemish art was also in decline. However, one continuous thread was in evidence in the prevailing attitudes to birds and other animals. They were regarded as God's creatures over whom man had dominion to hunt, eat and to cage, but they were also admired for their beauty, and even envied for their powers of flight.

In the eighteenth century many of these currents of thought underwent a profound change. Political upheavals drove artists from one country to seek refuge in another. Social conditions improved greatly in several European countries so that increasing wealth and prosperity gave rise to new life-styles. Artistically, there was a movement toward more decorative, lighter pictures than formerly. In addition, knowledge of a wider world, including the natural world, expanded at an unprecedented rate with the circumnavigatory voyages of discovery in the final quarter of the century. The means for the dissemination of that knowledge was significantly broadened by new illustrative techniques fuelled by a growing demand from a better educated public. Connoisseurship spread, assisted by newly created academies which held art exhibitions. Visits to other countries in order to view paintings were undertaken, not just by artists as in previous centuries, but by educated young men on the 'Grand Tour'. They went in search of art and architecture, literature conveying new philosophies, reasoning and analysis, and new vistas also in the sense of observing the scenery and nature. The various disciplines of science and the arts were not fragmented then, as now, and this is also true on the smaller scale where a naturalist was well versed in botany, zoology, geology and antiquities. It is, therefore, somewhat artificial to isolate the work of 'bird artists' at this period, because they were frequently also painting wonderful flower pieces among other still life compositions and, almost without exception, they were good landscapists. The choice of pictures in this volume demonstrates, to some degree, these other elements and it is hoped that the commentaries will help maintain a more balanced perspective on the artists' wider skills.

In common with other painters, the bird artists were affected by all the political, social and artistic movements. Cross fertilisation of artistic ideas was one of the spin-offs from political strife in Europe during the eighteenth century. England was a more stable country under the rule of Dutch William, Queen Anne and the Georgians and attracted several artists from continental Europe. On the death of William III, the Dutch artists Jan and Robert Griffier and the Flemish painter, Pieter Casteels, fled the subsequent wars with the Austrians and Spaniards and English art was greatly enriched by them. Bogdani left a Hungary divided between Hapsburg and Turkish rule and with his son-in-law, Tobias Stranover, introduced a rich colour sense and greater spaciousness in painting to England. Philip Reinagle with his family also quit Hungary, though reportedly as adherents of James Stuart of Scotland, the Young Pretender to the throne of England. Going in the reverse direction, the Hamilton family left Scotland circa 1664 and settled in Brussels.

Among the artists who stayed at home, some continued to paint in the traditional manner of the previous era, for example the Dutchmen van Royen, Bisschop, Valckenburg, but

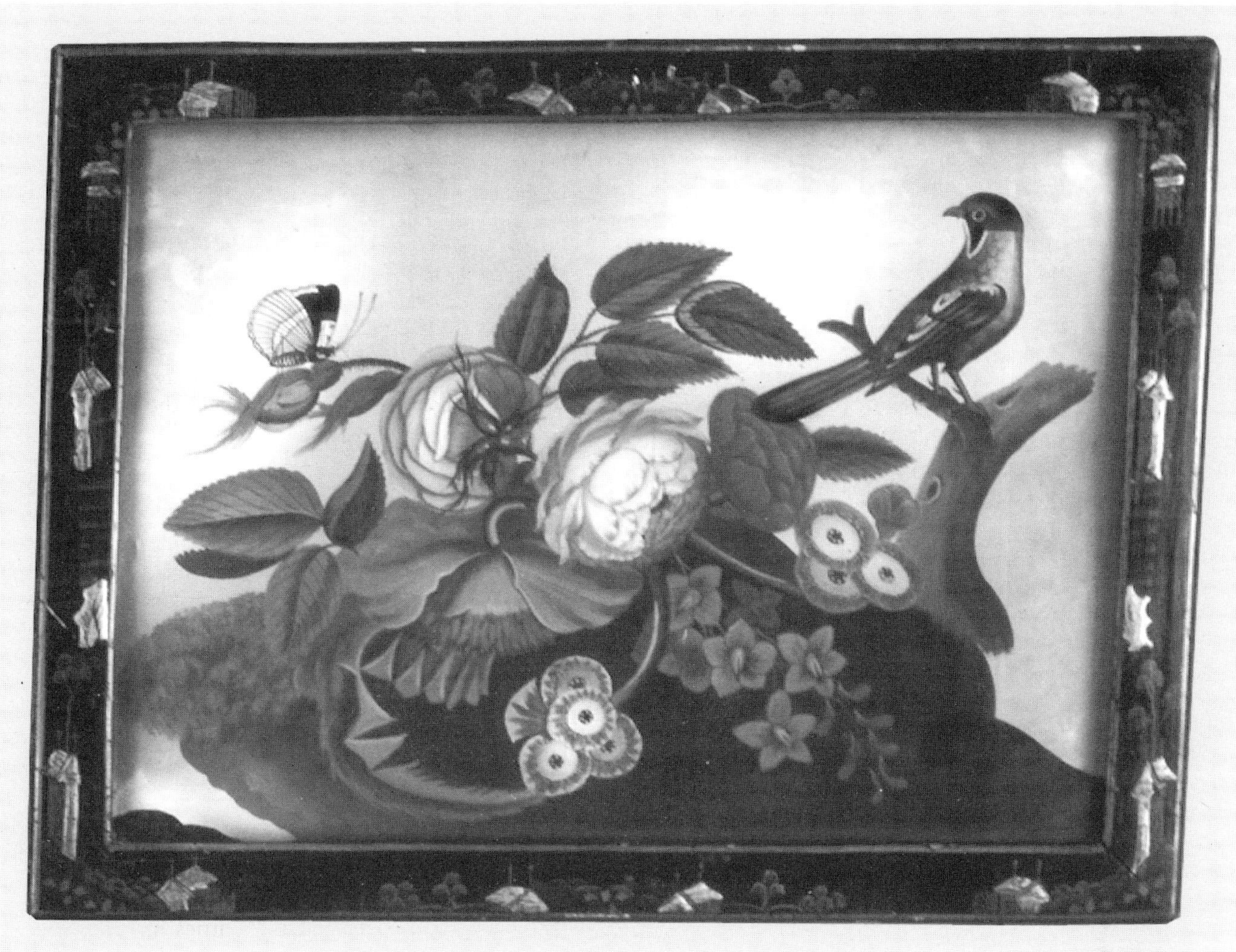

Weenix, van Huysum and Schouman, and later Vonck and Uytter-Limmege show evidence
of adopting new features and painting canvases that were less crowded and lighter in tone.
For them, as for the Italians and Spaniards, the greatest influence was French. The taste for
rococo, first in evidence in France as the rule of Louis XIV gave way to the Regency, spread
quickly. The old, heavy and dark elements were replaced by lightness, playfulness, and witty
frivolity. It stemmed from the aristocracy building new town houses, graceful in structure
with french windows letting in more daylight which was reflected in large mirrors, while in
the evening glittering chandeliers provided more light. Enjoyment and pleasure replaced
the authoritarian atmosphere of the seventeenth century and this included a delight in
nature in all its manifestations. Whereas a stern God had been worshipped, now homage
was paid to nature in a rational and intellectually free manner hitherto unknown. Sensibility
was given recognition and freely expressed.

  The Italian influence on artists and visitors to Rome in particular was still strong, but now,
as well as the classical style being admired, the bold, vigorous, even exuberant style called
'baroque' where decoration and ornament appealed to the emotions, became very popular.
Examples here are the paintings of Jan Griffier and George Edwards. Inevitably, fashion
changed again, and by the end of the century the classical style was appreciated once more
as patrons tired of the frivolities of the rococo style. Neo-classicism replaced it. During the
period of the French rococo, some artists attempted to copy Chinese decoration. There
were three distinct periods when the taste for chinoiserie was in vogue, the middle one
being in the late l730s to 1750s. Samuel Dixon's embossed bird pictures catered for this
taste.

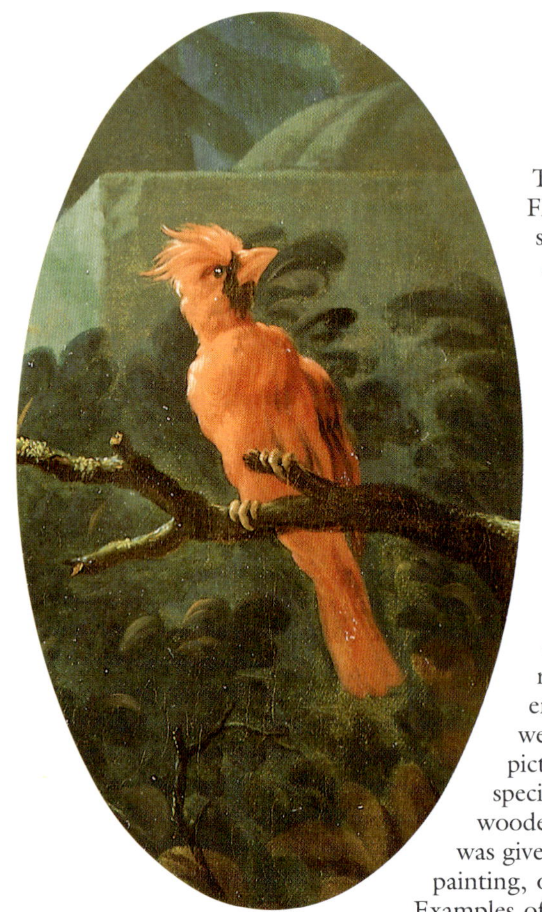

The northern cardinal (so named on account of its scarlet plumage) was a favourite cage bird in the 18th century.

The glorious age of French still life painting superseded that of the Dutch and Flemish. Desportes, Oudry and Chardin feature largely as the main exponents of still life painting and each painted many canvases incorporating birds. *Trompe-l'oeil* was acceptable, but no longer received as enthusiastically and Oudry's *The White Duck* (page 71) is more illusionist than intended as a full *trompe-l'oeil* painting.

Mainly for social reasons, the large canvases, crowded with birds from all parts of the known world, fell out of favour. Patrons still occasionally asked for these, but, generally speaking, smaller canvases were requested to suit smaller homes or to decorate the private, more intimate rooms in palaces. Grand topics such as classical and historic scenes once required for imposing entrance halls and banquetting rooms, were being replaced by paintings of large vistas of land and a stately new home, with portraits of the owner, his wife, horses and dogs. This celebration of increasing wealth and prosperity, not just for the old aristocratic families but a new landed gentry, affected the demand, or lack of demand, for genre subjects painted in the grand manner. Smaller and more charming pictures were wanted for the boudoir, the retiring room and the rooms where the family spent the evenings together when not entertaining. If the master of the house had sporting interests, still life pictures were purchased. If he had an interest in science and natural history, live animal pictures were bought. Frequently, the exact dimensions of these paintings were specified, so that they were designed to decorate a given space in the fashionable wooden panelling or wainscots, on the wall, over the door and fireplace. The artist was given clear instructions as to the requirements with regard to size and shape of the painting, oval, or square with a curved top, or oblong either horizontally or vertically. Examples of bird paintings executed to these requirements by Aert Schouman (pages 90 and 91) and Bogdani (*Bird Concert*, page 31) are reproduced here.

The patrons may have changed, fewer royalty and nobles, but the restrictions on the artists with regard to choice of size, shape and even content remained. The advantages of this, however, lay in the artist sometimes being commissioned not just for a single canvas, but often a pair, or even, like Reinagle, for three matching pictures (pages 106 and 107). Collins and Casteels painted a series of a dozen small pictures and then increased their income by having them etched and sold as sets of prints.

As the eighteenth century progressed, all the arts flourished and the demand for books and prints, as well as pictures, increased. Following the publication in 1731 of the first colour illustrated bird book, by Eleazar Albin, an ever increasing interest in natural history encouraged the production of a further thirty colour illustrated European bird books by the year 1800. It was in this area that science exerted the greatest influence on eighteenth century bird art.

Intellectual curiosity concerning the world encouraged exploration of new countries in order to discover what their people were like, their plants and animals and the landscapes they inhabited. A few bird artists travelled outside Europe, notably Eleazar Albin who went to Jamaica in 1701 and subsequently included five Jamaican birds in his books, but the most remarkable lone artist who travelled in the early part of the century was Mark Catesby, whose subsequent pictorial record of North American plants and animals set a standard and pattern of publishing that was copied for well over a century.

For the stay-at-home bird artist, models were found in several repositories. By and large, the most eminent artists were in royal service and thus had access to the menageries of the French kings (Desportes and Oudry at Versailles), the Dutch Prince Willem V (Schouman at Het Loo, Apeldoorn), the Spanish monarchs (Paret) the Hapsburgs (Hamilton at Schönbrunn in Vienna), The Grand Duke Cosimo III (Bimbi at the Boboli menagerie) and the Elector Palatine (Weenix, who worked at Düsseldorf).

Without access to royal and aristocratic menageries artists were deprived of exotic foreign birds during the first part of the century. However, as the landed gentry began to form collections, artists such as Bogdani in Admiral Churchill's menagerie were able to see newly imported species. Some artists had to be content with native species and the occasional foreign bird exhibited in coffee shops and inns, where they formed an added attraction for clients; in the private homes of men connected with the navy and merchant shipping; or they could go down to the docks when an East Indiaman docked, climb on board and buy a live bird or skin for themselves. Pet shops increased in number throughout the eighteenth century. Dead specimens were sought on poultry market stalls and then in museums, once taxidermists had overcome some of the difficulties of preserving skins. In the eighteenth century, both bird artists and illustrators (see Reinagle and Sarah Stone) used Sir Ashton Lever's public museum in London from 1774 to 1806.

Importation of foreign species to Europe was haphazard until the organisers of voyages of exploration and discovery followed the example set by Sir Joseph Banks on Captain Cook's circumnavigations in the 1770s. The consequences of sending trained artists, botanists and zoologists on voyages of discovery were profound. The roles of the draughtsmen on board ship were clearly defined. The professional artist painted landscapes, topographical artists drew the shoreline and recorded the territory. The naturalists drew the plants, animals, insects, amphibians and fishes, while both attempted to record the natives and their artefacts. Ever since artists painted pictures on canvas, from the end of the fifteenth century, live bird pictures had been landscape scenes with the birds depicted pursuing their lives within some habitat framework. Sometimes the birds were painted in correct proportions to the trees and rocks, sometimes they were over-large figures superimposed on the backgrounds, but to paint a bird picture had meant the artist provided either a landscape or an indoor setting as a background. The lost opportunity to provide New Zealand landscapes for the New Zealand birds recorded by Georg Forster on Cook's second voyage, or Australian scenery for the Australian species by the First Fleet artists, stems at least partly from this division of labour between the landscapist and the topographical and natural history draughtsmen.

By far the greatest influence on those draughtsmen who painted newly discovered birds was the demands made on them by scientists. The tradition of providing an imaginary italianate landscape for birds assembled from South America, Africa, Asia and Europe became unacceptable. Sensibly, Peter Paillou painted a slice of English countryside for his English birds and Collins painted groups of European species without being tempted to introduce foreign birds. But the old habits died slowly, as several pictures illustrated here demonstrate. Several other groups of native birds had just one exotic species among them, a peacock, but the peacock had been established for such a long time in the parks of country houses, it was almost, by this date considered to be a naturalised species.

Professional bird artists had greater freedom in painting backgrounds, to place the birds in correct relation with regard to size within the background, and to give a distant impression of the bird which was easily recognisable, even though small. All professional bird artists attempted to paint their birds looking alive and moving naturally, whether working from live specimens (very rarely), or mounted models. Reinagle worked on oil paintings, using bird specimens in Sir Ashton Lever's museum, many brought back from Cook's voyages. So did a number of bird illustrators, but the difference between their finished results are quite startling.

A scientific illustrator, recording the appearance of any species for the first time, had a heavy responsibility. All future imports of similar birds would be placed beside the book plate based on his drawing to see whether they were the same species, or different. The onus was on him to map the bird's plumage totally accurately in respect of size, shape and colours of all markings on the plumage. He was required to get the shape and size of the body correct, often drawing the outline in ink life-size before hand-painting it in watercolours. He approached each bird as a single, isolated specimen and drew it, alone (occasionally with

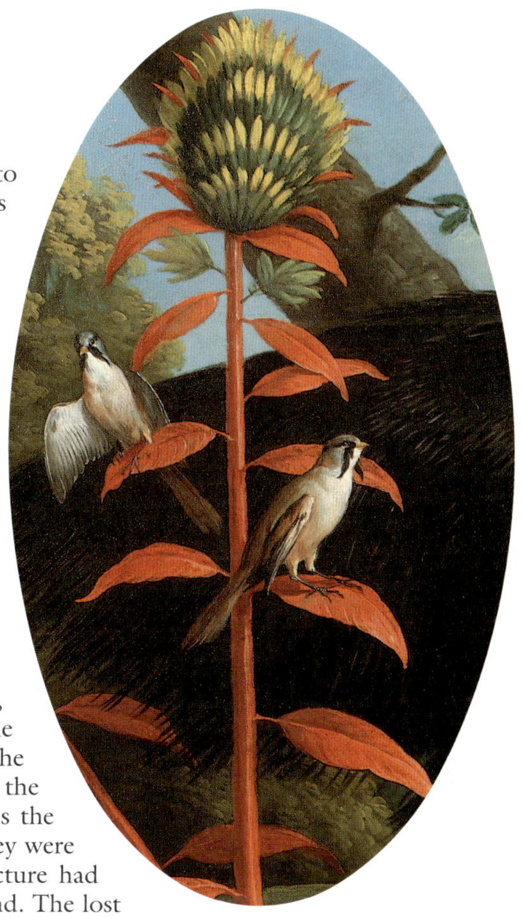

Bearded reedlings, first depicted in a book in 1731 by Eleazar Albin as 'The Beard Manica from Juteland, or Bearded Titmouse' following the arrival of a cageful of these birds from Denmark.

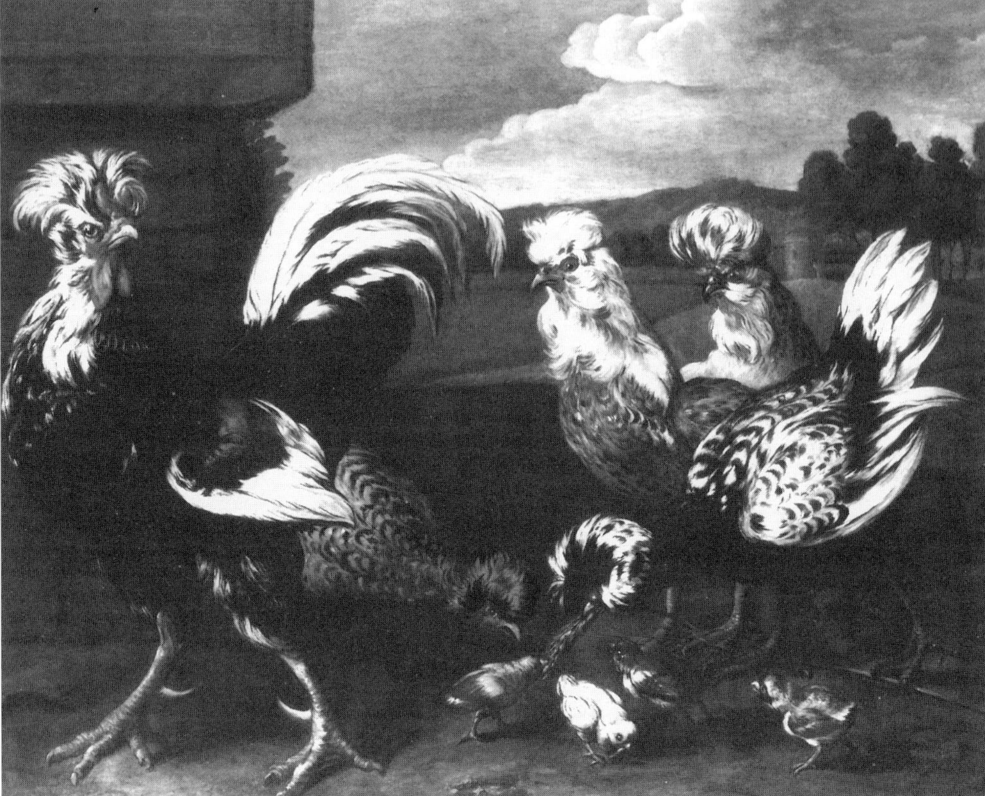

its mate if available), on the sheet of paper. While the scientists wanted a 'faithful record', as they liked to call it, the state of the mounted specimen frequently made that impossible for him to achieve. Skins were taken to Europe packed flat, then plumped out with wadding, regardless of where the underlying muscles would occur in real life. Indeed, that was not even well known and certainly not taught to artists until after the end of the century when George Stubbs published his researches into the anatomy of the chicken. Ill-stuffed birds in incorrect poses, crowded on to shelves with their beaks twisted over their backs in order to save space, were the basic materials from which a lively, accurate painting of the species had to be done. The impossible was asked of the illustrator.

The professional bird artist, trained in composition, perspective, and a knowledge of the effects of light and shade, approached his task differently. Even though seeing birds correctly within their environment is a modern concept in bird art, the artists of this early period nevertheless had some idea of relating the bird to its surroundings, and of painting it in terms of the effects of sunlight on the plumage, which enabled them to paint a more naturalistic picture. The bird artist was nearly always also a landscapist. This brings us full circle to the distinctions between a bird artist and the bird illustrator – a division largely, though not entirely, created by the social and scientific circumstances of the eighteenth century.

In the nineteenth century the dilemma, how to achieve scientific accuracy within a picture by the professional bird artist, and how to bring artistry into a printed illustration by the bird draughtsman, exercised the minds of both oil painters and watercolourists. Few came close to resolving it, but the gap that had opened up in the eighteenth century was narrowed.

The favourite bird subjects in the eighteenth century were still live domestic poultry, followed by dead partridges. This situation, however, was becoming more complex. Among the domestic birds, new breeds were being developed and pyle, hamburg and bantam cocks begin to appear. Hens with their chickens were very popular, although the young of almost every other species (with the exception of ducklings and goslings) were ignored. 'Polish' ducks with topknots were joined by 'upright ducks'. The favourite of the barnyard, however, was still the goose which formed such an important role in the rural economy that it far outnumbered chickens, which were rarely eaten in England, but kept for their eggs and feathers. Around the dovecotes of Dutch, French and English eighteenth century bird pictures there were pouters, jacobins and pigeons with crests. Peacocks were plentiful and formed the focal point in many paintings at the beginning of the century. Rivalling them, later, was the common variety of pheasant without the ring round the neck. Ring-necked pheasants were not introduced from China until circa 1768. Further introductions were the golden and silver pheasants which eventually were to become feral, but at this stage they, along with the common pheasant, were not in the open fields but kept in aviaries. Both albino and semi-albinistic peacocks and pheasants were proudly displayed as important features in pictures of the early years.

The table bird *par excellence* was still the partridge, which appeared in countless still life paintings. Grouse (see Elmer page 83) are seen less frequently, but the demand for sporting pictures grew apace once the sporting gun was made safer and more efficient and came into the hands of land owning squires. Woodcocks and snipes, familiar in numerous still life paintings in the previous centuries, now appeared fleeing from the guns.

Pet birds continued to be painted, in portraits of women and children in particular. Sir Joshua Reynolds had a pet macaw which he frequently incorporated in his portraits. Canaries were by now common as cage birds and bearded reedlings, which featured in Desportes' paintings, were also caged. A firm favourite among cage birds, owing to its brilliant red plumage, was the cardinal from North America, called the 'Virginian nightingale'. Birds that could survive the long sea journeys to Europe from North America, the Indies and Africa, to be bred in cages in Europe, were almost exclusively seed-eaters or, like the sailors, dry tack eaters. No doubt the odd weevil was welcome to the birds, if not the sailors, but exclusive insect eaters did not survive the long voyages.

Looking through the plates in this book it is possible to find a small selection of the recent imports of birds to Europe. The bird artists recorded the presence of some remarkable species from three-quarters of the globe until 1770 and all parts of the world thereafter. With these imports and the impetus given to the recording, listing and classification of birds by Carl Linnaeus' systematic list, the tenth edition of which recorded 444 bird species in 1758, the number of birds described and named for science grew to three thousand by 1801. Today, we are aware of some 8,650 bird species, but a score of those known in the eighteenth century have become extinct. The detailed descriptions and naming of birds became a branch of ornithology which absorbed a good deal of the attention of late eighteenth century naturalists. It was they who needed detailed drawings from book illustrators. Curiously, they and nearly all scientists since, have ignored the evidence, beautifully painted and presented in countless canvases, of a rich store of birds, frequently still un-named at the time they were painted. These pictures recorded a wonderful galaxy of exotic foreign and native European birds. They are aesthetically pleasing, of great scientific interest, and potentially of great value for our knowledge of which birds had been recorded pictorially by the end of the eighteenth century.

The work of the first recorders of Australasian natural history across the eighteenth/nineteenth century boundary has been included. The main surge of the discovery of the new avifauna, and the artists making drawings of them, occurred following Captain James Cook's voyage of 1768 through to 1820. The portraits of scores of new birds were painted in Australia, Norfolk Island, New Zealand and Tasmania, by George Forster, the Port Jackson Artist, George Raper and Ferdinand Bauer within this period. Luise Panhuys and Lady Gwillim were active in Surinam and India in the early years of the nineteenth century and they have been included as two of the finest of the European artists born in the eighteenth century but at work in foreign countries up to 1816.

Wenzel Peter, the final artist in this book, provided the opportunity to look back on some of the most influential developments of the eighteenth century that were to play a significant part in the artistic life of the nineteenth, the establishment of art academies and schools, with their accompanying exhibitions and patronage.

BARTOLOMEO BIMBI
born near Florence 1648, died Florence 1729

Bimbi was a pupil of Lorenso Lippi from 1661-65 and then specialised in painting flowers, fruit and rare animals. He was employed to paint the birds and mammals in the Grand Duke Cosimo III's menagerie for some time. The Boboli menagerie was built in 1677 and had large rooms for monkeys and other rare mammals, besides pheasant and poultry houses. Bimbi's paintings of the Grand Duke's exotic species were framed in black and gold and hung on the walls of the Villa Ambrogiana, a hunting-lodge near Empoli. Cosimo sometimes wrote notes on Bimbi's paintings indicating the place and date of the specimens' discovery. Among many of Bimbi's pictures that have been preserved are oil paintings of a gyrfalcon, flamingo, eagle owl with a barn owl, three studies of a golden pheasant, a woodcock with a merganser and ruddy shelduck, a capercaillie, two black-crowned night herons and an Egyptian vulture.

SALMON-CRESTED COCKATOO
oil on canvas, 86.5 x 72.5 cm
Courtesy of Pitti Palace, Florence

Bimbi's work is distinctive because of the brush strokes he used to simulate soft feathering and the manner in which he curls the feathers sideways, rather than painting them straight and overlapping one another neatly. He paid some attention to the birds' anatomy and could put life into his models even when commanded to paint them from stuffed specimens. There was an area in the menagerie set aside for the display of mounted specimens which had been set up to look like live animals. Of greater importance, at this date in bird art, was Bimbi's unusually thoughtful attention to anatomical details such as feet and legs, combs and wattles, and beaks.

It is thought that Bimbi's painting of the *Salmon-crested Cockatoo* was made in 1716, shortly after a live specimen had been delivered to the Grand Duke Cosimo. It was brought from Amsterdam. Dutch spice traders had been importing live cockatoos from the Moluccas for a century or longer before this bird was captured. A salmon-crested cockatoo had been portrayed by Georg Hoefnagel and his son Jacob from a specimen in Emperor Rudolf II's menagerie (built at the Schloss Neugebau near Vienna in 1587) at the end of the sixteenth century, and again by Roelandt Savery (in his *A Forest Landscape with Birds*), who worked in Rudolf II's menageries until 1612. Bimbi's painting may have been the first detailed study in oils of *A Salmon-crested Cockatoo* by an Italian artist. He placed it within the parrot room at the Boboli menagerie, where mesh across the windows allowed fresh air to enter the room, but prevented the free flying birds from escaping. The cockatoo has its own special ornamental ironwork perch and ring perch.

The salmon-crested cockatoo is 52 centimetres in length and the general plumage of the adult birds is salmon pink but the crest is of a much deeper shade. The white eye-ring, so carefully painted here by Bimbi, surrounds the dark brown iris of the male and the reddish-brown iris of the female. The birds were originally found on the islands of Ceram, Saparu and Haruku in the southern Moluccas, Indonesia, but some birds have been introduced since to Amboina in the Moluccas. They live in deep forests where they find seeds, nuts, berries and some insect food, a diet correctly noted and provided for this bird in captivity which has pears, walnuts and hazelnuts under its perch. This attractively coloured bird also has a remarkable ability to imitate sounds, including the human voice.

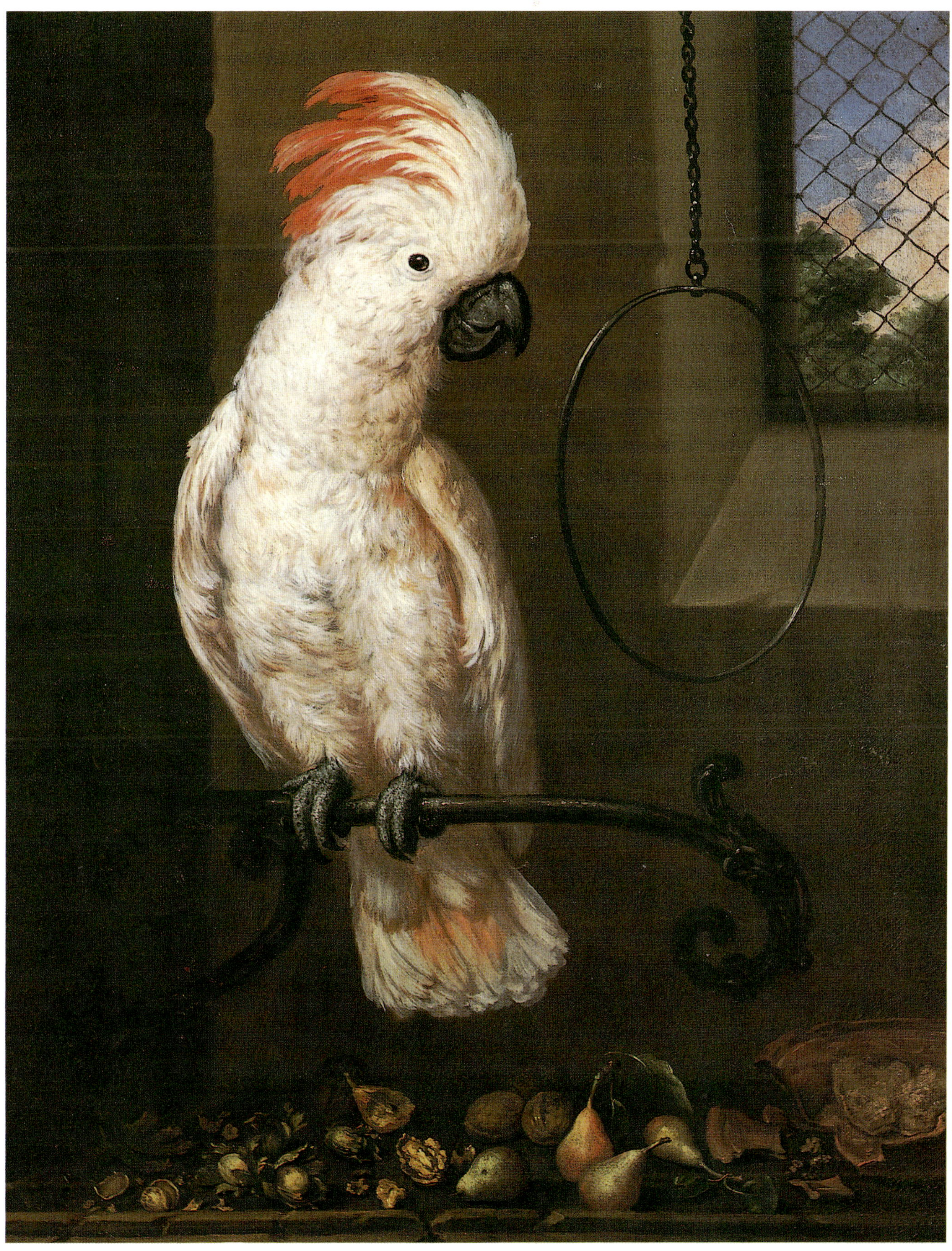

WILLEM FREDERIK VAN ROYEN
born Haarlem 1655, died Berlin 1723

This Dutch painter of still life was active first in Haarlem, then in The Hague where he was the pupil of J. Antonij van Ravensteyn, before being appointed a court painter to the Great Elector Frederick William, at Potsdam in 1669. He remained there for ten years before moving to Berlin where he was a founder member of the painting academy in 1696 and served as its director periodically between 1706 and 1716.

He painted many fruit and flower pieces, often with a live parrot or other bird in the composition, for which he used the menagerie at Kurfürsten belonging to Frederick III of Brandenburg. Royen also used the rare plants in Frederick's garden for decorative elements in his fruit and bird pictures.

A GOOSE AND OTHER WATERFOWL BY A FOUNTAIN
oil on canvas, 122 x 102 cm
Courtesy of Rafael Valls, London

Royen signed and dated this oil painting of *A Goose and other Waterfowl by a Fountain* in 1701. He has painted the bird, closely related to a pink-footed goose, greeting the dawn while standing on a splendid carved shell at the edge of a fountain with a landscape in the distance. The full early morning light falls on this bird, while its companions, a motley crowd of ducks and geese, are waking and beginning to preen their feathers for the first time that day. The painting of the feathers of the main goose, in a shaft of sunshine, and those still in the shade and so more subdued in tone, is masterly. The birds, the sunlight and the background all convince the viewer that this is the start of a new day that promises to be both fine and warm.

There are probably as many pictures of domestic fowl in existence as there are of all other bird species put together. Painting domestic birds has several advantages over trying to find and sketch wild birds. They are near at hand, either in the artist's own back yard, or in a neighbour's. They do not fly away the moment that an artist wishes to paint them. Even when not pinioned, they are slower in their movements, often being heavier than their counterparts in the wild. The mallard interbreeds with domestic ducks to produce a never-ending variety of plumage, though geese are more conservative in their choice of mates and so fewer variations in plumage occur. The goose in this picture has great self-possession and a solidity that is reassuring and makes one suspect that it is the leader of this particular group of geese, male mallard and white domestic duck.

Pictures of such familiar scenes of the barnyard with poultry or a village pond with tame geese and ducks have always been popular and still find a ready market. In the nineteenth century, the genre was developed to include a charming female figure who was feeding the birds, and numerous girls appeared in pictures with such titles as *Feeding the Ducks* or *The Goose Girl*. The interest in these later pictures is more concentrated on the female figure than the birds. Earlier pictures of domestic fowl have a simple, direct appeal emanating entirely from the birds, as in this painting of *A Goose and other Waterfowl by a Fountain*. Royen's picture is in the style, and follows the compositional pattern, of the Old Masters and has a definite seventeenth century Dutch atmosphere.

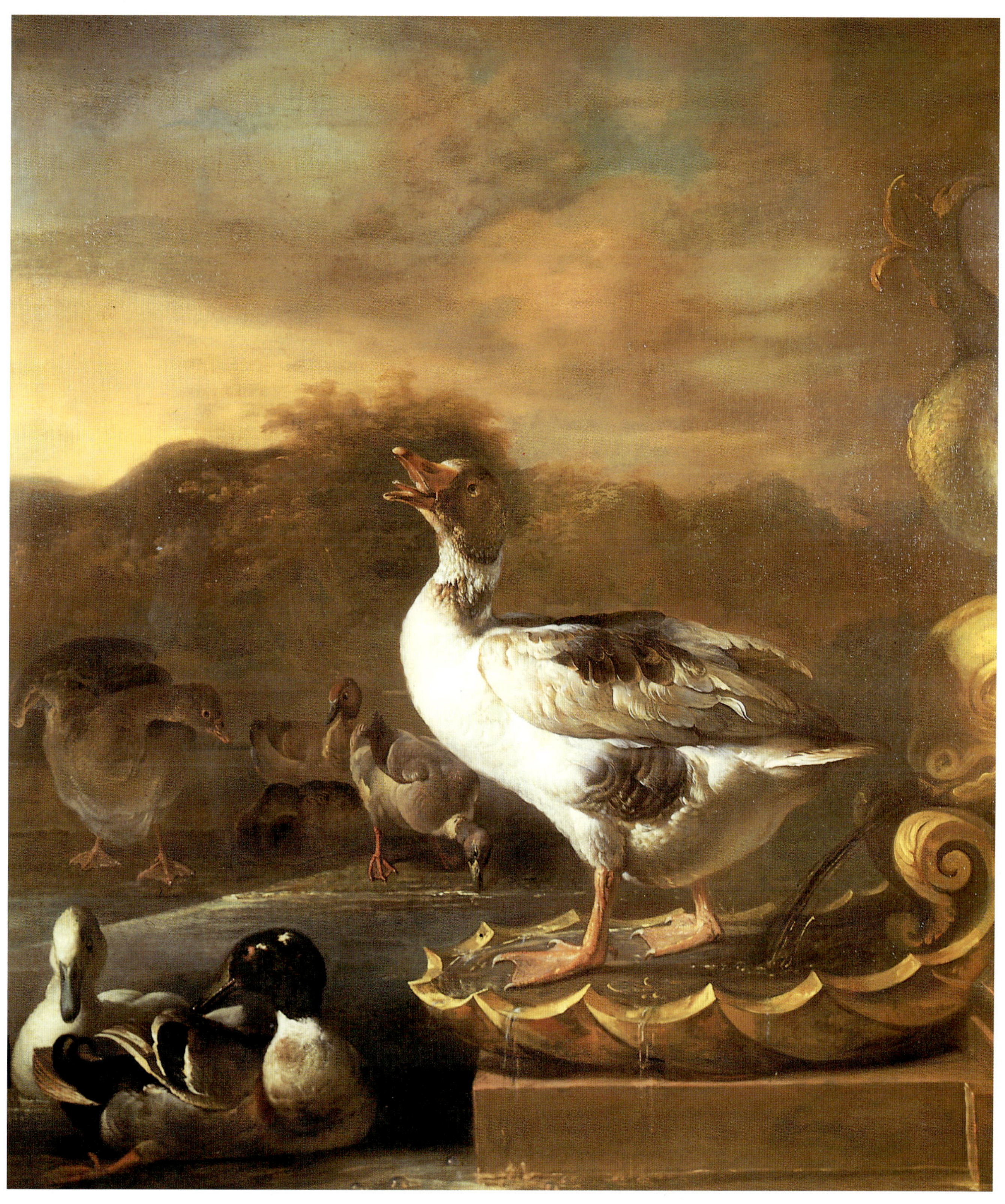

JAN WEENIX
born Amsterdam 1640, died 1719

Jan Weenix was the son and pupil of the famous Jan Baptist Weenix (1621-1663). Another pupil was Melchior de Hondecoeter, Jan's cousin. With two such gifted artists in the family, Jan might have been overshadowed, but his talent was such that this was not a possibility. Naturally, he began to paint like his father, his still lifes with flowers and animals and dead game subjects being set in Italianate scenes, but soon after his father's early death, Jan developed his own style and excelled in dead game and hunting pieces beyond any other artist of his time. Melchior de Hondecoeter died in 1695 and Jan lived on into the eighteenth century as the foremost Dutch painter of animals. He earned this esteem by the clear and brilliant colouring of his highly finished work which was excellent in every part, whether fur, feather, plants or landscape. The plumage of his birds is always in beautiful condition suggesting access to live birds or very new specimens that have not faded or become ruffled. This is quite likely to be the case, because Jan was court painter c.1702-16 to the Elector Palatine, Johann Wilhelm, and made a series of paintings of both live and dead game to decorate the Elector's baroque Schloss Bensberg, built near Cologne c.1706-13. He also worked in Düsseldorf during this period. Apart from these commissions, there are many other canvases, all of a high standard, which are now in European museums.

A TERN AND OTHER BIRDS IN A LANDSCAPE
Oil on canvas

Many years ago, this painting of a tern was reported as being in the 'Stschawinsky Collection, St Petersburg', but we have failed to trace its locality. The Russian connection, however, gives rise to speculation as to whether the painting was owned by Peter the Great (1672-1725), with whom Weenix was contemporary. Peter was founder of the capital (from 1712-1918) of the Russian empire, St Petersburg. He was also a great admirer of Dutch paintings.

The birds in this picture of *A Tern and Other Birds in a Landscape* were unusual choices and rarely painted in such detail before. Ringed plovers are common among waders on shallow shores where they live and nest. The fine feathers on the back are of the softest sandy brown and blend in with their surroundings, especially when the female is sitting on her eggs on the seashore.

Coots are familiar birds wherever a small stretch of water is available for them. The sooty black feathers of the body are relieved only by the bill and frontal shield which are startlingly white. At a distance, the coot looks as though it is has lost some head feathers, hence the expression 'as bald as a coot'. The male is a very aggressive bird, and very articulate when chasing away any other waterbirds from its pond. This is a solitary coot, but if it had a mate and was defending its territory, the ringed plovers would not be standing peacefully on the bank.

Which tern is this? Such a pronounced forked tail suggests a common or arctic tern. Bird-watchers nowadays, finding these two species hard to distinguish, dub them 'commic terns'. It is obvious in this painting why the old name 'sea-swallows' was given to terns. Their flight is light and aerobatic when idling, but when fishing they hover purposefully with bill pointing down on to the sea and eyes focused to catch any movement. They plunge swiftly to pluck a fish out of the water, using the bill. Paintings of seabirds are much rarer than of land birds, so this Weenix is a delightful composition for many different reasons.

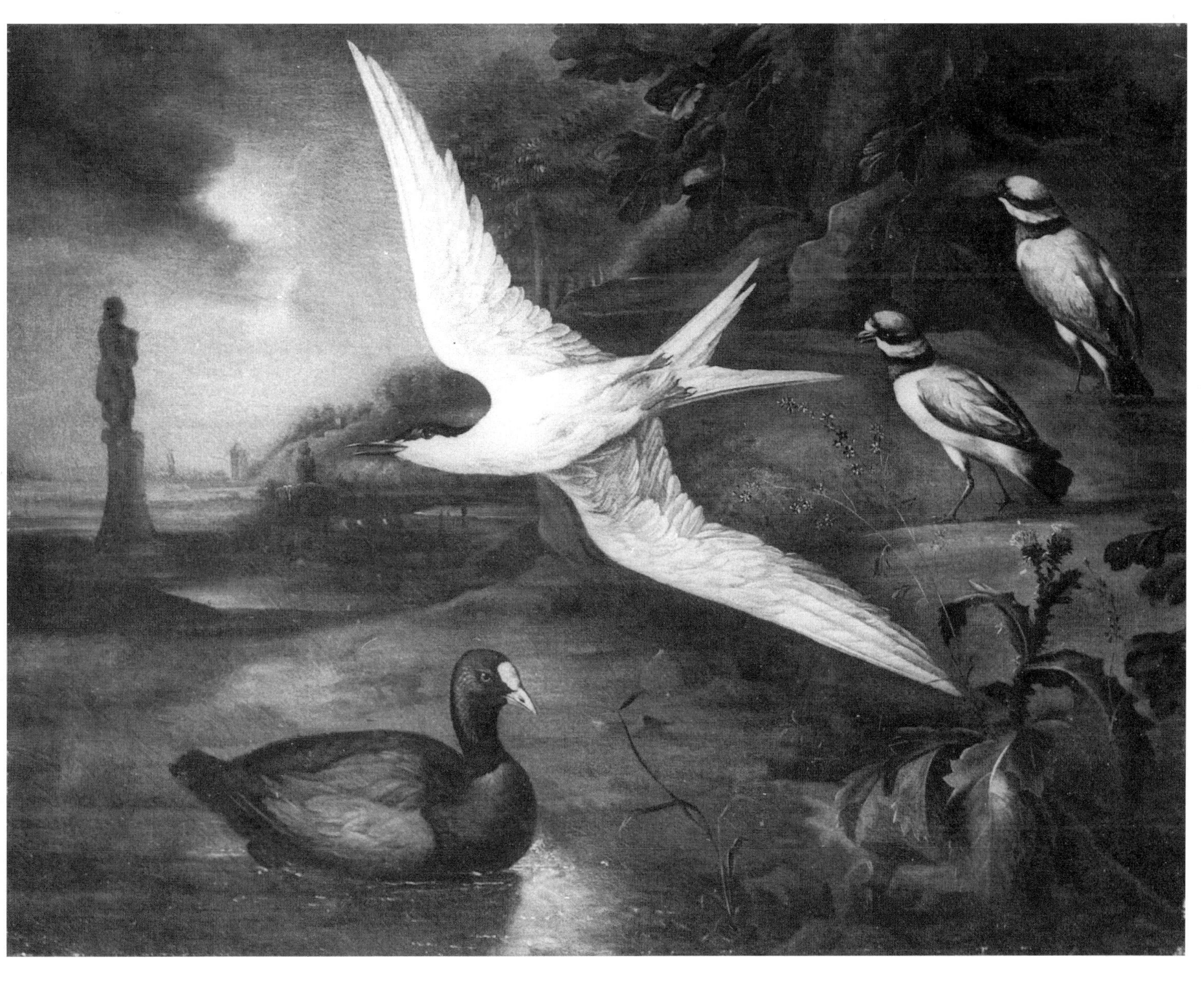

JAN GRIFFIER
born Amsterdam c.1652, died London 1718

Griffier went to London soon after 1666 and painted river scenes, ruins and picturesque castles in the Dutch style. He was one of several Dutch and Flemish artists of this period who chose to live in England for much of their lives and so influenced and enriched English art. In 1672 the French invaded the Low Countries and defeated the Dutch. French art became fashionable with rich patrons, and Dutch artists fled to England and elsewehere, hoping to earn a living when their pictures were no longer appreciated at home. Jan married Jane Gilborthorpe on 13 February 1673, at St Marylebone, London, and seemed to be settled in England. Then William of Orange ascended the English throne in 1689, and with greater freedom of movement established between England and the Low Countries, Griffier returned to Holland for a few years, c.1695-1705, before he settled permanently in London, where he died.

NOAH'S ARK
oil on canvas, 396 x 396 cm
Bristol Museum & Art Gallery

Several etchings by Griffier after other artists included pictures of birds, among them some by his friend Francis Barlow. Griffier used similar bird species in his own paintings as the ones that had appeared in pictures by Barlow. The ostrich and cassowary in this picture, *Noah's Ark*, are direct copies of one of Barlow's paintings, a drawing and published print (etched by Griffier) in Barlow's *Various Birds and Beasts drawn from*

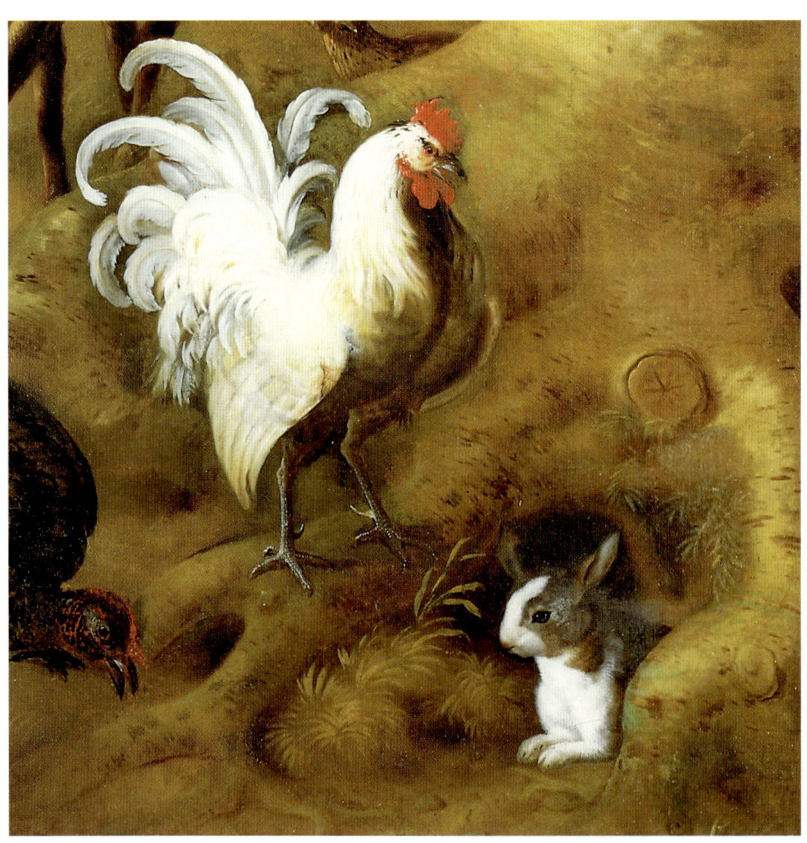

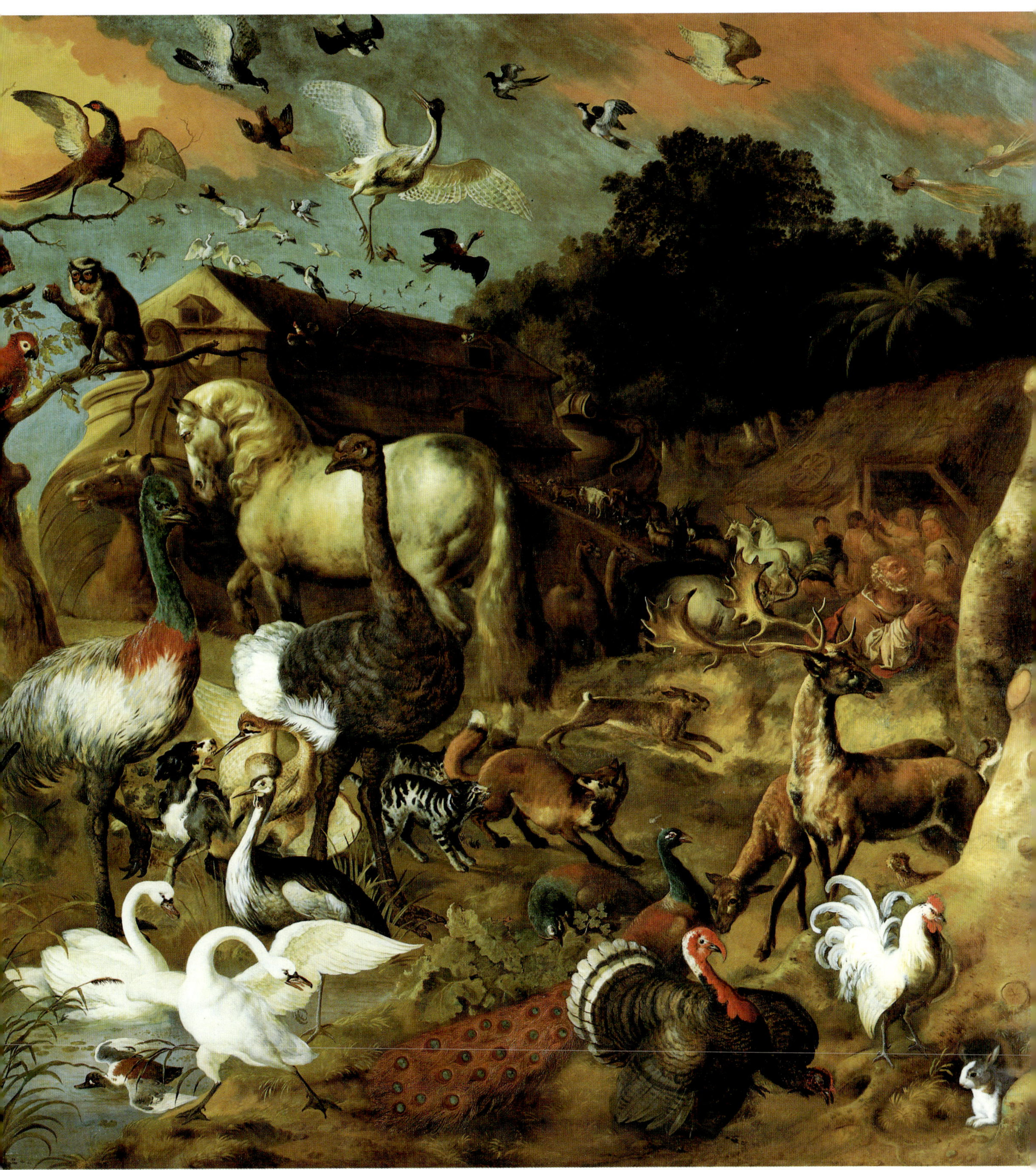

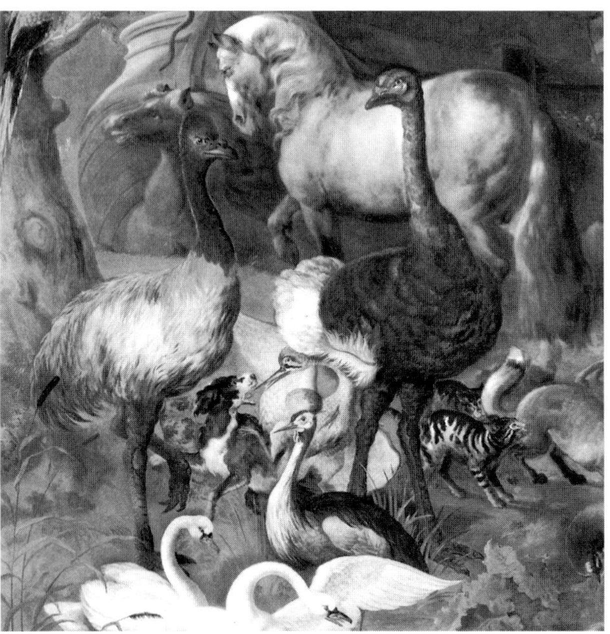

Detail of Griffier's Noah's Ark.

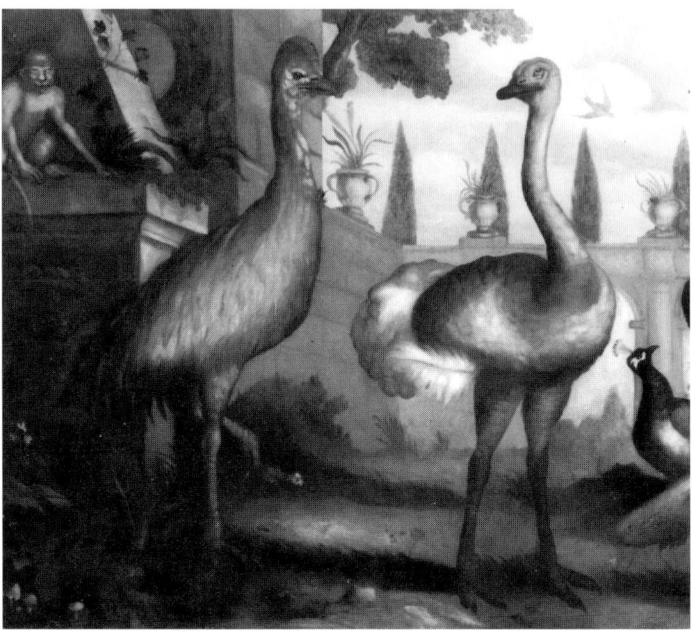

Detail of Barlow's Ostrich and a Cassowary *illustrated in* Bird Painting – The Old Masters. *Courtesy of Christopher Gibbs, London.*

the Life (1660-70, plate 14). They probably both worked 'from the life' by sketching the birds in Charles II's aviaries in St James's Park. This painting was done c. 1710, some twenty-five years after Charles II's death, so several birds are painted here from earlier sketches. The white horse is reminiscent of Brueghel's white horse in his pictures of Noah's ark and Garden of Eden. The self-assured rabbit, however, appears to be peculiarly Griffier's own animal. Many paintings of Noah's ark have a greater number of mammals and not as many birds, so Griffier's picture is a pleasant exception.

This *Noah's Ark* is an ark with a difference. Earlier Dutch and Flemish arks were painted after studying God's instructions to Noah. *The Book of Genesis* records that Noah used long planks of gophar wood to build a three-storeyed ark with one window and one door, all sealed with pitch. Griffier's ark is a figment of his eighteenth century Baroque imagination, all curves and curly embellishments.

The birds assembling are mostly familiar European species, e.g. the shelduck, hawk, lapwings, long-tailed duck, heron and bustard, all in flight. The birds of paradise are an exception. Two swans are perched on the roof of the ark, as well as a pair on the ground by the stream. In the tree, the pheasant is agitated by the presence of an owl with short ear tufts. The monkey and scarlet macaw were familiar pets in many households. The crowned crane, peacocks and turkeys, with a splendid white rooster, were common in parks surrounding country seats by this time.

Griffier took great pains to render fur and feathers in such a manner as to show their varying textures. His choice of colours was taken from the Dutch palette of browns, dark greens, and sky blue, while touches of bright red were used sparingly on the goldfinch, macaw and turkey.

Noah's Ark, a canvas over twelve feet square, hung in the great hall at Nettlecombe Court, Somerset, for almost three hundred years before it was sold in 1992.

MARMADUKE CRADOCK
born Somerton near Ilchester 1660, died London 1717

Cradock began his career as an apprentice house-painter in London, but determinedly practised painting in oils on canvas until he became sufficiently proficient to set up a studio and specialise in painting birds. He painted some still life pictures, but more often live birds in a landscape similar to those of Francis Barlow. The birds in his parkland pictures were mostly British species with the addition of a glamorous peacock in the foreground. He painted them for 'persons that pay'd him p. diem, or that dealt in pictures' and he had little to do with the 'Nobility and Quality' who did not pay promptly. This accounts for his not having access to the parks and menageries of the wealthy in which to paint exotic bird species. It also explains why he painted rapidly to supply demand and left many compositions that repeated the same motifs.

With Barlow, Cradock firmly established the English school of animal painting that has proved to be of continued popularity since the end of the seventeenth century. He painted his lively birds in beautiful colours against blue skies and within landscapes that were always bathed in sunlight. His colours are delicate, and the plants and trees thoughtfully chosen before being carefully positioned to decorate the scene and never to obscure the birds which are, in their turn, also carefully spaced to show their full beauty in terms of form and colours.

TWO PEACOCKS, DOVES, CHICKENS AND ROOSTER
oil on canvas, 89.5 x 127.7 cm
Courtesy of Rafael Valls, London

Two Peacocks, Doves, Chickens and Rooster in a Parkland Landscape is a deliberately composed picture to show off the birds to their best advantage. Cradock's birds when shown flying (and they are in the same pose in both the pictures reproduced here) are elegant. The same description may be given to the two swans on the lake and the manner in which the trees are painted. He is far more eighteenth century in spirit, anticipating the age we associate with elegance, refinement, good taste and called 'The Age of Enlightenment'.

There is an added element of charm to this painting. This may be attributed directly to the small chickens, particularly the two fluttering down from the wall. They are only a few days old, covered in fluffy down which will keep them warm and protect them while their flight feathers grow. They have spread their wings, but cannot yet fly, so are fluttering or parachuting down and may arrive with a bounce and a tumble, but will scramble to their feet unharmed.

One of the lesser known wonders of nature is the manner in which some very young chicks, not yet able to fly, make their first foray into the world outside their nests. Several ducks, including the mandarin duck, nest in holes in trees between ten and fifty feet up. The young drop from the nest within a day of hatching to fall on to the forest floor and follow the female to water. Puffin chicks, deep in burrows on the top of sea cliffs, are deserted by their parents after some forty days, and leave the nest to go to sea, alone at night, a week later. They have to take a leap into the unknown, and despite sometimes bouncing off ledges on the way down the rock face, they plop into the water and swim merrily out to sea. Guillemots leave the cliff for the sea when only partly grown and still cannot fly for another three weeks after leaving their rock ledge to flutter down to the sea far below. There are other young birds who perform this small miracle each nesting season. Cradock's chickens are but one example of multitudes of very small birds that launch themselves into the air before they can fly –

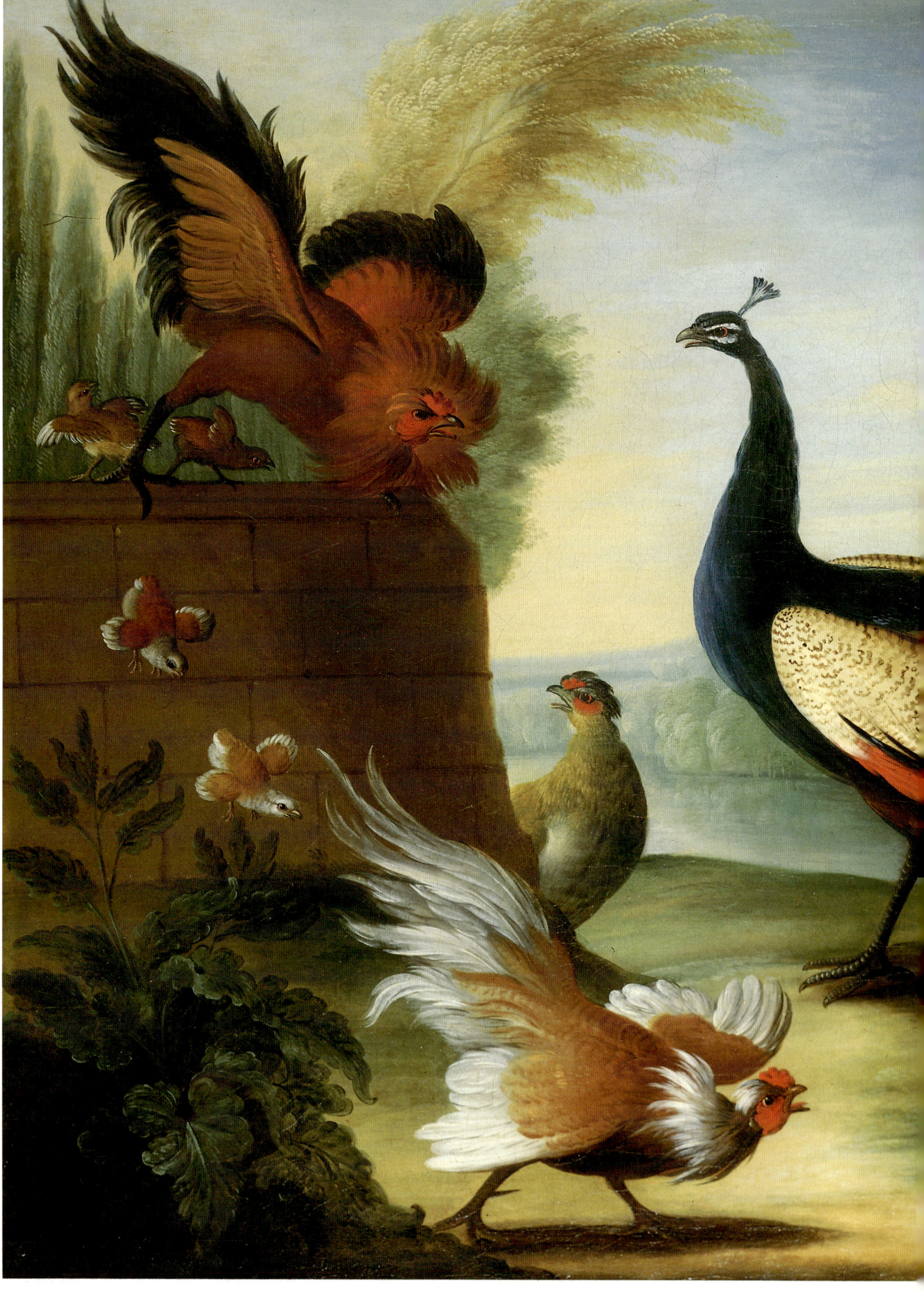

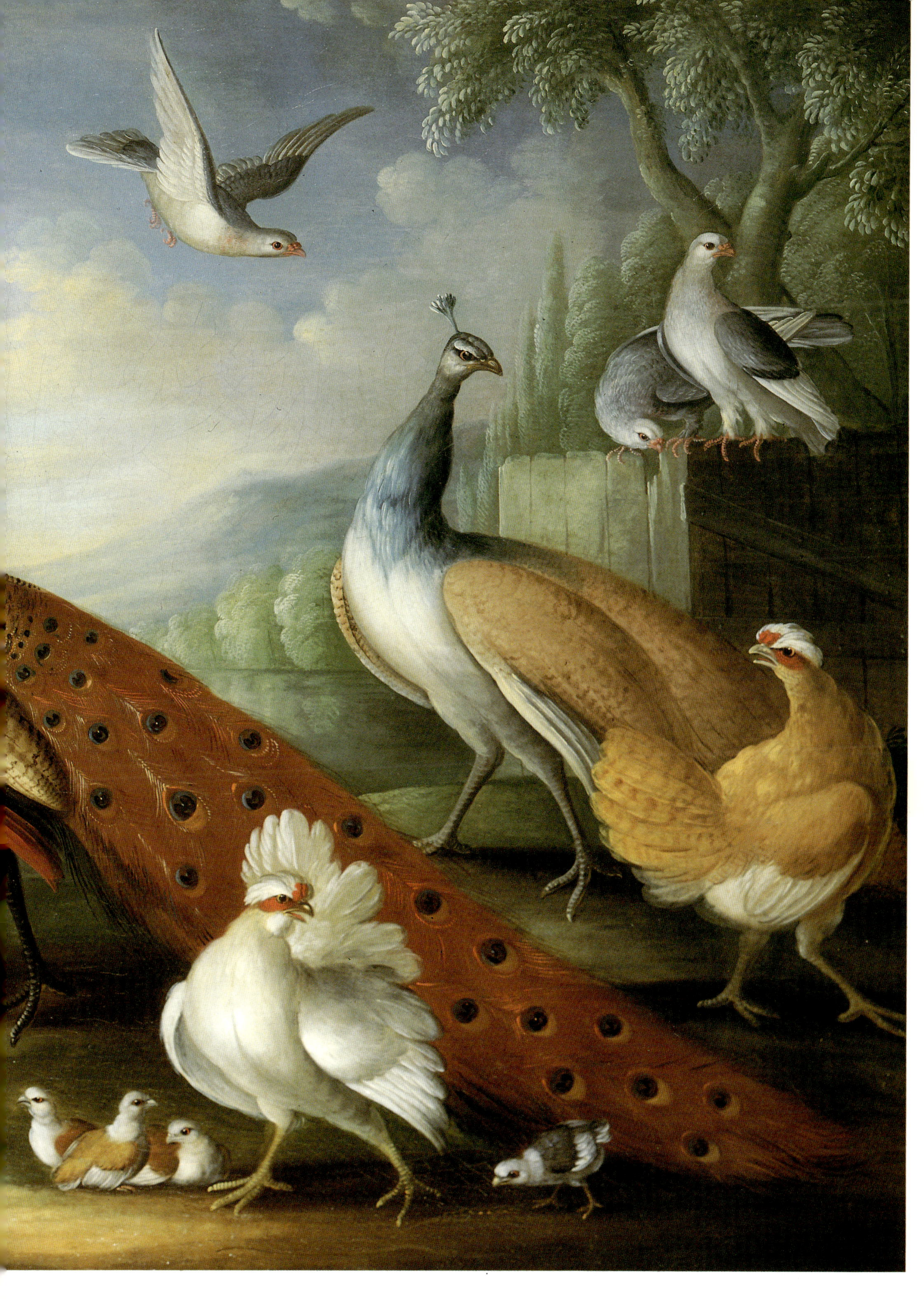

and land safely.

The Indian jungle fowl is the ancestor of the fighting cocks, barnyard fowl and all domestic varieties. Farmyard poultry has provided mankind with nutritious eggs and meat, as well as soft bedding, for thousands of years. By tradition, looking after the poultry was the housewife's responsibility, and for centuries the selective breeding of poultry in order to improve egg or meat production was ignored.

Cock-fighting is a very old sport and was well-established in Britain when Caesar invaded in 55 BC. Men bred game fowl specifically for fighting purposes. Eventually, the lessons learned in mating game fowl in order to produce the desired characteristics were adapted to breeding for meat and egg-laying qualities. Equally, plumage colour varieties were produced for both game and poultry. By the early 1600s, seven or eight different kinds of domestic fowl were known. Thomas Bewick, at the end of the eighteenth century, knew and illustrated the crested cock, hamburg cock, bantam or dwarf cock, frizzled cock, silk fowl and rumpless cocks in his *British Birds* of 1797. These were distinct from the game cocks and ordinary barnyard fowl.

Poultry breeding became of even greater interest after cock-fighting was declared illegal in Britain in 1849. Then, men who had bred the fighting cocks turned their attention to poultry, and developed distinctive named breeds. Poultry shows and clubs followed the increase in interest in distinctive types of poultry.

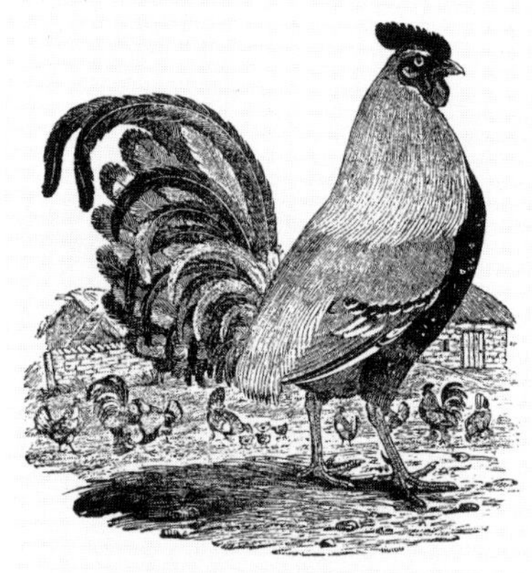

Thomas Bewick's Farmyard cock, 1797

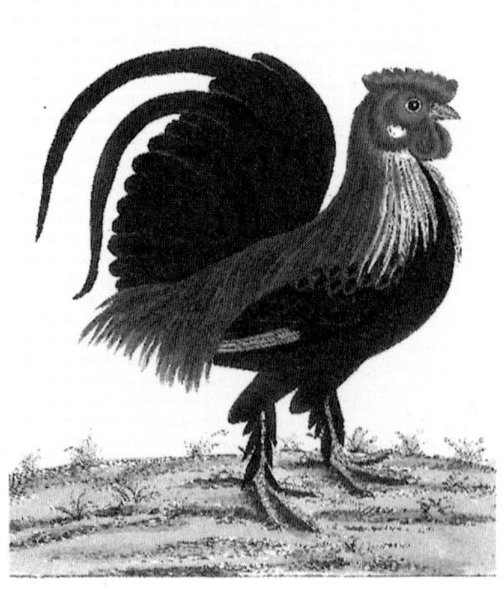

Eleazar Albin's Bantam cock, 1738

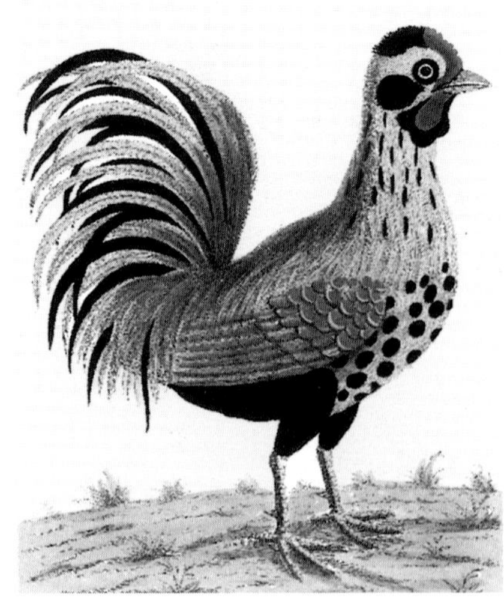

Eleazar Albin's Hamburg cock, 1738

Marmaduke Cradock
DOVECOTE AND BIRDS IN A LANDSCAPE
oil on canvas
Courtesy of Rafael Valls, London

Cradock has brought together several favourite subjects when he was painting bird
pictures at the beginning of the eighteenth century. The peacock is prominent, the
shelduck is included for its rich colouring, the cockerel for his glamorous glossy
plumage, his hen with a woolly crest matching that of the duck with a clear mallard
ancestry, and some ducklings and chickens to add charm to the scene. He has a light
background with a romantic castle and in the foreground some masonry suggestive of
a garden temple. His trees and the flowering plant, as usual, are carefully positioned
and painted both to clothe the foreground and to make the scene more intimate by
closing it in at the sides. What is different in this typical and traditional composition is
the thatched dovecote. It is made of wood, supported by a stout central pillar and
stabilised by two struts.

Hundreds of dovecotes may be seen in villages all over England, but they are more
substantial constructions built in stone and brick. These are the successors to the earlier
type of wooden dovecote which is shown in Cradock's painting. Most dovecotes are
circular in plan, perhaps following this early pattern. Wooden dovecotes of similar
design feature in Dutch and French paintings of this period. They were very significant
buildings for our ancestors and an important part of the rural economy at a time when
most of the large livestock had to be killed in the autumn before the onset of winter
when there was no fodder available for them. As a change from the salted meat during
the cold months of the year, fresh food was obtained from rabbit warrens, fish ponds
and the dovehouse.

The pigeons or doves shown here are, like all feral or domesticated doves, descended
from the common rock dove, but selective breeding has produced a pouter pigeon and
some other varieties. The terms pigeon and dove have no technical significance and are
used interchangeably throughout their world-wide range in temperate and tropical

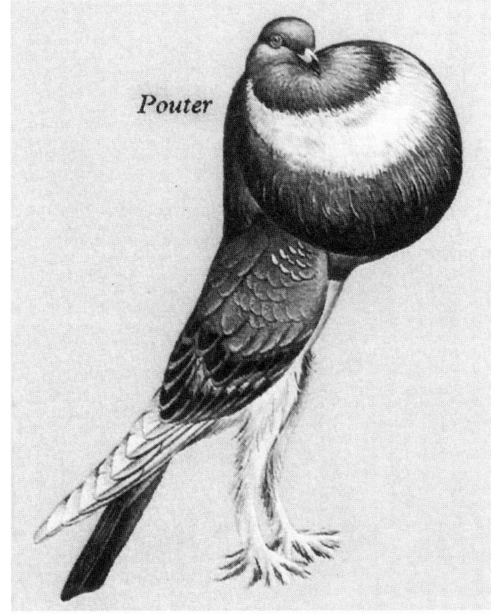

Present day pouter

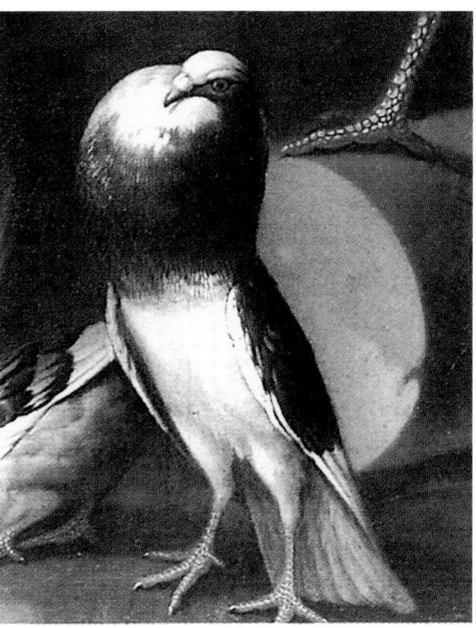

Pouter painted by Cradock

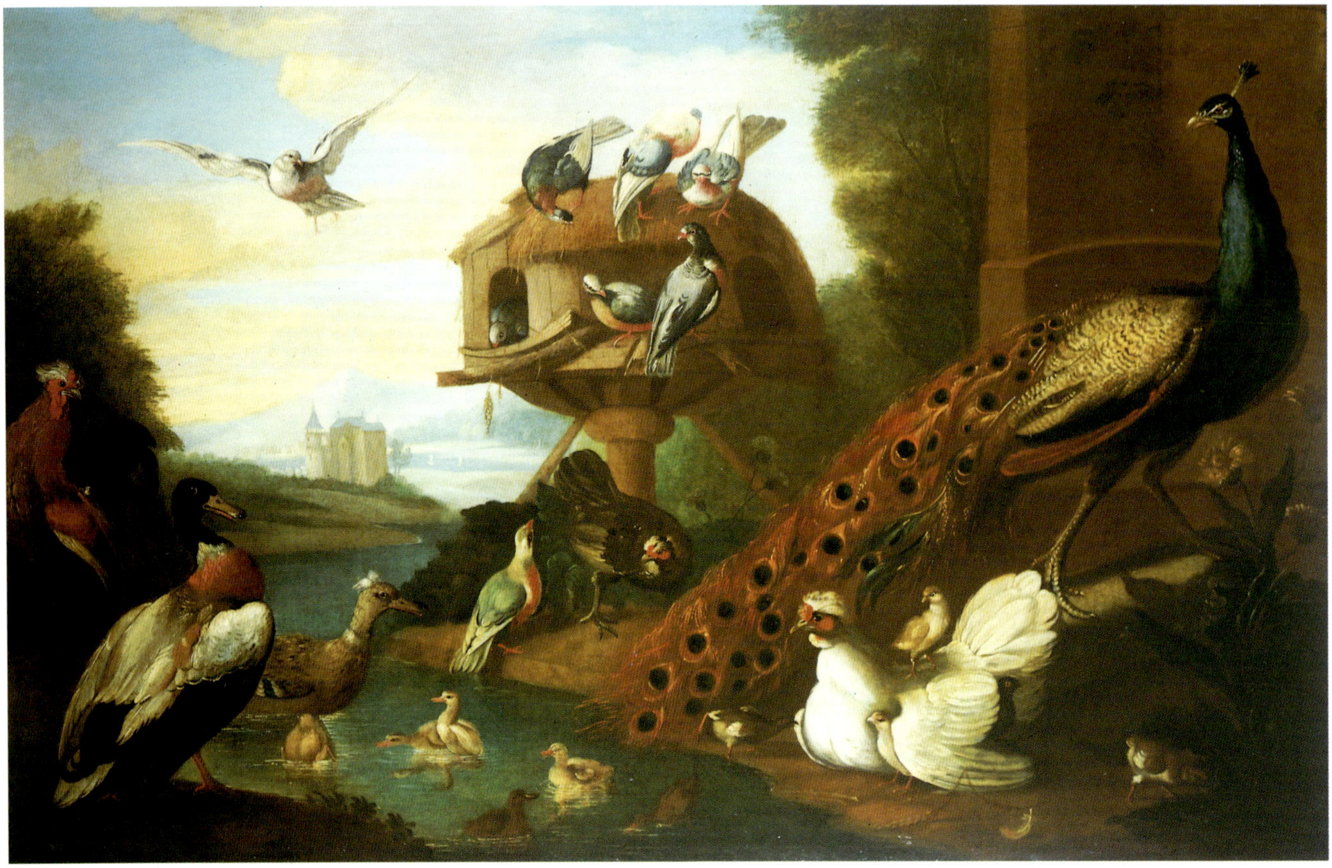

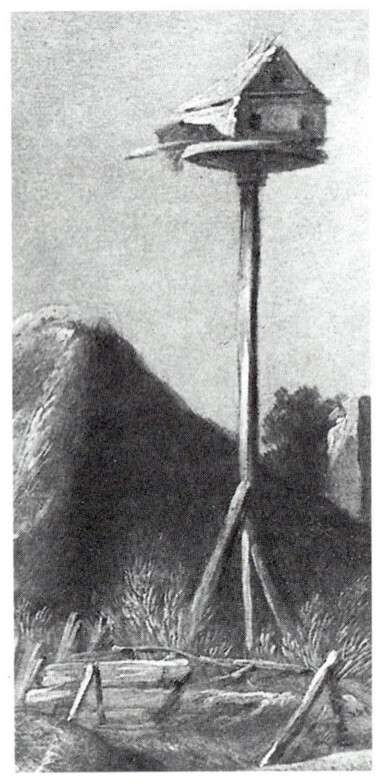

This Dutch dovecote (or 'polecote') is a 17th century wooden dove house, a much simpler design than the English one painted by Cradock or the French one painted by Oudry (page 69).

regions. They are useful birds, because they domesticate easily, and though usually only laying two eggs, they make up for this by rearing two or three broods each year. Their young when newly hatched are called squabs and are a delicate food given to invalids. Slightly older birds, before leaving the nest when they are nearly three weeks old, are 'squeakers'. They begin to breed at about nine months old and both parents brood the chicks and feed the young with a kind of curdled milk which exudes from their crop linings.

Apart from the cockerel, pigeons were probably the first birds to be domesticated. They have been raised for food, bred for the beauty of their colours and feathering and have even had their shape altered to produce bizarre forms. They have been used as carriers of messages because of their homing instincts noted in the story of Noah's sending out the dove to test whether the flood waters had subsided. They have carried messages for thousands of years, some under fire in war conditions and deserved, and got, medals for their achievements. Caesar's conquest of Gaul was notified to the Romans by means of carrier pigeons. The news of Napoleon's downfall at the Battle of Waterloo reached England in a message attached to a pigeon, four days before the human courier could cover the distance over land and sea. Sieges have been lifted when news of the plight of cities has reached the outside, carried by pigeons.

In addition pigeon posts have a very long history. Unofficially, they have been used by commercial houses, later officially by national post offices. The pigeons' urge to return home as quickly as possible, especially when they had young, was exploited to transport messages in the speediest way before aeroplanes could do this job. The homing pigeon was introduced to England by Dutch sailors in the early part of the eighteenth century and these birds were first used by stockbrokers and financiers to get market news for their businesses. Sportsmen, especially prize-fighters and gamblers, used pigeons for swift news of meetings. These were just the beginnings of the use of pigeons which expanded greatly in the next century.

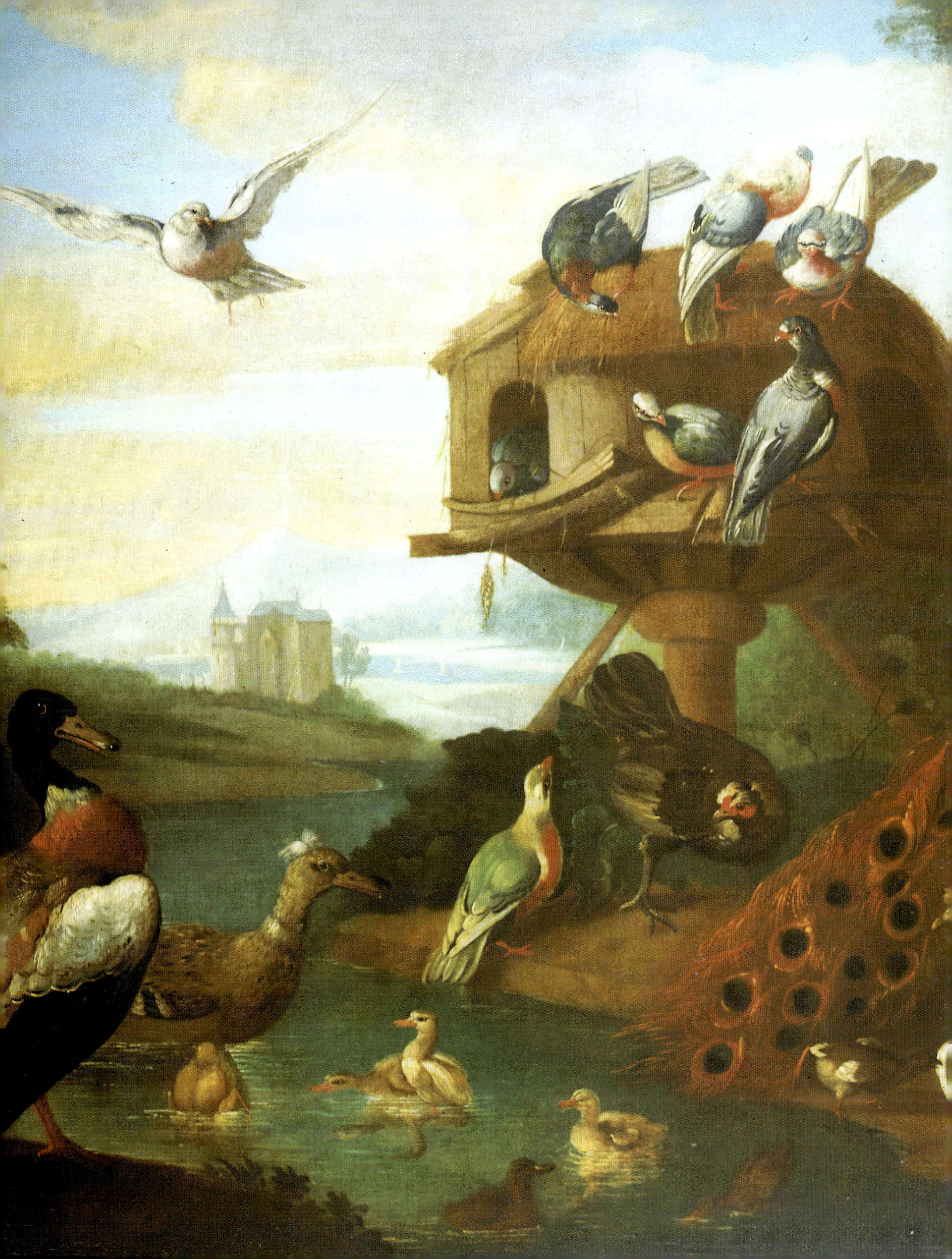

JAKOB BOGDANI
born Eperjes, Saros, Hungary 1660, died London 1724

Bogdani was reputedly a good tempered, courteous and civil man who worked in a very methodical manner, according to the season. His method was to paint 'in the Spring flowers & in the Somer flowers & Fruits when they are out Lobsters and oyster pieces. In the Winter pieces of Fowell & plate.' These were the components of his lively and very colourful canvases which were bought by kings and aristocrats in Europe, more particularly in England.

Bogdani was a Protestant and had lived in the part of Hungary which was under Catholic Hapsburg rule, while another large part of Hungary lay under Turkish rule. This may be why he left his home when he was aged twenty-three to travel to Amsterdam. He remained in Holland for about five years and learned much about the Dutch style of painting still life. He then went to England in 1688, married an Englishwoman, Elizabeth Hemmings, in 1693, and became a naturalized Englishman in 1700. He was buried at St Mary's, Finchley in north London, on 11 February 1724, two years after the death of his wife.

Bogdani assembled groups of exotic birds from all known parts of the world, placed them within an English country park setting, and painted their bright colours in a spirited, cheerful manner. His birds are flying, calling, walking, interacting one with another and present a lively group for the observer to enjoy. He used and re-used specimens, both alive and stuffed, so that at an exhibition of his paintings one soon comes to recognise the residents in captivity in English aviaries at that time. Curiously, the exotic macaws and parrots, painted from life in such a lively manner, contrast strangely with some common British species which Bogdani could have seen alive in most English gardens, yet he obviously painted them from stuffed models. He repeatedly used a stuffed great titmouse, a poor specimen, hanging upside-down from a branch; and his model bullfinch had been in his studio for some time too. They were destined to be preserved for use after Bogdani's death, because he wrote in his Will, 'all my modells I give to my said son William Bogdani and to my said son in law Tobias Stranovius and his wife and I will that the same may be divided between them by Lots and not be publickly disposed of'.

Several features of Bogdani's painting are hallmarks by which his work may be recognised. His fruits, especially the peaches and grapes frequently incorporated in his bird paintings, are so realistic as to be mouth-watering. The feathering on his birds is meticulously finely painted. His care over their anatomy and especially their legs is exemplary. But it is the eyes of his birds that are the most remarkable feature. They are painted with a *trompe-l'oeil* effect and look like small beads that could easily be picked off the canvas. In many cases, it is his manner of painting the actual small glass beads with which mounted specimens were provided for eyes which gave cause for this effect. However, even the eyes in Bogdani's living models have the same appearance.

BIRD CONCERT
oil on panel

The title of this Bogdani study of fifty European birds is *The Birds of Britain* in the National Trust brochure. However, it is so clearly a *Bird Concert*, with the long-eared owl holding a baton in its raised foot, and the notes of the music on the scroll of paper on the forest floor is so clear, that this is the title used here.

By the year 1600 the list of birds known to be British (that is they lived in Britain or spent part of the year in the British Isles) numbered 150, and by 1700 it was just over two hundred species. Bogdani's bird identification picture contained only a quarter of the birds an ornithologist could have seen and named at that date.

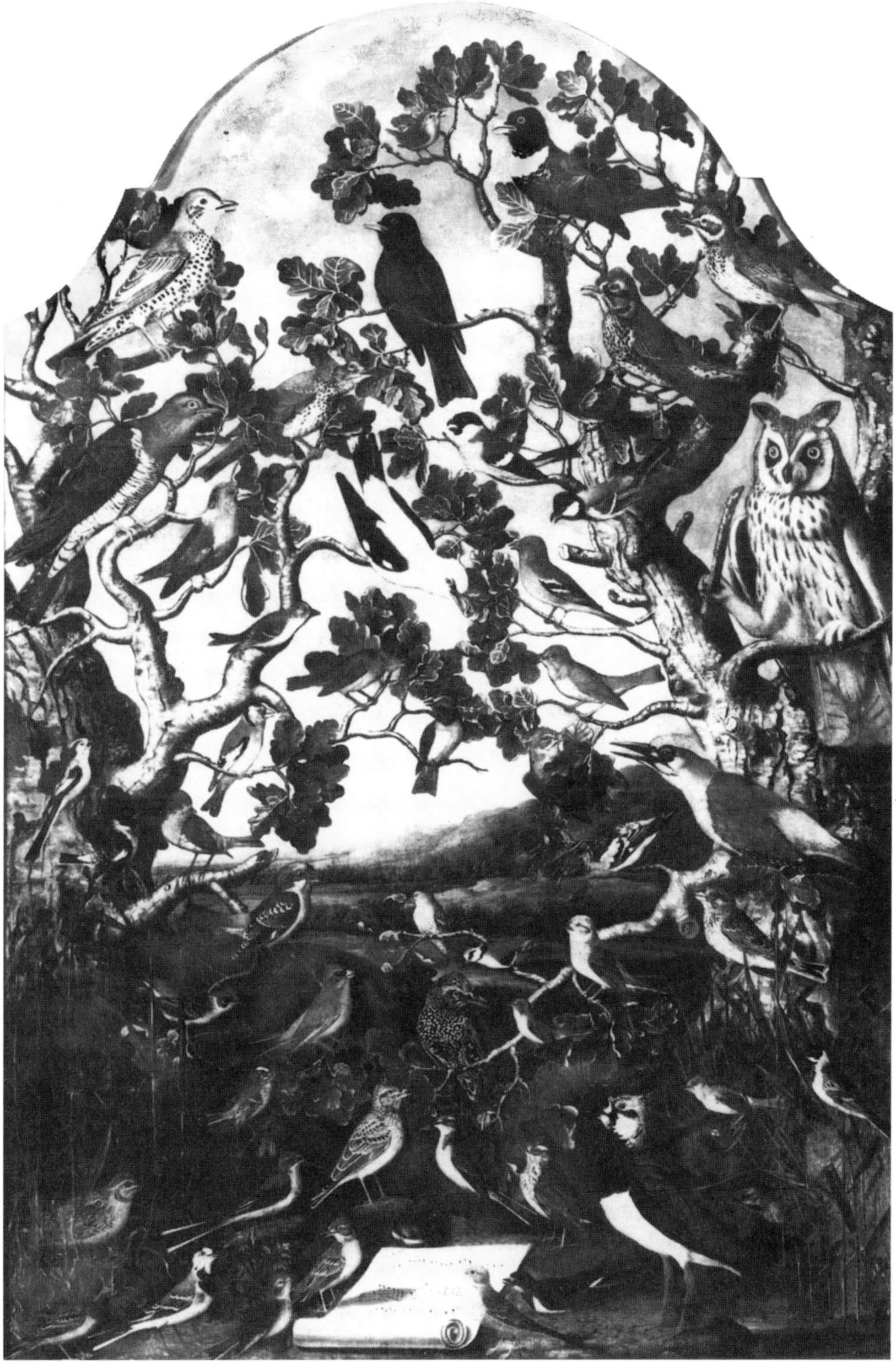

Wren
Mistle thrush
Blackbird
Fieldfare
Cuckoo
Hawfinch
Golden oriole male
Spotted flycatcher
Blackcap
Goldfinch
Long-tailed tit
Robin
Stonechat male
Red-backed shrike
Greenfinch male
Tree sparrow
Starling
Goldcrest
Skylark
Blue-headed wagtail
Grey wagtail
Quail
Meadow pipit
Pied wagtail
Linnet
Ortolan bunting female
Ring ouzel
Redwing
Song thrush
Bullfinch male
Great tit
Long-eared owl with baton
Chaffinch male
Nightingale
Redstart male
Wood warbler
Green woodpecker
Brambling male
Siskin
Corn bunting
Blue tit
Yellowhammer male
Willow warbler male
Reed bunting male
Whitethroat
Lapwing
Woodlark
Reed bunting female
Sand martin
Swallow
Cirl bunting

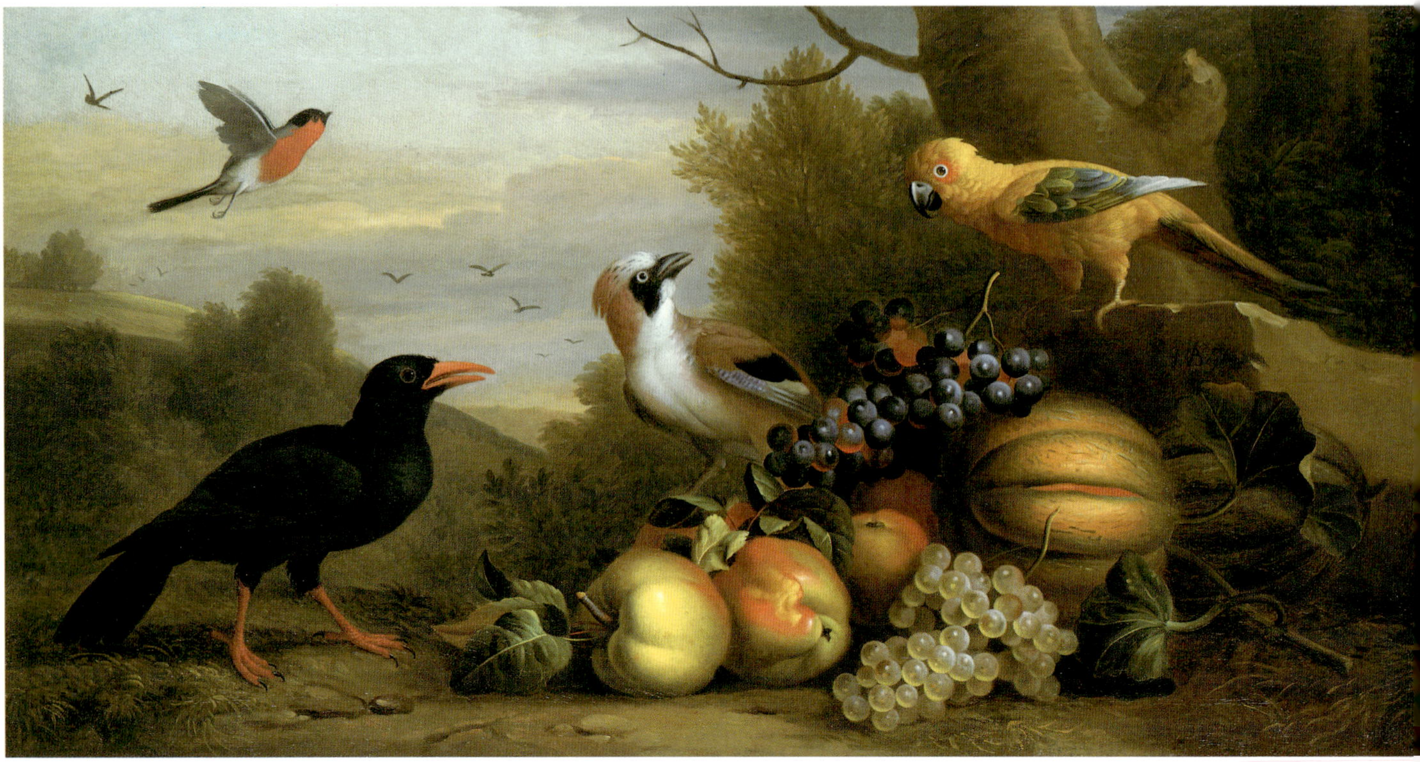

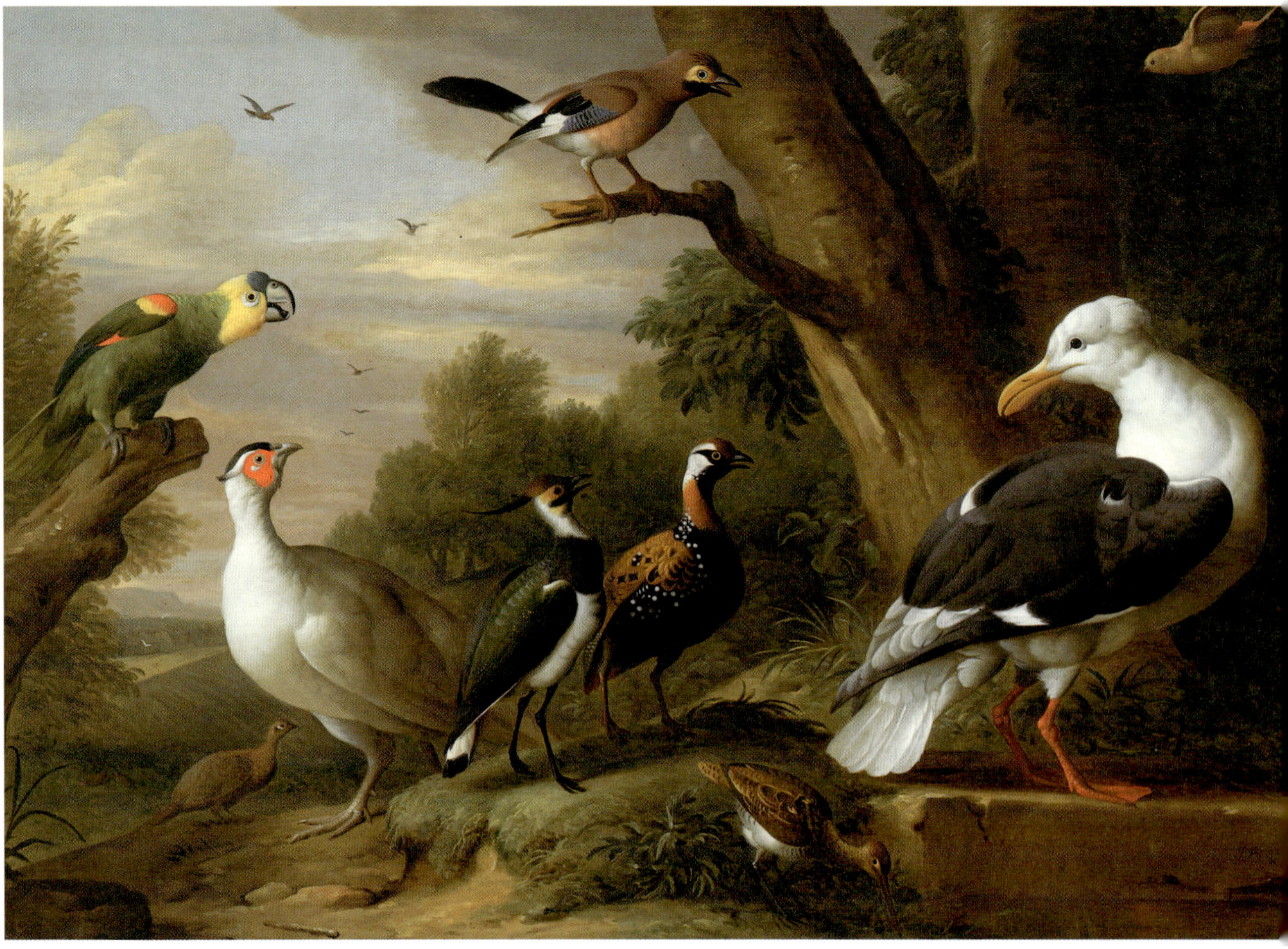

Jakob Bogdani
STILL LIFE OF FRUIT AND BIRDS IN A LANDSCAPE
signed, oil on canvas, 109 x 56 cm
Courtesy of Richard Green, London

Bogdani's fruit is always exquisitely painted, and here he groups four birds near it, complementing and accentuating the colours of the grapes, apples and pumpkin. The brightly coloured bullfinch enlivens a cloudy sky. The blue-black plumage of the chough subtly echoes the bloom on the black grapes. The jay is painted with soft colouring and feathers, but the strong beak will make short work of picking off the grapes and swallowing them whole. A sun conure is standing on the stone which bears the signature 'J Bogdani'. The yellow of the conure's plumage is carried through from the pumpkin, across the apples, and in a slender touch of sunlight on the top of the hill at the left of the picture. The reds form a curve in the opposite direction, down from the bullfinch, beak and legs of the chough, across the apples and up to the vine leaves and feathers round the eye of the conure.

The sun conure is one of the most spectacular of the neotropical parrots. When the sun catches the feathers they look like pure gold. They feed on fruit, nuts, berries and seeds in savannahs and forests along the banks of the Amazon. They are usually seen in small parties, feeding together and calling with loud screeches. Bogdani has managed to capture the glowing yellow plumage when seen in the sunlight, as well as the clear blue and green of the wings.

Jakob Bogdani
A GREAT BLACK-BACKED GULL AND OTHER BIRDS
signed, oil on canvas, 91 x 130 cm
Courtesy of Richard Green, London

In this group of *A Great Black-backed Gull and other Birds* the magnificent study of the gull is accompanied by a native snipe, lapwing, jay and a pair of pheasants, the male of which is an albino. The foreign species are a blue-fronted amazon parrot and a francolin. Black francolins or black partridges are handsome birds from Asia, and had been kept in Dutch aviaries from the middle of the previous century. The blue-fronted amazon already had a long history as a popular, good, talking pet. It was included in a painting by Hans Eworth (c.1520-1574) of William Brooke's children. It was one of the first parrots to be taken to Europe from its native South American forests.

Bogdani places items of interest at all points of the canvas, delighting the eye with colour and activity, as well as creating curiosity as to what each bird is doing. He also focuses our attention by getting us to join in with the other birds to look at the main bird in his composition. Here, all the birds which normally inhabit open fields and the edge of woodland, turn towards the seagull, as though wondering how it got where it is standing. However, the fact that the snipe has its bill half immersed in mud, and the clever manner in which Bogdani has shown the gull's red legs reflected in some water, show that it is not entirely out of its natural element. Several gulls fly inland to feed, especially in hard winters, and the great black-backed gull may be seen feeding in fields alongside black-headed, lesser black-backed, herring and common gulls in European meadows.

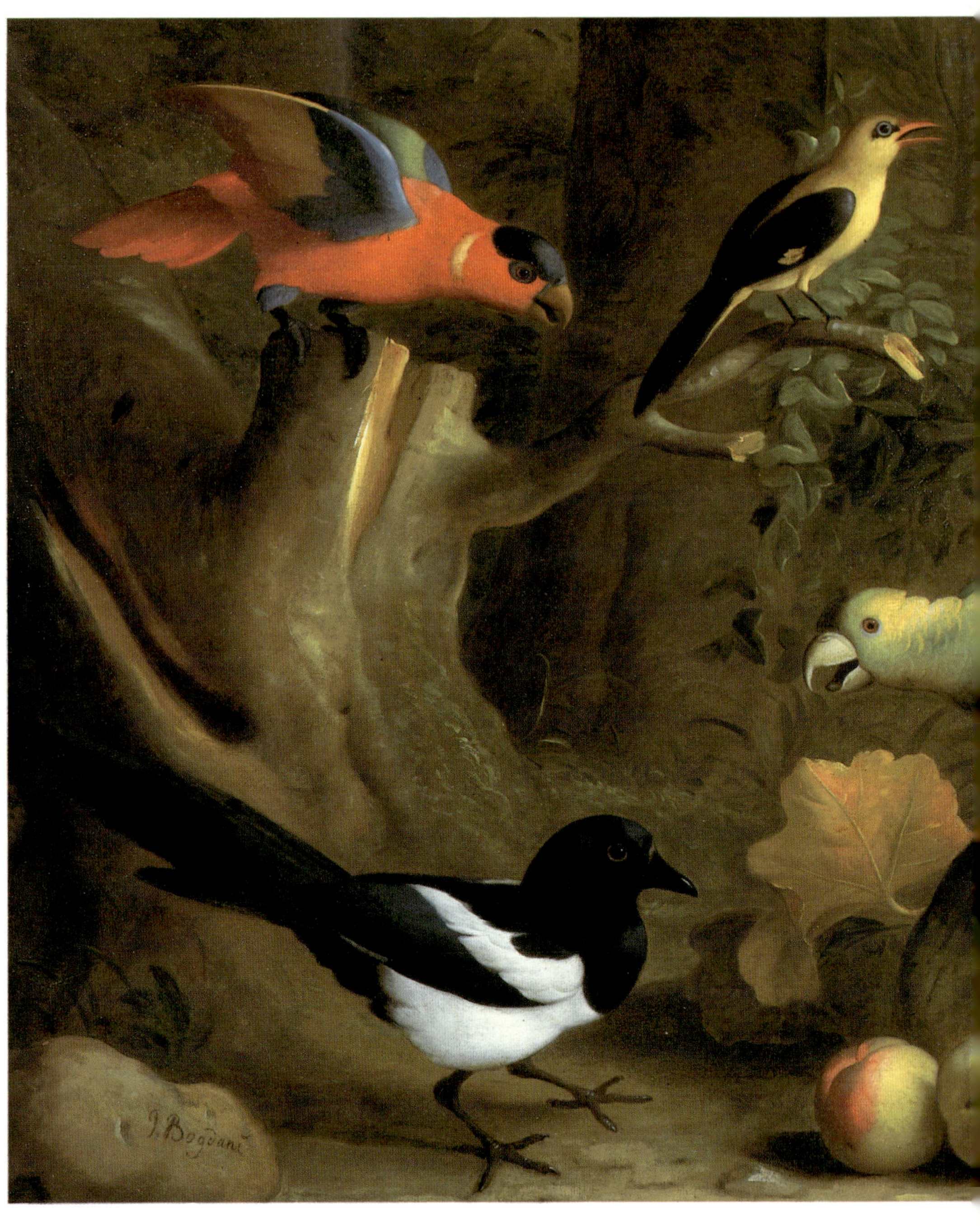

Jakob Bogdani

A SALMON-CRESTED COCKATOO WITH OTHER BIRDS, IN A
LANDSCAPE
signed, oil on canvas, 70 x 142 cm
Courtesy of Richard Green, London

Bogdani specialised in painting exotic fowls, doing some work for William III, both in
Holland and England. His bird pictures were designed for positions in the King's new
apartments at Hampton Court. Queen Anne also purchased pictures from him. She
was 'pleas'd with his performances, and encourag'd him much'. Another important
patron, who ordered a series of large canvases, was the art collector and menagerie-
keeper, Admiral George Churchill (1654-1710), a younger brother of John, Duke of

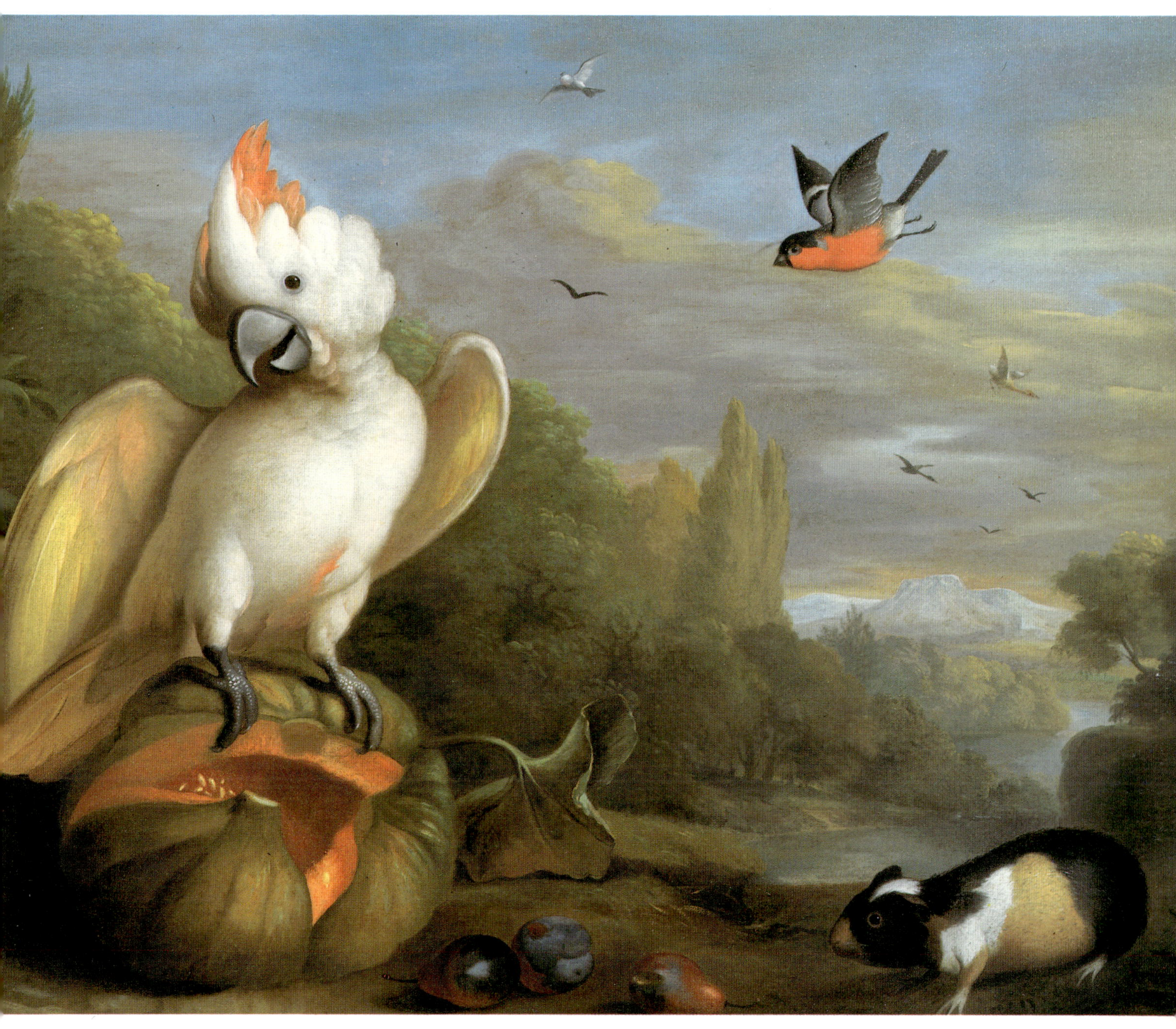

Marlborough. This series forms a unique record of George Churchill's aviary and its numerous foreign birds brought to England by the Admiral's naval friends and contacts. Churchill retired from the navy in 1708 and constructed his aviaries at his house, Ranger's Lodge, in the Little Park near Frogmore, Windsor, which had been lent to him about December 1706 by his sister-in-law, Sarah, Duchess of Marlborough. Unfortunately, he only lived two years to enjoy what was almost certainly the best collection in England of live foreign species, apart from the royal collection of Charles II, in the seventeenth or eighteenth centuries. When Churchill died on 8 May 1710 his menagerie was bequeathed to his two friends, James Butler, 2nd Duke of Ormonde and Arthur Herbert, the Earl of Torrington and a fellow Admiral of the Fleet. Queen Anne then purchased a series of seven or more canvases recording the birds in his aviary from Churchill's executors. In consequence, there is a wonderful collection of Bogdani's bird paintings in the English royal collection.

A Salmon-crested Cockatoo with other Birds is not definitely a canvas known to have been painted to record Churchill's birds. However, because Bogdani repeated the same birds, often in exactly the same poses, it is possible to compare the birds in this painting with those in Churchill's paintings in the royal collection and discover the aviary birds. Among the exotics, we know there were peacocks, guineafowl, macaws and several species of the parrot family, guan, curassow, touraco, troupial, the northern cardinal and chachalaca. Bogdani loved to paint parrots and had a superb choice of subjects from which to choose. He painted four amazons, yellow-billed, yellow-crowned, yellow-naped and blue-fronted. He had blue and gold as well as scarlet macaws and painted these with great panache. Among the lories were purple-naped and chattering lories. He also recorded sun and jandaya conures, ring-necked parakeet and red-faced lovebirds.

In this picture, with its charming landscape background, the salmon-crested cockatoo takes the centre stage. Its feathering is painted in the conventional manner and can be compared with Bimbi's unusual way of painting the feathers of the same species. Bogdani painted fruit in a most realistic manner and often included some pieces in his composition, here legitimately, for parrots are fruit-eaters. The head and neck of a blue-fronted amazon appear to the left of the cockatoo, and a magpie stands on the ground. Above it, a purple-naped lory, which came from the Indonesian islands of Ceram and Amboina, was carefully positioned so as to reveal the purple cap, red body with a variable yellow band across the breast, purple thigh feathering and, very astutely, both the underwing and top wing feathers. The green wings have underwing coverts of blue.

Apart from the bullfinch flying uncomfortably in from the right, Bogdani has painted another brilliantly coloured European species, the golden oriole, a very shy bird. It is widely distributed in Europe and breeds in very small numbers locally in south-eastern England.

Guinea pigs, long bred in Peru, were introduced into Europe in the mid-1500s and charmed their way into flower paintings, bird paintings and other genre scenes very soon afterwards.

ALEXANDRE FRANCOIS DESPORTES
born Champagne 1661, died Paris 1743

Desportes, Oudry and Chardin were the three great French still life painters of birds in the eighteenth century. By the age of twelve, Desportes was in Paris to stay with an uncle and while there was seriously ill. During his convalescence a talent for drawing became apparent and he was placed in the studio of Nicasius Bernaert. At this date, the court, with the Paris Academy of Painting (founded by the King in 1648) held the monopoly of teaching and exhibitions following a decree by the King in 1663 that all the King's painters must enroll in the Academy. Several flower and animal specialists enrolled, among them Bernaert. Desportes entered the Academy in 1699 and was destined to inaugurate the golden period of French still life painting which was later continued by Oudry and then given its final and most glorious period by Chardin.

Desportes travelled for a while and served a period at the court of King Jan Sobieski in Poland, painting portraits of the King's family. He obtained French royal favour when he returned to Paris in 1696 and became a councillor at the Academy in 1704. Still wishing to widen his experience, he obtained permission to work in England and was employed by Lord Burlington in 1712. On his return to Paris, he was commissioned by the king to record the rare animals in the royal menagerie. When seeking exotic backgrounds, he visited the gardens of the Jardin des Plantes and included some remarkable tropical plants growing there in these two pictures.

There was a regency under the Duc d'Orléans following the death of Louis XIV in 1715 which lasted until the young Louis XV began his reign in 1723. Desportes continued to serve the crown and he also helped to decorate the châteaux at Auet, Chantilly, Muette, Bouillon, Clichy and Marly as well as continuing his work in the menagerie. He was considered to be eccentric when he worked in the open air among the animals. Another distinction (which he shared with J. B. Oudry) was that he was one of the first French painters to introduce landscapes behind his fruit and game.

BIRDS IN EXOTIC LANDSCAPES
Pair of oval oils on panel, 113 x 133.4 cm
Courtesy of Richard Green, London

The two oval paintings reproduced here show several of these characteristics. The birds have been given an open air situation, with rocks, trees and water, with a romantic landscape and beautiful sunny blue sky. The presentation is purely decorative with the birds being fitted into the oval shape and exotic setting regardless of whether they would normally associate in the wild. They have been painted with a true French feeling for elegant rhythm and graceful lines.

Working to a commission sometimes restricted the artist not just to the subject, in this case portraits of several new birds added to the menagerie, but frequently the patron also stated that he wanted a matching pair of pictures of a given dimension to fit spaces in a room he needed to decorate. These could either be large canvases or lesser 'cabinet' paintings as they were called when required to fill a space on the wall of a smaller room such as a boudoir. Desportes' two oval pictures were of this last type.

For reasons of prestige and prices charged, artists often preferred to paint the large canvases which hung in the main rooms and demanded correspondingly 'important' subjects like heroic battle scenes and historical events. The cabinet pictures were for less important, more private rooms and their subjects became associated in people's minds with 'less important' motifs – birds included. During the eighteenth century the huge canvases of birds which de Hondecoeter and other seventeenth century artists had been commissioned to paint were less frequently in demand as fashions changed. Bird

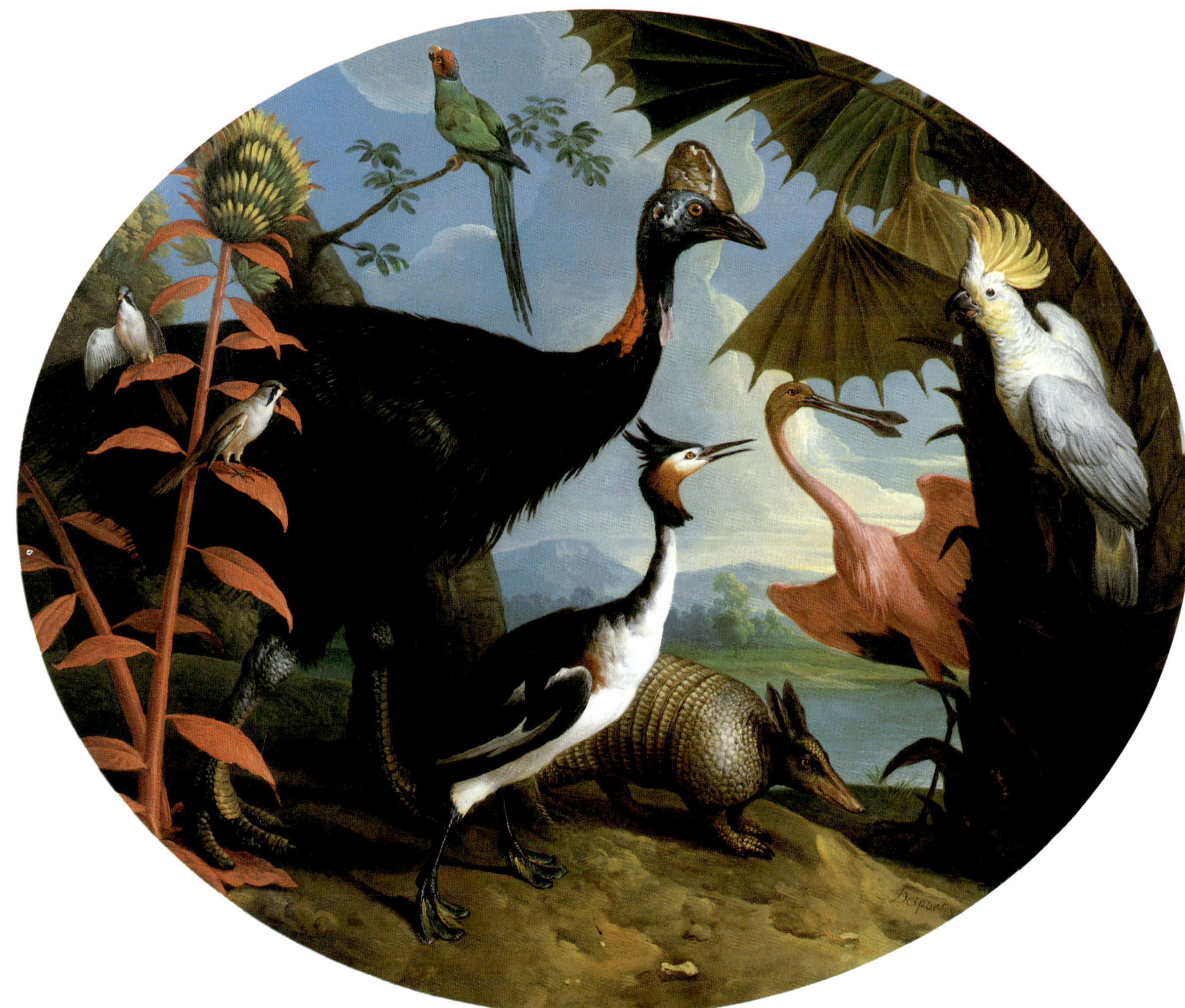

pictures became associated with other 'genre' pictures on a smaller scale. The seeds were sown here for many of the bird artists' later problems in being classed as less important painters than portraitists, landscapists and painters of history. When bird artists struggled to remedy this situation in the nineteenth century, only those who were also proficient landscapists had any chance of selling or exhibiting a large painting with birds in it.

Louis XV took little interest in the royal menagerie and Desportes became more involved in designing for the Gobelins factory. There he incorporated designs for some very dramatic tapestries with a large number of animal and vegetable species from both the Old World and the New.

In the painting of *A Flamingo and King Vulture*, it is the vulture which is the most extraordinary bird to our eyes. The greater flamingo is a European bird, and one of the

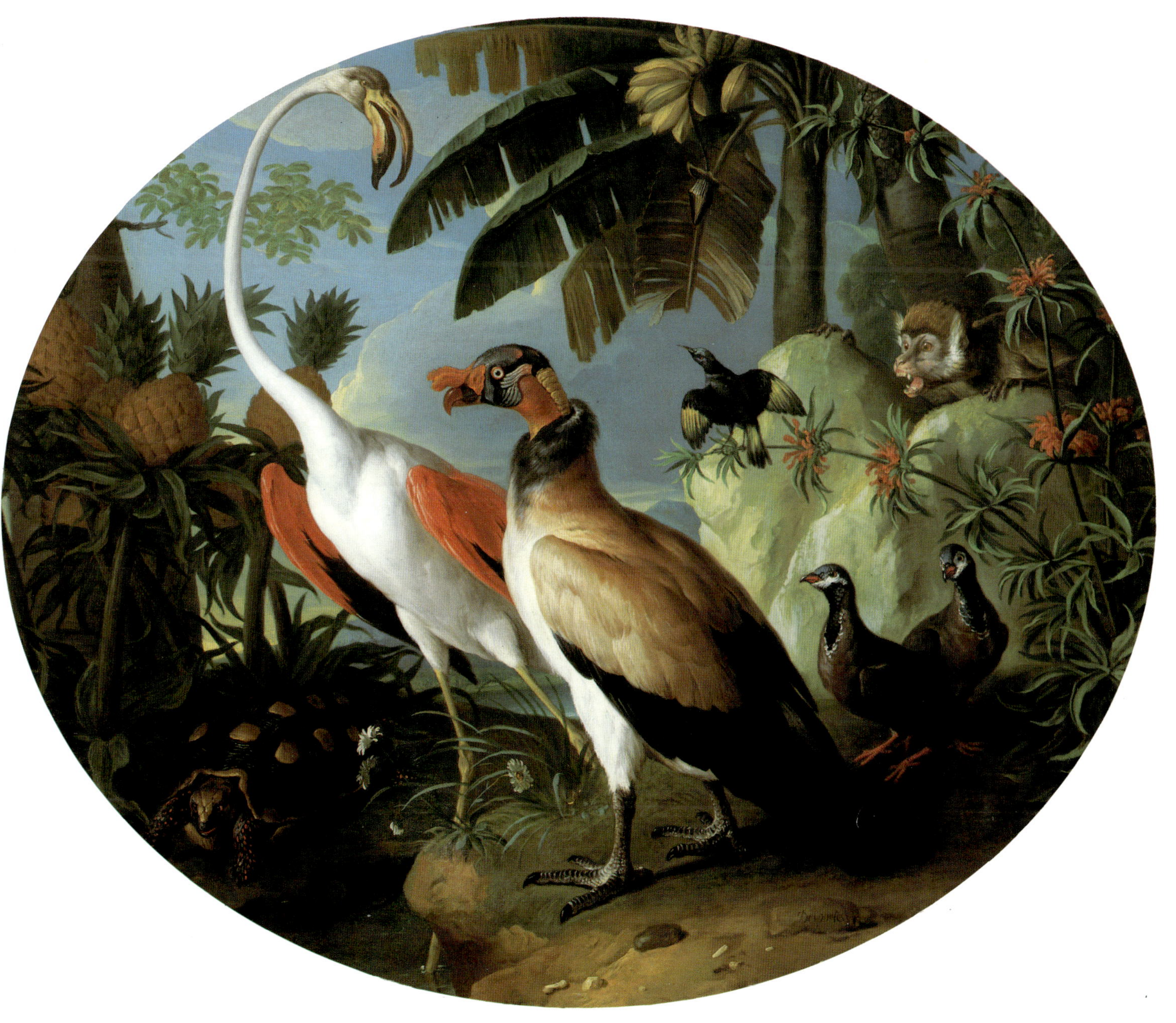

most unusual of all birds because its neck and legs are longer in proportion to its body than that of any other species. However, it would have been more familiar to the French, even in the eighteenth century when it was painted, than the king vulture from South America. So great was the impact of this bird on those who were allowed to see it in the menagerie that two other eminent bird artists painted it. Jean Baptiste Oudry's *Flamingo and Condor* (*sic*, king vulture) is in the Muséum National d'Histoire Naturelle, Paris, and Jan Weenix's *Japanese Crane and King Vulture* is in the National Gallery of Ireland. Weenix made it the central figure in at least two more of his canvases. This king vulture is in excellent condition, and Desportes has painted the fine feathering almost as though it were soft hair. He has paid great attention to the naked head where the skin is brilliantly coloured in purples, greens and yellows, with the addition of a wattle over its beak, none of which shows until the bird is in its full adult plumage which it acquires when three to four years old. It lives in tropical rain forests from southern Mexico down to Argentina. At 82.1 cm (32 ins) long, it is the third largest of the New World vultures, only being exceeded by two species of condor.

The cassowary would have been taken to France from New Guinea, along with the sulphur-crested cockatoo, while the plum-headed parakeet would have been picked up at a port en route home. These were all, by now, well recorded pictorially. The bearded reedlings and great crested grebe were native French birds, but the lovely roseate spoonbill was a rarity indeed, brought from the eastern coast of the Americas or the West Indies. It migrated down the eastern coast to winter in the south, returning to Florida each spring to nest in colonies, thousands strong.

The birds, monkey, armadillo and tortoise were choice exhibits in the menagerie and an interesting record of their presence there. Not intended to be a record of species from a specific region, they were grouped on purely decorative lines. Similarly the plants, including a fan palm, banana tree and pineapples growing on exceedingly long stalks, had been selected on account of their interesting shapes and colours, besides their rarity. Art triumphs over science in these compositions.

CARL WILHELM DE HAMILTON
born Brussels 1668, died Augsburg 1754

Carl Wilhelm was the third son of James de Hamilton who emigrated to Brussels, and was the brother of Ferdinand Philipp (see page 45). He was taught by his father and became a painter of mammals, and birds which he painted as the main subject in his pictures, with small lizards and insects for additional interest. He placed plants in the foreground and was especially fond of large clumps of sea-kale.

He worked for many years at Baden-Baden before moving to Augsburg where he became a court painter to Bishop Alexander Sigismund and is renowned for his paintings of the Bishop's horses. Dozens of his oil sketches are preserved in Karlsruhe and this is the medium in which he preferred to work, whether making small studies or large paintings.

THE PARLIAMENT OF BIRDS

The subjects for the paintings, *Parliament of Birds*, *Mobbing the Owl*, and *Concert of Birds*, are all based on the observation that many birds are highly sociable and because they sing, and also otherwise communicate by chattering, whistling and calling, they, like us, will occasionally gather together for a discussion. This may have been in order to select a king (see *The Fable of the Raven*, page 55), to be mischievous or protective (see *Mobbing the Owl*, page 63) or for communal singing (see *Bird Concert*, page 31), or to discuss more weighty matters as in this *Parliament of Birds*. Geoffrey Chaucer wrote a seven hundred line poem with this same title, about 1380, in which he described a vision of the 'court of nature' on St Valentine's day 'when every fowl cometh there to choose his mate'. It was an orderly affair with the birds knowing their proper places. Chaucer said that the birds of the raven-kind sat in the highest position, just as Hamilton has the magpie and crow at the top of the tree in his picture. Next came small birds, seen here in the branches of the tree. Chaucer's 'foul that liveth by seed sat on the grene', while the water fowl 'sat lowest in the dale'. Chaucer itemised thirty-six species, giving preference to the royal bird, the eagle, who would choose his mate first, and then 'by order shall the rest' choose. Before they departed, the small birds sang:

> 'Now welcome summer, with thy sun soft
> That has this winter's storms shaken off
> And driven away the long nights black.'

Gathering to select a mate would suggest both males and females would be present, and in some numbers if a true choice were to be made. However, that did not suit the purpose of a bird painter, for he wanted to include as many different species as possible. Hamilton's *Parliament of Birds*, with a Speaker or President in charge of proceedings in the form of an eagle (ably assisted by a scribe, an owl), looks more like a debate. Judging from the number of birds with their beaks open, this is a lively discussion with several birds speaking at once. The result must have been something like 'Question Time' in the British Parliament's House of Commons.

In Hamilton's picture, the two non-European species are the two Chaucer also included in his poem, the peacock and the 'popinjay' or parrot, in this case a scarlet and a blue and gold macaw. Through much of the eighteenth century, the scarlet macaw was regarded as the male and the blue and gold macaw the female of the same macaw species.

Hamilton has over sixty bird species in his versions of *Parliament of Birds*, all astonishingly well posed and painted so that they can be identified.

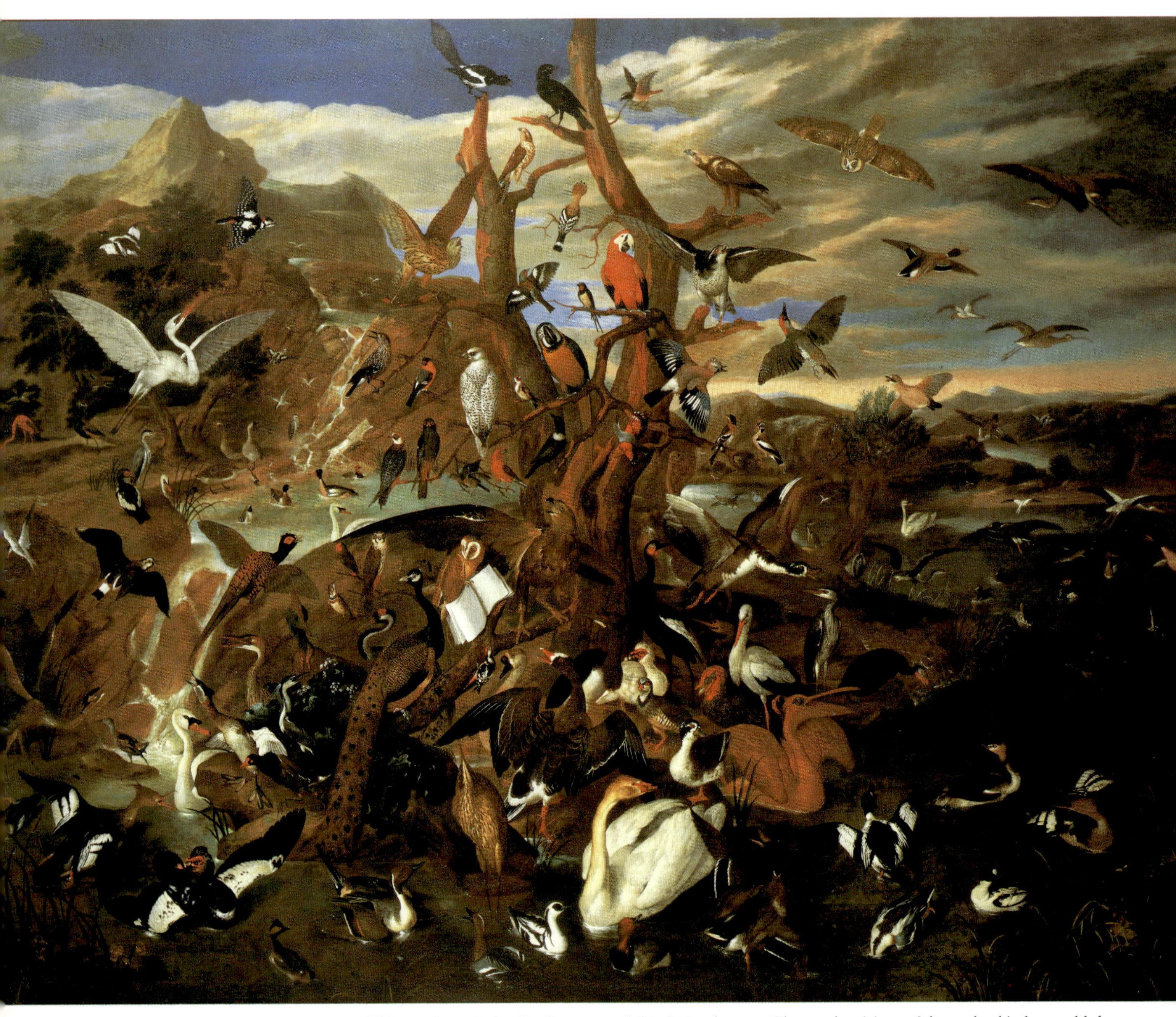

This version of the Parliament of Birds is close to Chaucer's vision of how the birds would be assembled, with the members of the crow family at the top of the tree, small song birds in lower branches, 'seed-eaters' on the ground, and waterfowl at the bottom of the picture. The wise owl is the secretary to this parliament, presided over by the eagle who is speaking vigorously on some subject.

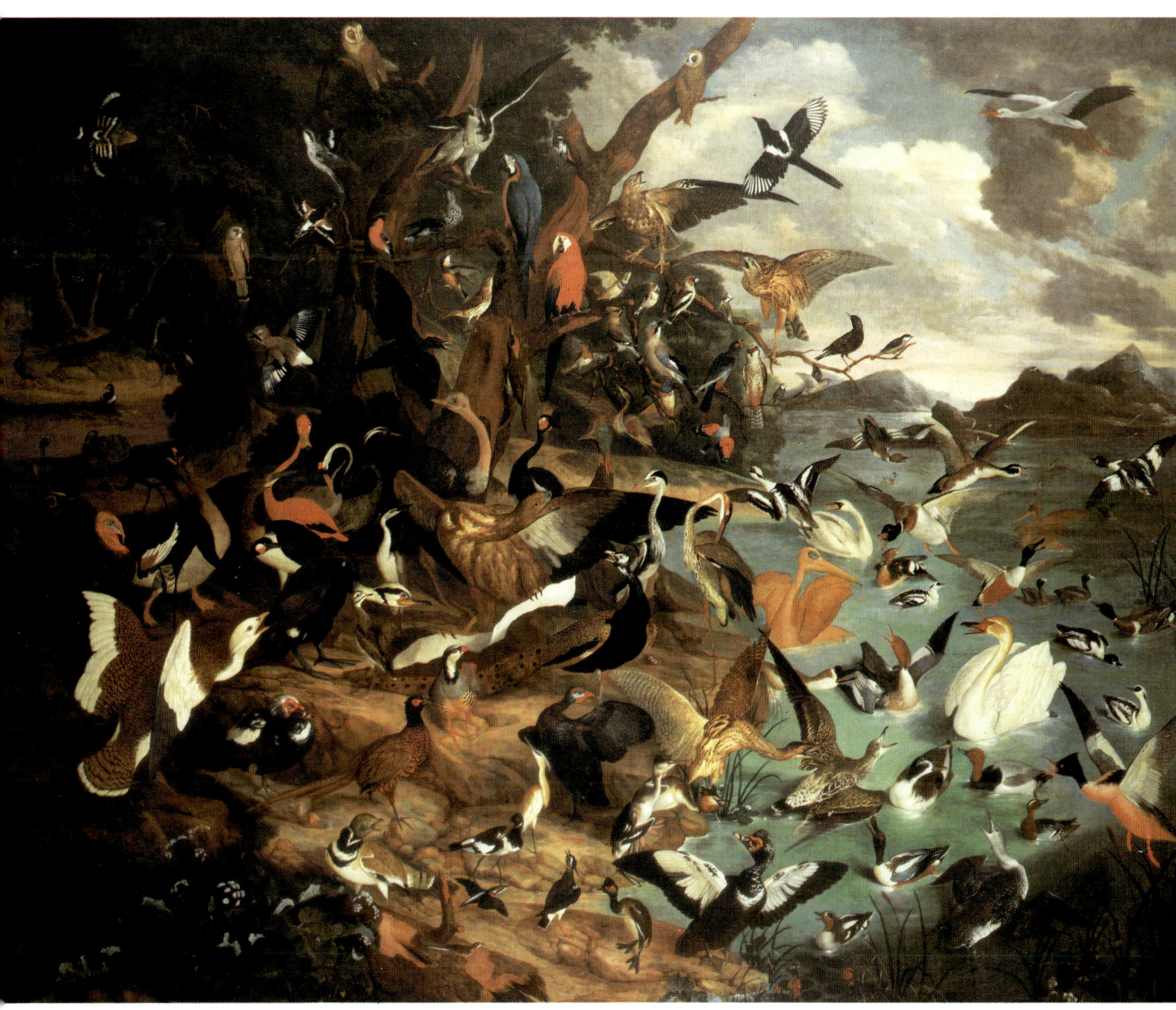

To paint some seventy different birds of varying sizes, and take into account their relative distance from the viewer, in addition to making them lively, recognisable species, is no mean feat. This is the work of an accomplished bird artist, and, in addition, a good landscapist.

1. Magpie 2. Crow 3. Redstart
4. Goldeneye 5. Spotted Woodpecker
6. Kite 7. Hawk 8. Hoopoe
9. Black kite 10. Long-eared owl
11. Purple heron 12. Curlew
13. Ring ouzel 14. Mallard
1 5. Goshawk 16. Scarlet macaw
17. Swallow 18. Chaffinch
19. White stork 20. Flamingo
21. Heron 22. Nutcracker
23. Bullfinch 24. Gyrfalcon
25. Goldfinch 26. Blue and gold
macaw 27. Jay 28. Green
woodpecker 29. Brambling
30. Wallcreeper 31. Hawfinch
32. Hobby 33. Red-footed falcon
34. Crossbill 35. Goosander
36. Mute swans 37. Red-faced
lovebird 38. Barn owl President
39. Pheasant 40. Bluethroat
41. Crane 42. Cassowary head
43. Peacock 44. Lapwing 45. Tern
46. Great crested grebe 47. Water
rail 48. Red-breasted merganser
49. Muscovy duck 50. Black-necked
grebe 51. Pintail duck
52. Garganey 53. Smew 54. Pochard
55. Mallard 56. Goldeneyes 57. Swan
58. Goose 59. Bittern 60. Pelican
61. Rock partridge 62. Crowned
crane 63. Guinea fowl 64. White
stork 65. Heron 66. Eagle

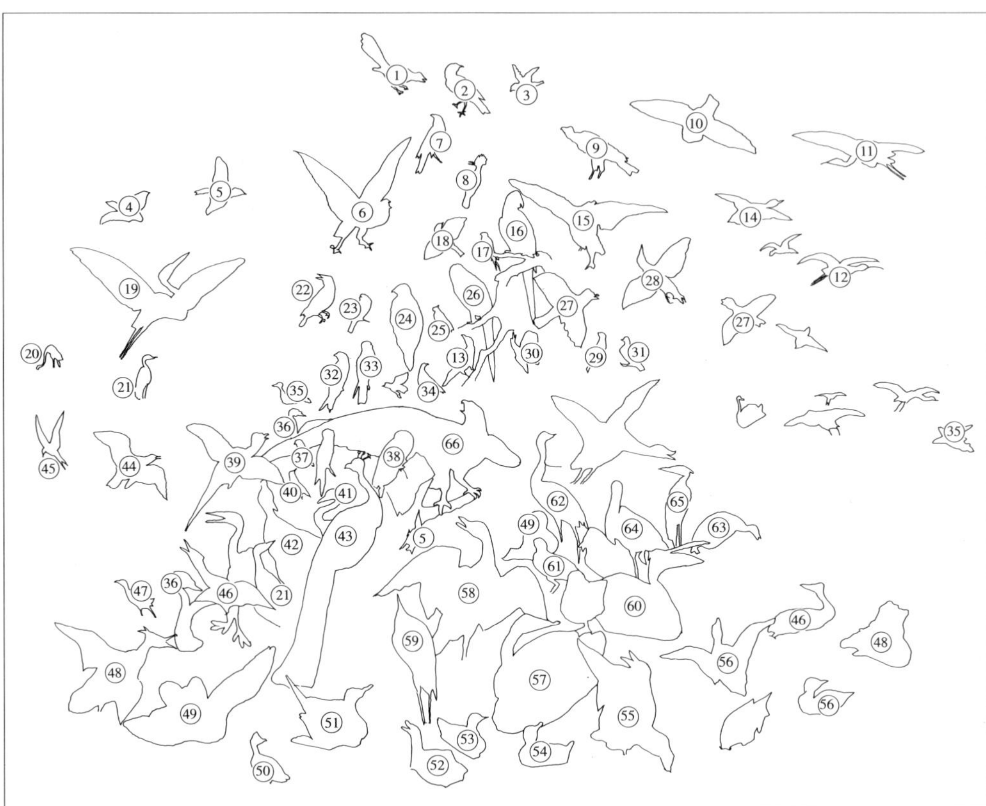

Hamilton Parliament of birds (see page 42)

1. Hoopoe 2. Barn owl 3. Great
grey shrike 4. Brambling 5. Kestrel
6. Jay 7. Black woodpecker 8.Bullfinch
9. Song thrush 10. Nutcracker
11. Osprey 12. Blue and gold macaw
13. Scarlet macaw 14. Woodpecker
15. Long-eared owl 16. Magpie
17. White stork 18. Eagle 19. Kite
20. Bluethroat 21. Goldfinch
22. Hawfinch 23. Crested tit
24. Robin 25. Waxwing 26. Smew
27. Red-footed falcon 28. Hobby
29. Starling 30. Great tit
31. Wallcreeper 32. Purple heron
33. Cassowary head 34. Crowned
crane 35. Green woodpecker 36. Ostrich
37. Demoiselle crane 38. Crane
39. Flamingo 40. Goose 41. Turkey
42. Bustard 43. Muscovy 44. Pheasant
45. Rock partridge 46. Golden
Eagle President 47. Little bustard
48. Wagtail 49. Kingfisher
50. Oystercatcher 51. Squacco heron
52. Black-necked grebe 53. Guineafowl
54. Lapwing 55. Great crested
grebes 56. Bittern 57. Gull (immature)
58. Teal 59. Shoveller 60. Garganey
61. Pochard 62. Goosander
63. Goldeneye 64. Mute sawn
65. Pelican 66. Mallard 67. Pair
of coots 68. Grey heron 69. Peacock
70. Cormorant

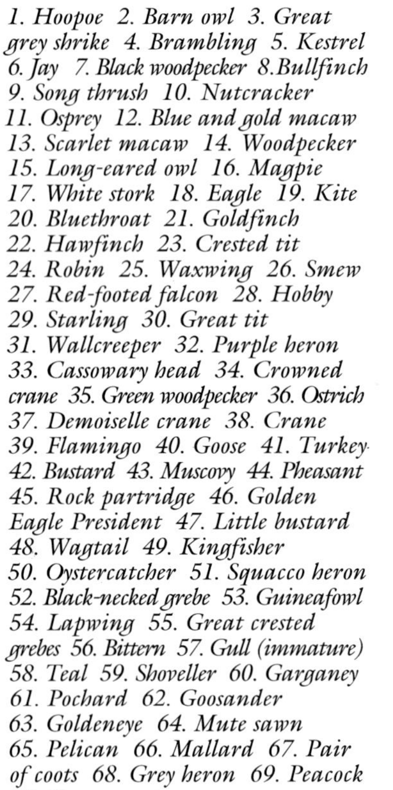
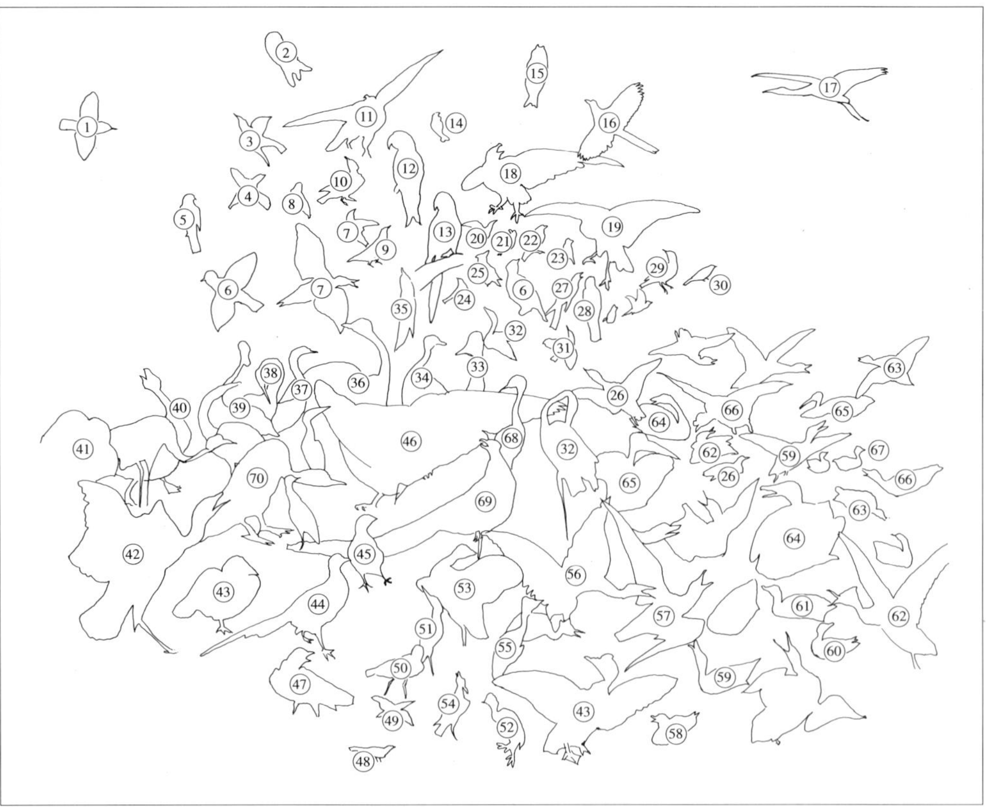

Hamilton Parliament of birds (see page 43)

FERDINAND PHILIPP DE HAMILTON
born Brussels 1664, died Vienna 1750

Ferdinand was the eldest son of James Hamilton (1640-1720), a Scotsman of Fife who fled to Brussels a little while before 1664. Two more sons were born in Brussels, Johann Georg and Carl Wilhelm, and all three adopted the Flemish/Dutch form of their names and were trained by their father to become still life painters. The subject matter and style of their pictures reflected their upbringing among the numerous examples of Dutch still life masterpieces.

They painted fruit and insects, and game, including birds, both live and dead. Ferdinand is considered to be the most talented of the family and his work is widely represented in European museums following his employment by three monarchs in Vienna. With his brother Johann, he was appointed court painter to Joseph I (reigned 1705-11), and then Charles VI (1711-40), finally to the Empress Maria Theresa (reigned 1740-80).

SHELDUCK, EURASIAN PURPLE GALLINULE, KINGFISHER
AND WHITE-HEADED DUCKS
oil on canvas, 122.2 x 142.8 cm

Courtesy of Rafael Valls, London

Ferdinand Hamilton's choice of birds is different from the usual selection of peacocks, hens and ducks. This picture of *Shelduck, Eurasian Purple Gallinule...* is a lively painting with only four species of birds, but one of them is of particular interest. The shelduck and kingfisher had already featured in many paintings, and the Eurasian purple gallinule had been represented in Brueghel's *Noah's Ark* over a century before this. The glowing deep blue purple of these birds attracted several artists who found that the red legs and facial shield, also the contrasting white undertail coverts, provided valuable colour points in their compositions.

Several features make the shelduck a distinctive and thus easily recognisable bird. It is boldly marked, and so large a duck that it is almost a goose in size. Male shelduck have a glossy green head and neck with a red bill that has a knob at the base. A wide band of chestnut coloured feathers around the breast and back breaks up the largely white body. Some more glossy green plumage occurs on the belly and leading edge of the wing.

Shelducks are seen mostly on flat, sandy shores in bays and estuaries but also occur on lakes near to the sea. In the brackish water they find small lobsters, shrimps, worms and molluscs. They also eat grass and weeds, which they find close to the shore on coastal fields.

They usually nest in rabbit burrows in dunes, sometimes as much as eight to ten feet at the end of the tunnel. They also nest under hollow trees or under rocks. The female incubates eight to fifteen creamy-white, glossy eggs, while the male remains on guard nearby. When the ducklings hatch, they are covered in black and white down. While all ducklings are totally delightful little birds, young shelducks are among the most attractively patterned. As soon as all the ducklings have hatched, a matter of hours, they are led out of the burrow and marched, sometimes on a long hike, to the nearest water and saltings where they can find food. The parents remain with them for a while, then a crèche is formed from many families and only a few adults remain with the young birds. At the end of a couple of months they are independent. This is the time when the adults flock together in safe areas in order to moult. In July, large flocks build up in Bridgwater Bay, Somerset and in the Waddenzee area. They disperse for the winter, when they can fly again, but may re-congregate in hard weather in more favourable,

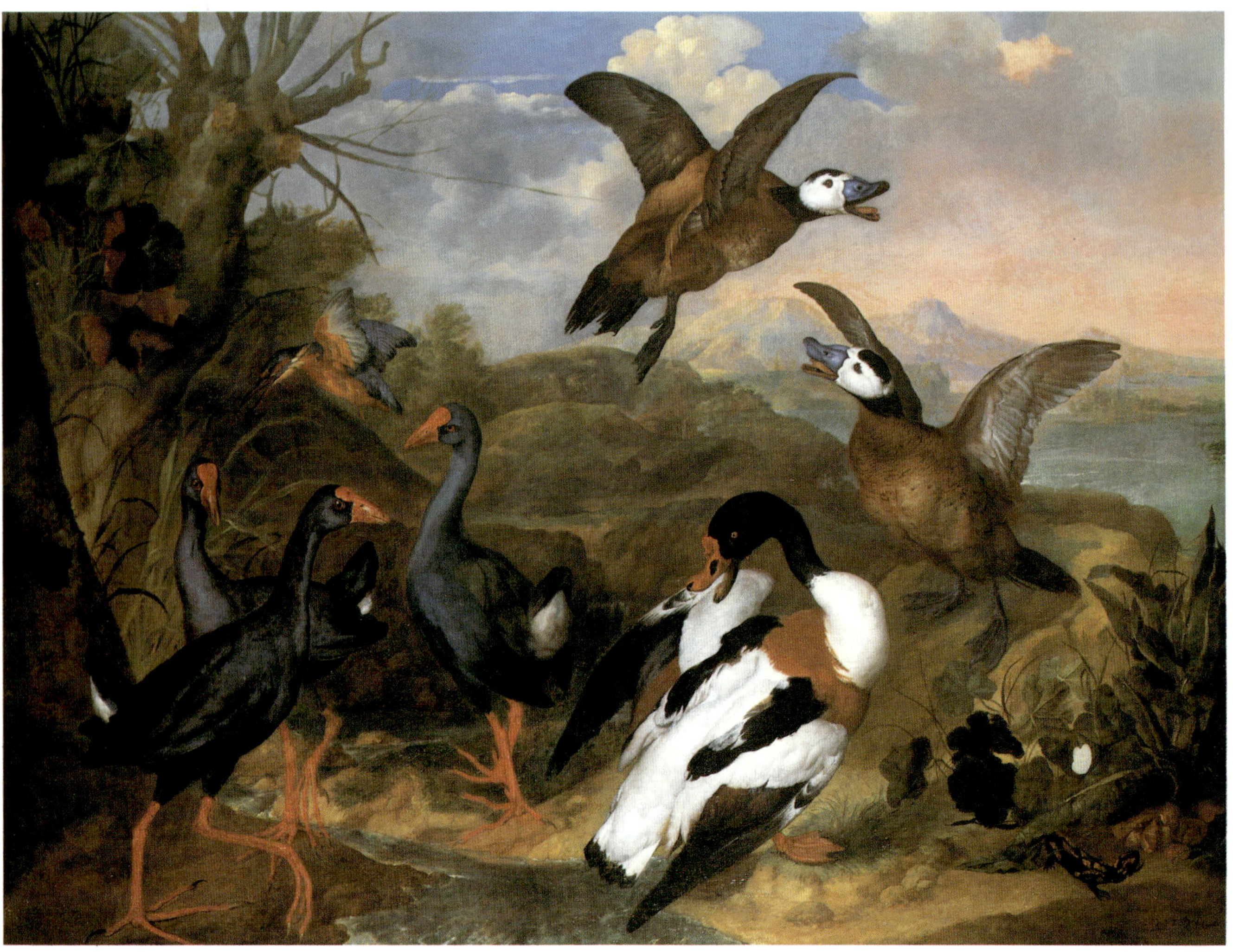

southern parts of Europe and the east, as far as north-western India. In North America this species is called the northern shelduck and is kept in aviaries among other exotic waterfowl, but has not become established in the wild.

In this mellow painting with its soft light, the birds which first demand attention are the white-headed ducks, particularly the one on the wing. This diving duck occurs very locally in southern Spain, Sicily, and north Africa across to Asia, frequenting freshwater lakes. It can submerge for long periods should danger threaten, and it needs this way of escape because on the surface it requires a long take-off run. It is one of a group of ducks called 'stiff tails' because the stiff-feathered tail is held upright when the bird is at rest. When swimming, their tails are thought to have an underwater control function. The drake has the clear diagnostic feature of the swollen-based blue bill and mostly white head. However, the bright blue fades to grey when he is in eclipse. Like most duck species, his moult begins once the female has a young brood. He goes off to moult in the company of other males, leaving her to rear the ducklings alone. The females do not moult until their offspring are fully grown and can feed and fend for themselves.

Hamilton has contrasted the red and warm ruddy brown colours with cool blues. The whites relieve this subtle palette, including a tiny white flower in the bottom right foreground. Apart from the interesting birds, it is a pleasing picture in form and colour.

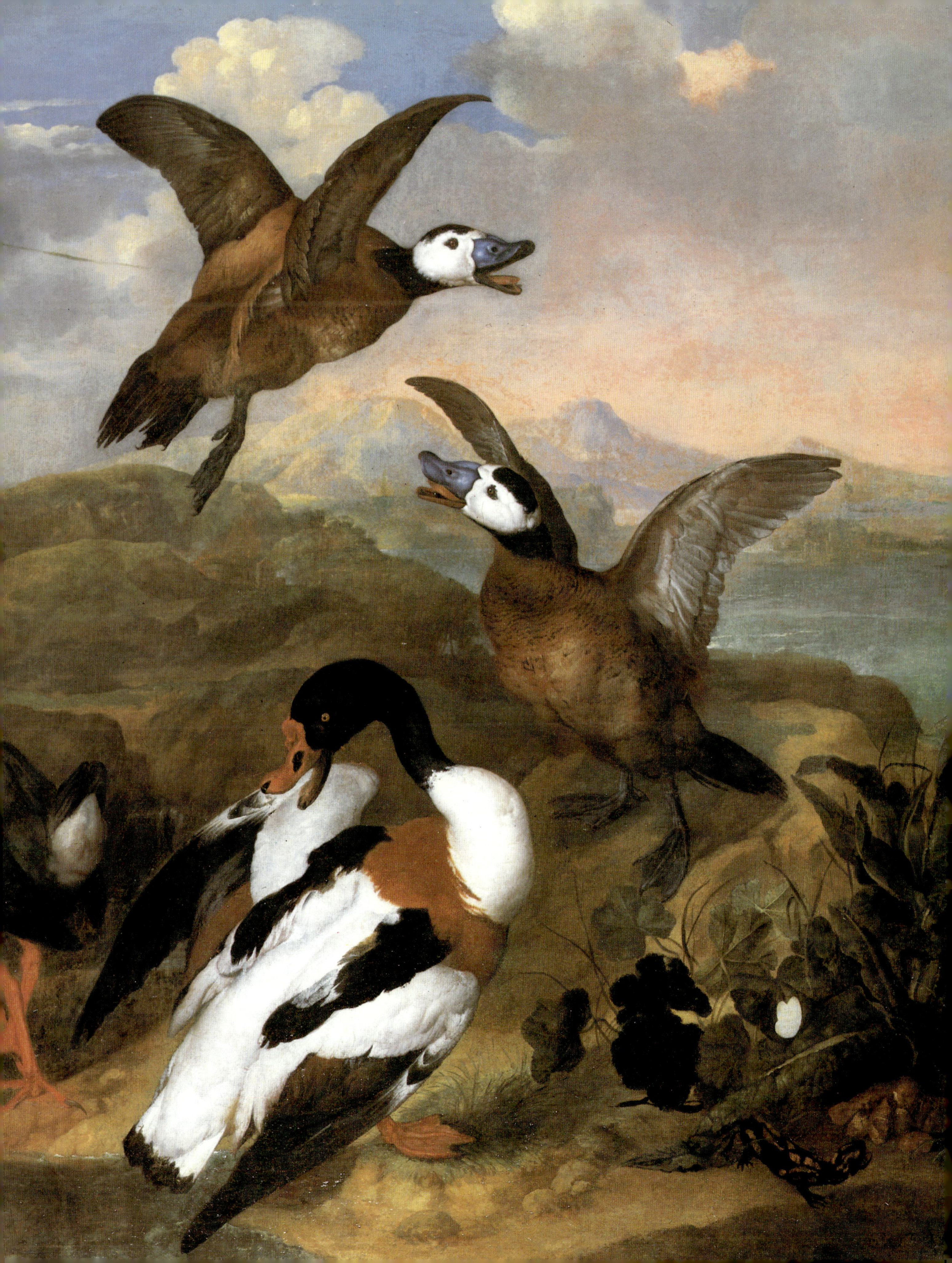

ABRAHAM BISSCHOP
born Dordrecht 1670, died Middelburg 1731

Abraham Bisschop was a Dutch painter of birds in Italianate landscapes, of portraits, and room decorations for large houses in Holland. He was the youngest son of Cornelis Bisschop (1630-1674), a court painter to the King of Denmark. The majority of his oil paintings are large canvases of both familiar and exotic birds, usually in landscapes with classical ruins and urns. Little is known of his movements, but he was elected a member of the painters' guild of Middelburg in 1715. He died in Middelburg, the capital of the province of Zeeland, and may have lived there during the last years of his life.

A WHITE PHEASANT AND OTHER FOWL IN A CLASSICAL LANDSCAPE
signed, oil on canvas, 96 x 107 cm
Courtesy of Rafael Valls, London

Bisschop painted in the old Dutch bird masters' style while he was active at the end of the seventeenth and beginning of the eighteenth centuries. His signed painting of *A White Pheasant* is not dated, but shows the characteristics of seventeenth century Dutch paintings. He shared an ability to paint feathers of great softness, careful pattern and good colouring, with such great masters as Vonck and the d'Hondecoeters. His canvases are not so thickly populated, however, and the choice of species is smaller. In this picture he has painted the familiar farmyard fowl and lapwing, but introduced an unusually feathered or coloured pheasant, and one exotic bird, a cardinal from North America.

Throughout the history of menagerie ownership, there seems to be a recurring predilection for the bizarre or unusual form of animal, which is comparable with a stamp collector who values an aberrant form more highly than the normal example. In this painting of a pheasant, there are more white feathers than coloured. Albinism, or the lack of pigment resulting in white feathers instead of coloured, may be partial, as in this so-called *White Pheasant*, or total. Totally albinistic birds lack pigment in all the feathers, the bill and feet. It does not affect the health of the bird, though it may make it look pale and strange. Not all the brilliant colours in a pheasant's plumage are from pigments, some are due to refracted light. The red colour of the wattles (retained in this partially albinistic bird) is provided by an organic compound. In its normal state, this would have been a copper-coloured pheasant without a ring of white feathers round its neck. This was the only species of pheasant present at this time in aviaries in Europe. It was not until the second half of the eighteenth century that the ring-necked pheasant was introduced (see the painting by Bewick, page 113).

The northern cardinal, or the 'red bird' of many early writers, is one of the best known of North American birds and lives throughout most of the States (except in the west) and south through Mexico to Belize. They were favourite cage birds, taken to Europe prior to 1601 when the Italian author Aldrovandus wrote of them. They were present in the menagerie of the splendid Villa Pratolino near Florence, built by Francisco I, Grand Duke of Tuscany.

Cardinals were known as Virginian nightingales, from their place of origin when first exported to Europe, and on account of the clearness and strength, rather than the variety, of their notes. The brilliant scarlet feathers of the male bird in breeding plumage are well set off by the black facial and bib feathers, to make this an extremely handsome bird, as much admired for its plumage as its clear, loud, liquid whistle.

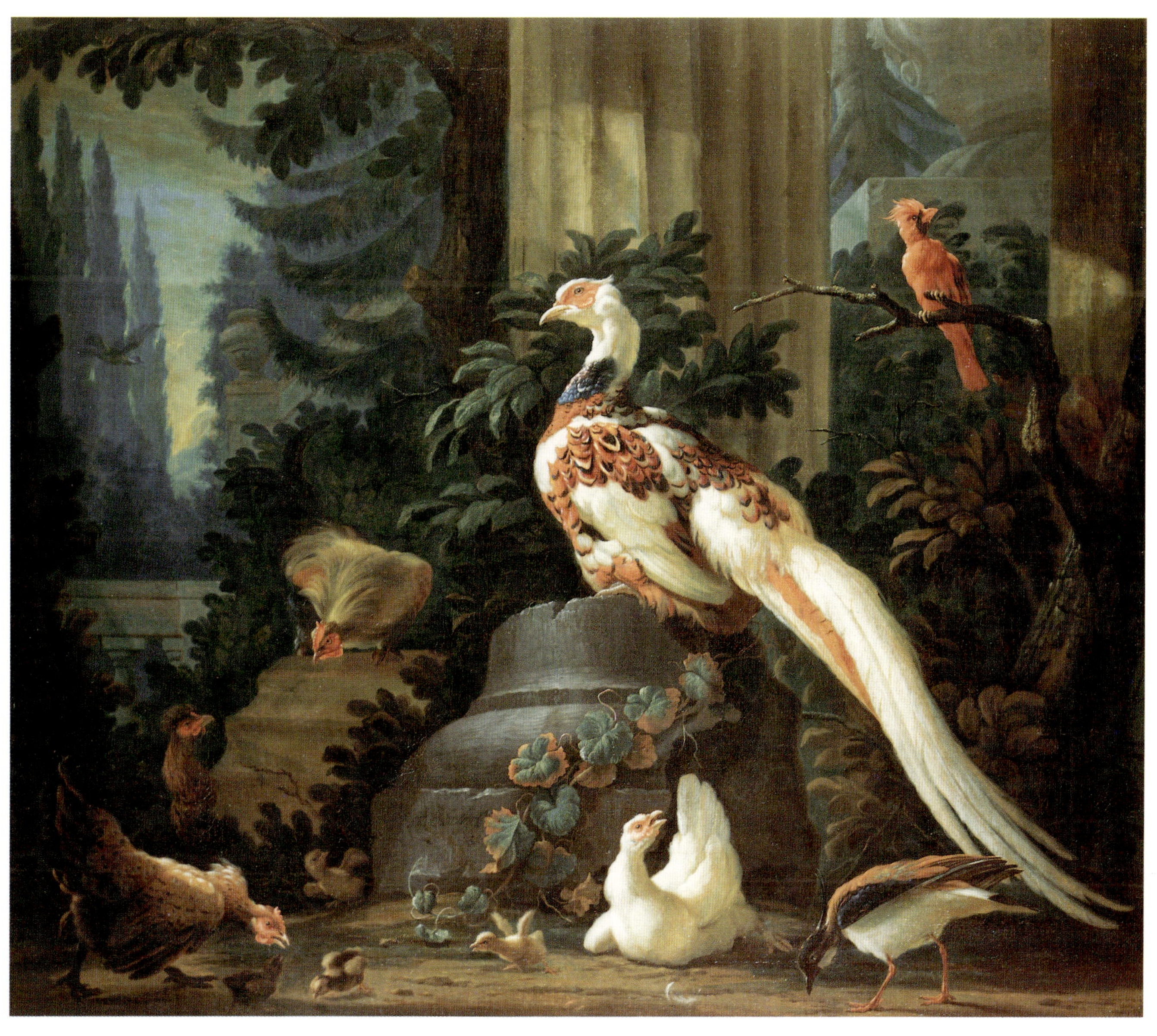

CHARLES COLLINS
born c. l680, died London 1744

Charles Collins was a painter of dogs, birds and dead game whose original work is rarely seen. There were few references to Charles Collins in contemporary literature but George Vertue said that he 'painted all sorts of fowl and game. He drew a piece of a hare and birds and his own portrait in a hat'.

Watercolour paintings of birds, dated between 1736 and 1744, show his skill at painting feathers with soft, rich colours and delicate highlights. He used gouache or bodycolour for the bird and painted in the slight background and foreground with clear watercolours. He and Peter Paillou were engaged to paint aquarelles of as many species of birds and mammals present in Britain, from c.l736, for the collector Taylor White. Some of the subjects were in White's menagerie in London, but many were in other collections. Collins signed about two hundred studies, he also dated a few others among the 659 in White's collection. These watercolours executed for Taylor White are now preserved in the library of the McGill University, Montreal, Canada. Several more bird paintings by Collins have been sold recently in art auctions, and a few are preserved in museums in England.

Collins painted bird still life pictures for the sheer pleasure of representing the texture, markings and contours of feathers. He was skilled at painting the texture of the hard primaries and of the soft wing linings and breast feathers, as well as reproducing the beautiful colours.

THE COMMON BUZZARD
signed and dated 1739, watercolours, 13 x 19.2 cm
Courtesy of The Trustees, Cecil Higgins Art Gallery, Bedford

The buzzard is a predominantly dark brown bird of prey with pale patches on the wing and breast feathers and underwing. It is not an exciting bird to paint, for it has neither the magnificent fierce presence of an eagle nor the dash and verve of a falcon. Nevertheless, it is a very competent hunter, either through treetops or on the ground and is versatile enough to take rodents, birds, snakes, frogs and insects. It is one of the most widespread and abundant birds of prey in Europe, to be seen soaring in wooded hill country and perching on good lookout posts. Collins has captured its essential characteristics, as a bird of prey well-equipped in beak and claw, strong breast muscles and large wings for the job of flying down and seizing prey. He has also given it a softer touch by concentrating attention so strongly on the beautiful variation in the plumage markings. In 1761 Peter Mazell etched a very close copy of Collins' watercolour of 1739 for the print in Pennant's folio edition of *British Zoology* (figure 28). Pennant was friendly with Taylor White, but this watercolour was not borrowed by Pennant from the White collection. It was sold separately, by Sotheby's, London in 1960 for £28.

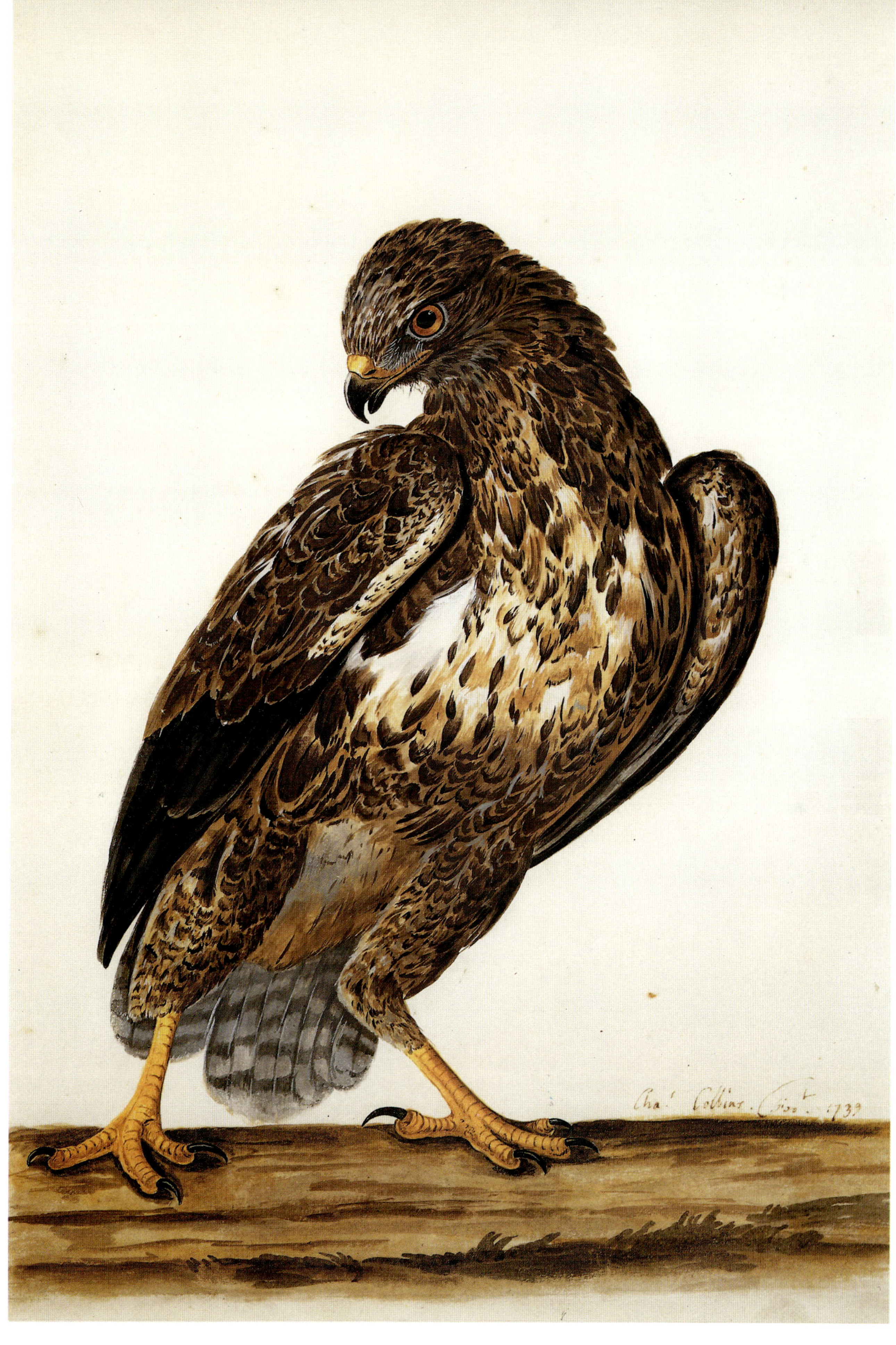

Cha.ˢ Collins. Pinxt. 1739

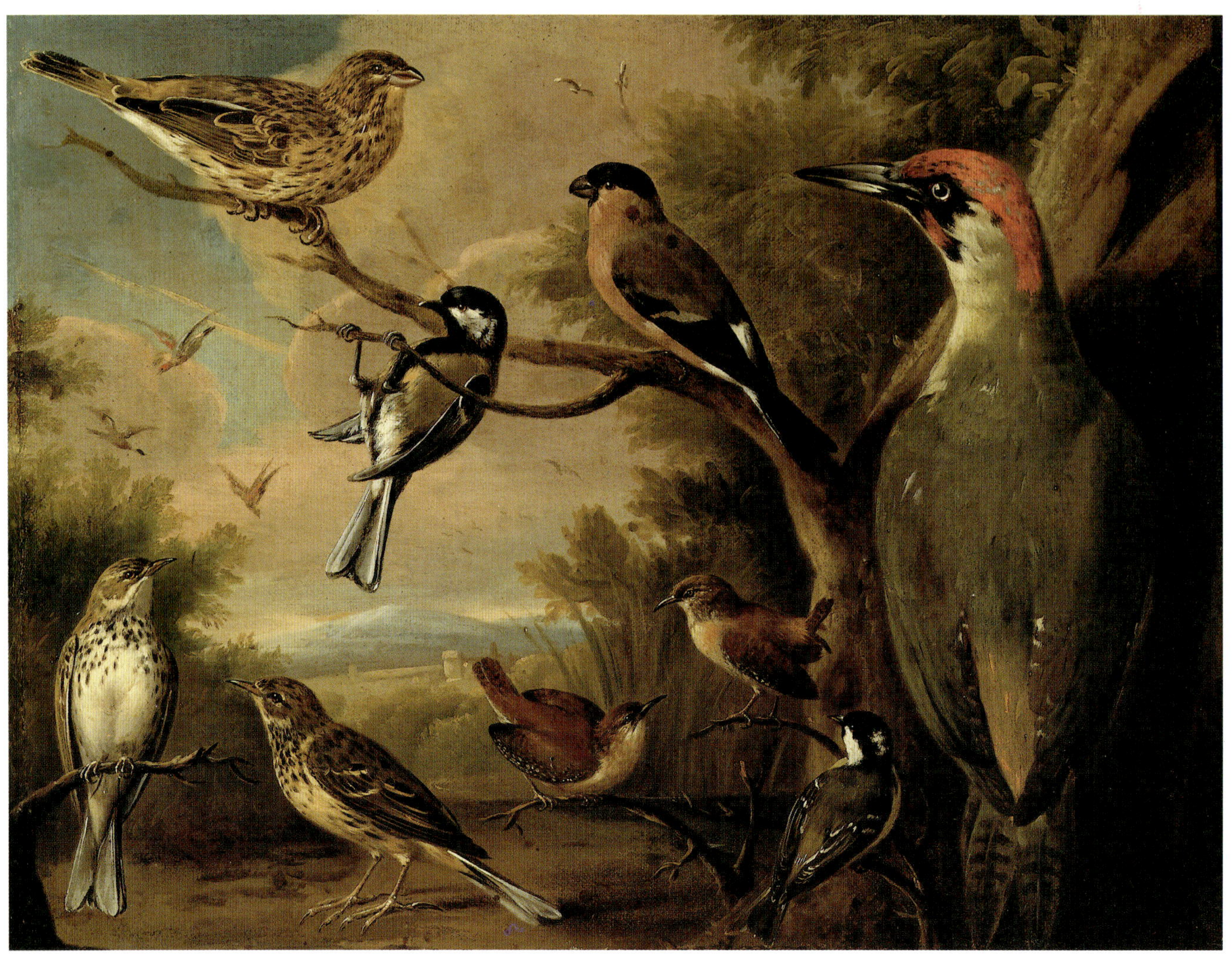

The oil painting for plate 5 of Icones Avium *with a green woodpecker, female corn bunting, a bullfinch, great tit, pair of meadow pipits, pair of wrens and a coaltit.*

Charles Collins

BRITISH BIRDS, A SERIES OF 12 OIL PAINTINGS

A set of nine oil paintings of British birds, each with a detailed foreground of trees and distant background with water and sometimes a building, is in a National Trust property. There were twelve of these uniformly sized pictures, signed and dated 1736, which together had 115 figures of fifty-eight species. Each picture has nine or ten birds, often the pair of a species, one flying close to the viewer, others in the distance, all carefully spaced and relatively active. Three of the canvases are at present unlocated, but we know exactly what they look like because Collins followed the example of Barlow and Peter Casteels before him, and had them etched in order to sell them as a set of prints.

It took an artist days to produce even a small canvas with carefully painted birds and an intricate setting such as Collins has used. At the end of that time, having sold the picture and got a price, the artist then had to start again and create another scene and spend more time arranging his birds and painting them. By copying the painting on to a sheet of metal, either by engraving or etching, and then printing multiple copies, the artist could sell the same design repeatedly. The print could be left uncoloured, or tinted by hand using watercolour paints.

In the seventeenth century, Francis Barlow had issued sets of prints, without any text,

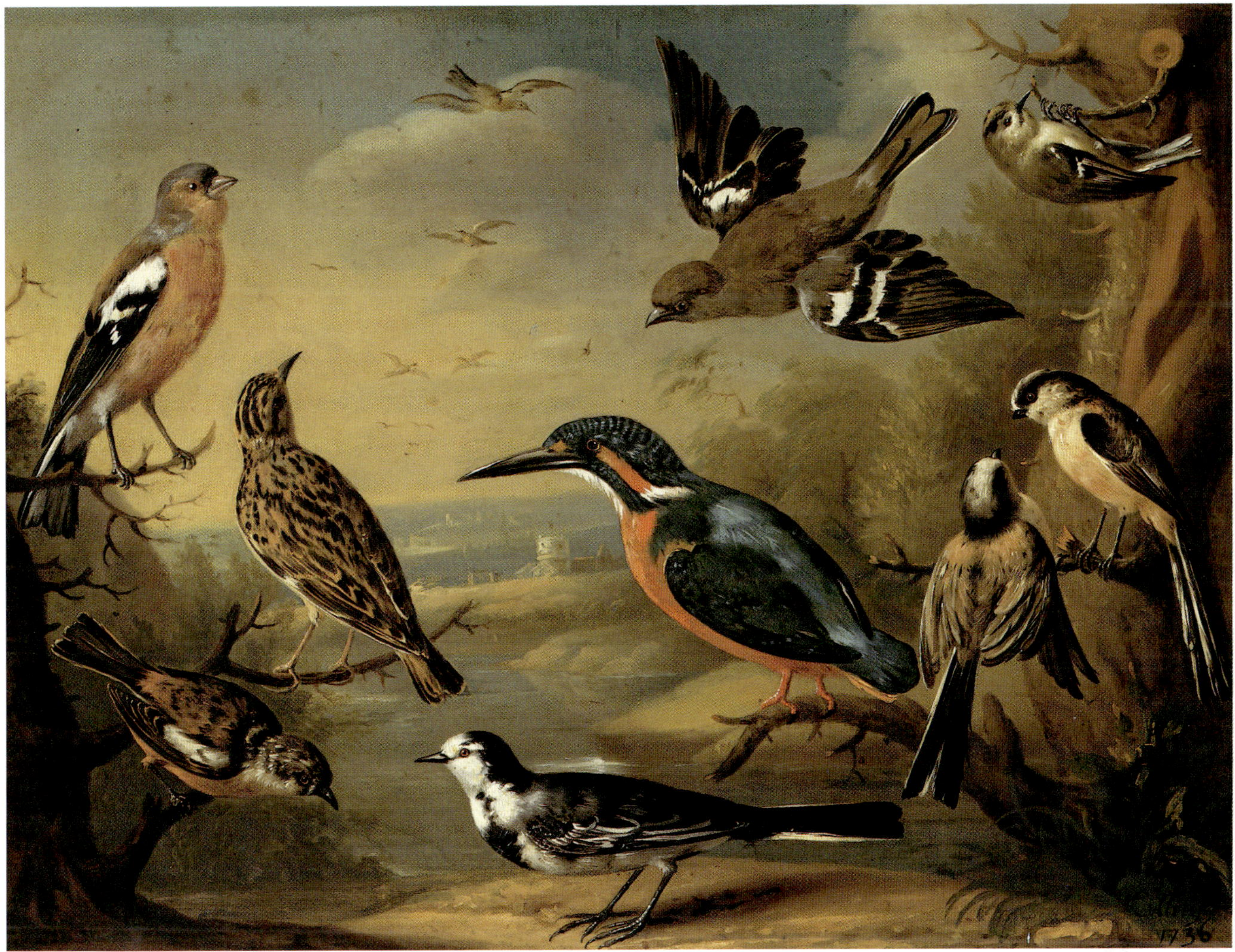

The oil painting and plate 2 of Icones Avium *shows a pair of chaffinches, goldcrest, woodlark, kingfisher, long-tailed tits, stonechat and wagtail.*

and these had sold well. In 1726, Peter Casteels also sold a set of twelve of his paintings, similar in composition to those by Collins, having birds in the foreground and a house or other building in the background. Casteels' prints were folio size, while Collins chose to turn the paper round and issued his oblong folio (48.3 x 61 cm, 19 x 24 ins). Both men called their set of prints *Icones Avium*. Collins' prints, published in a set of twelve in 1736, include exact copies of the nine canvases at the National Trust house. They must have sold well, because the oblong folio prints were reissued and then printed in a smaller size for which the plates had to be re-etched by the two etchers, James Mynde and Henry Fletcher.

The set of canvases is entirely devoted to British species of birds, but the settings are not British landscapes. Collins has a romantic view of landscape painting and more of an Italianate colouring of sky with golden light than one would normally see in England. He has not relinquished the composition of the bird paintings of the Old Masters, but he has changed the choice of birds so that they are all genuinely native species. This is in contrast to Paillou, who has painted native birds in countryside that could be part of an English landscape. Paillou painted his scene forty years after Collins painted this series of canvases.

PIETER CASTEELS
born Antwerp 1684, died Richmond Surrey 1749

Pieter Casteels was the son and pupil of another Pieter Casteels. He was trained in the Flemish school of painting before emigrating to England, in 1708, with his brother-in-law Pieter Tillemans, a painter of sporting scenes. Apart from a brief return to Antwerp in 1713 in order to enrol as a master painter in the guild, Casteels lived in England for the rest of his life. He succeeded Francis Barlow in the painting of canvases filled with colourful birds, usually in parkland settings, or landscapes. Although he painted the birds confidently, whether on the ground or in the air, they are static by comparison with those of Barlow. Like Charles Collins, and Barlow before him, Casteels had a set of uncoloured etchings printed, copied from his oil paintings of assemblies of birds. He was successful, but not outstanding, and sets of prints increased the sales of his work. In 1740 a large canvas, catalogued at Knowsley Hall, had been purchased for £3.10s. At this period, the canvas for this picture would have cost the artist at least £1 and he would have charged about 40 guineas had he painted a full-length human portrait rather than birds. Casteels' large canvases sell for about £30,000 today, which is one third of the price of a Melchior d'Hondecoeter canvas. Casteels' pictures are highly colourful and well painted, but the composition is less skilful and more haphazard than similar pictures by the Old Masters. Casteels gave up painting pictures of birds in 1735, preferring to earn a steady living by designing for a firm of calico printers in Tooting.

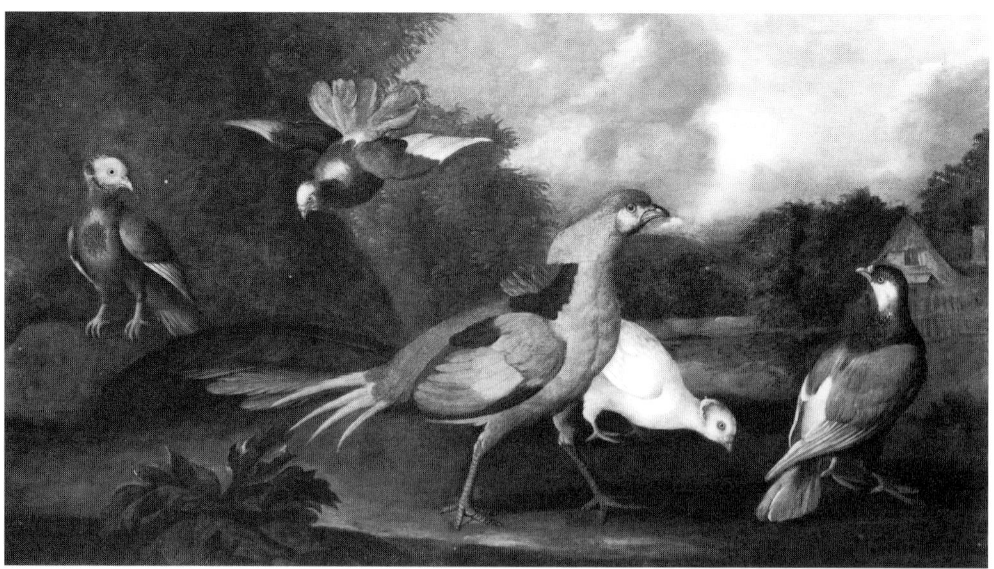

Casteels has painted a canvas to fit a place of given dimensions, wider than high, probably intended to be hung over a mantelpiece or door. He, like Cradock, is interested in the development of different breeds of pigeons and poultry. 'Fan-tails' have been bred to the point where their tails have as many as forty-two feathers instead of the normal twelve. Courtesy of Rafael Valls, London.

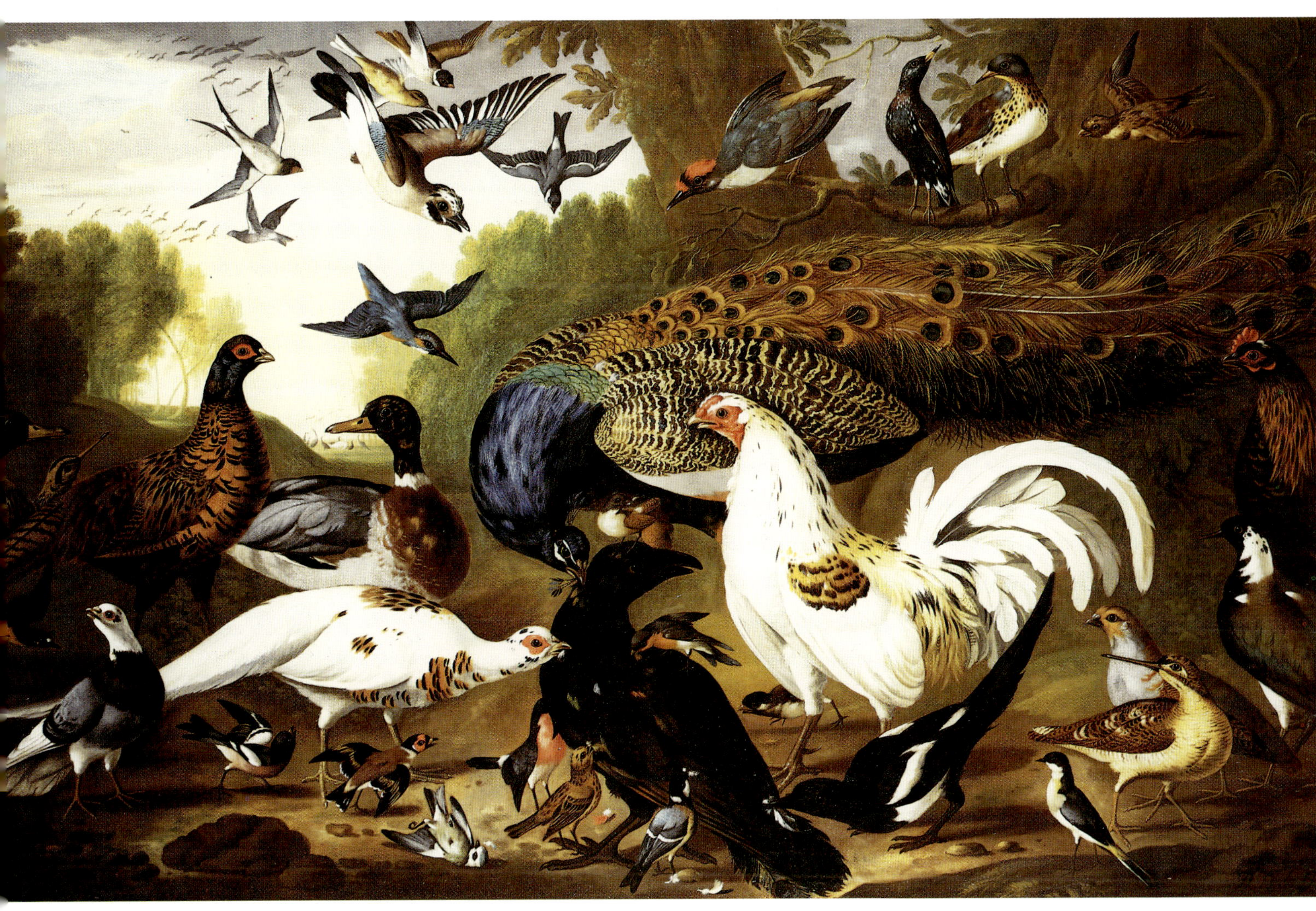

FABLE OF THE RAVEN

signed and dated 1719, oil on canvas, 113 x 174 cm.
Courtesy of Rafael Valls, London

The Fable of the Raven is a story from Aesop, the great fabulist who lived in the last half
of the sixth century BC. Fables bearing his name have been popular ever since that
time, because of their wit and underlying truths. In this story Zeus, the king of the
gods, decided to choose a king to reign over the birds. He appointed a day on which
they were all to appear before him for election. The raven (sometimes the story-teller
said it was a jackdaw, but a black-plumaged member of the crow family is intended),
realised how plain and dull was his appearance, and so he collected up all the discarded,
colourful feathers he could find and adorned himself with them. Zeus surveyed all the
birds gathered before him and was about to award the throne to the raven when the
other birds spotted the deception and indignantly stripped him of his false feathers.
Each bird retrieved his own moulted, colourful feather. Casteels has painted the scene
at this point, where the peacock, robin, bullfinch, magpie, albino pheasant and great
titmouse are extracting their own feathers. Other birds are standing near, waiting to
claim theirs. A small blue titmouse has been knocked over on to its back and is lying
on the ground. The moral of this tale is that men in debt, like the raven, cut a dash
with other people's money. Make them pay up, and you see them for the nobodies they
really are.

Pieter Casteels

ORNAMENTAL FOWL IN A GARDEN
signed and dated 1719, oil on canvas, 122 x 134.5 cm
Courtesy of Rafael Valls, London

Casteels has painted a large picture with a massive urn, distant temple and fountains and a glowing yellow light over all the canvas. He learned to paint similar compositions in Antwerp before moving to England. His country was then under Spanish rule and when an English picture dealer discovered him in Antwerp in 1708 and assured him that his pictures would sell in England at a profit, Casteels had two motives for emigrating. He continued to paint in the Flemish Old Masters' style and there is little in his paintings to suggest that his home was in England.

Apart from a resplendent peacock, his birds were homely but he managed to paint sparrows as though they were something special and gave every nuance of shading and markings on the plumage full importance. The rock dove on the ledge appears to be associating with a feral pigeon. The fancy pigeon has been brought to the foreground to make sure every feature and colouring is noticed. The displaying turkey takes the eye to the background where the full extent and magnificence of this garden is to be enjoyed. There are two fountains playing and more urns on low walls where birds can perch and pose. Casteels is obviously interested in the different breeds of pigeon, turkeys and poultry. At this date, few Englishmen were interested in breeding programmes, unlike Casteels' Flemish countrymen. Poultry were kept in England for their eggs and feathers, and few chickens were eaten. The people of Brussels were referred to, quite contemptuously, as 'chicken eaters' – an attitude which Casteels must have found very strange. Casteels has hidden most of the gloriously feathered black cockerel behind the peacock, but he has captured the deep blue-black of its tail very well, and this provides the base to a triangle of blues, completed by the neck of the peacock and the nesting blue titmice.

The little bluetits in the tree-hole are ready to take their first flight. Four fully feathered nestlings are visible and there will probably be another nine beneath them. This small bird lays one of the largest clutches of any European species, averaging a clutch of thirteen eggs. When nearly ready to fly, the nestlings take turns to clamber to the entrance in order to exercise their wing muscles and to receive food brought to them by their parents. Over the previous two to three weeks since they hatched from their tiny white reddish-spotted eggs, the adult birds have brought at least ten thousand caterpillars to the nest. During the fifteen to sixteen hours of daylight, the parents will have made a thousand feeding visits to their chicks. After this enormous effort, only one or two birds of the new generation will survive the following winter, which is just as well, or the countryside would be overwhelmed by bluetits.

Although bluetits nest in trees, as Casteels has indicated, they would have preferred a less open cavity with a much smaller entrance hole. They nest from mid-April to May, when the leaves on the oak trees are not as fully developed as in this painting. However, an oak tree is a perfect site for bluetits, providing a mixed diet from caterpillars and the larvae of other insects when they are at their most abundant. Few trees are host to so many insect species as the oak. Did Casteels know this, or observe bluetits nesting in an oak tree? Or was it pure chance that he placed an oak tree in this painting?

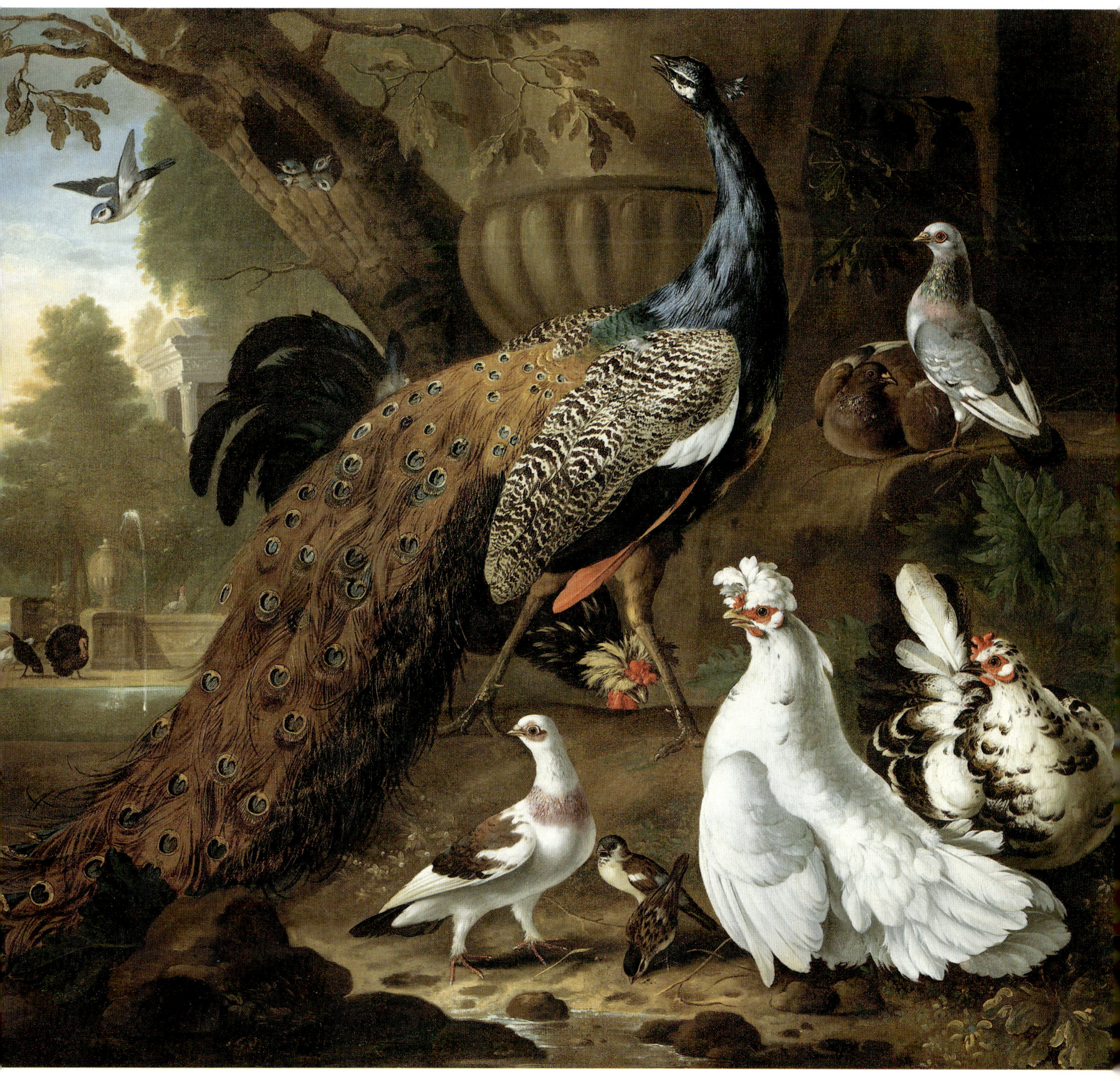

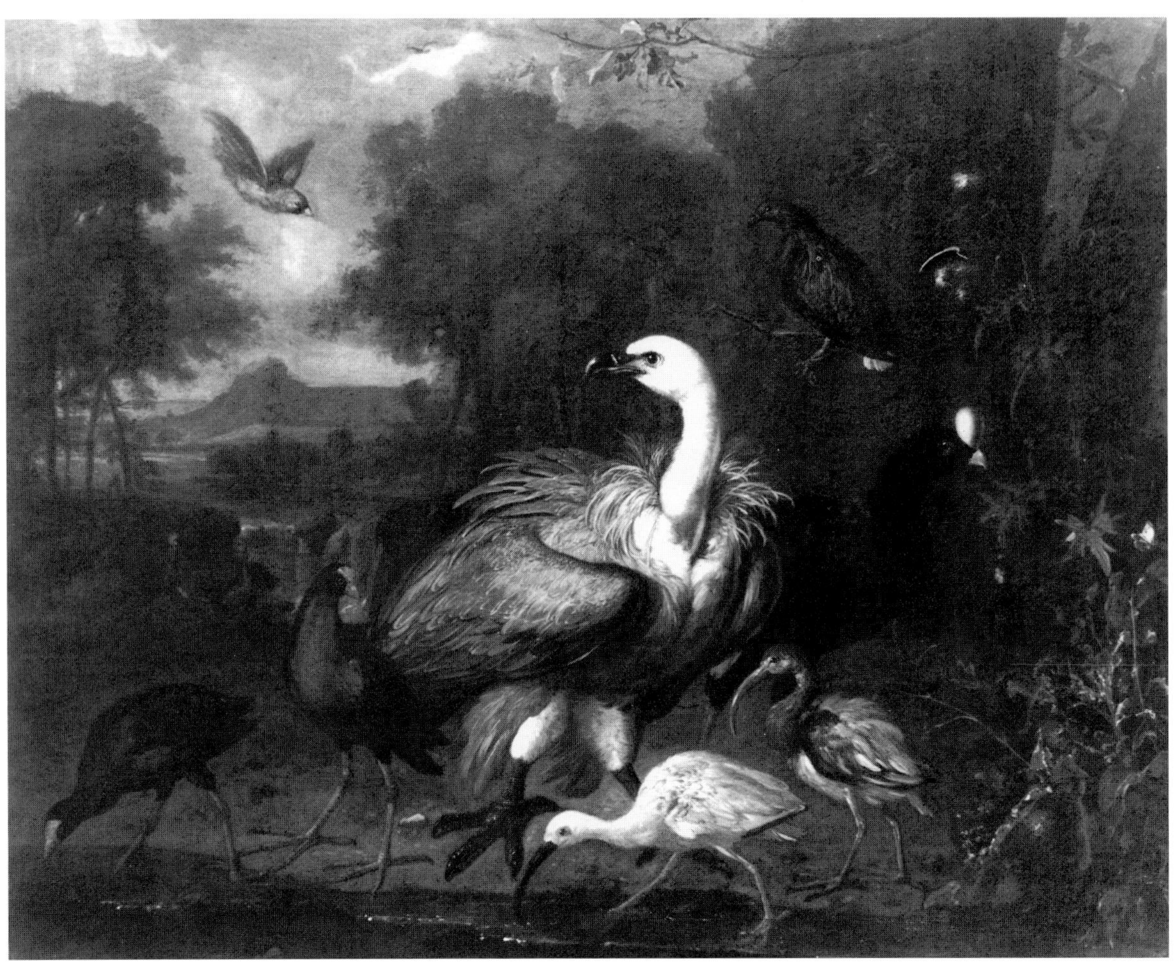

DIRK VALCKENBURG
born Amsterdam 1675, died Amsterdam 1721

Valckenburg was a Dutch painter of high repute whose skill was well repaid both by his own countrymen and other European patrons. He was the pupil of four Dutch painters, including Jan Weenix whose influence may be seen in the subjects of his still life pictures, though Valckenburg's composition is less well balanced. Following his training, in 1696 he set off for Italy, but he never arrived. He travelled via Frankfurt and Augsburg and worked for the Duke of Bade, then Prince Johann Adam of Lichtenstein in Vienna, where he painted four important canvases in 1698-99 which firmly established his reputation and gave him a good financial start to his career. He returned home to Amsterdam, and was employed by William of Orange at Het Loo, and married in 1702. Four years later he travelled to Surinam and painted tropical plants and animals on the plantation of Jonas Witsen.

BIRDS OF THE WEST INDIES
signed and dated 1701, oil on canvas, 150 x 176 cm

This picture was painted when Valckenburg was living in Holland and had access to the menagerie at Het Loo. The purple gallinules, two ibises, great curassow and cardinal all occur in the West Indies, but the Nicobar pigeon is an oriental and East Indies species. The central figure, the griffon vulture, inhabits mountainous regions in Southern Europe and North Africa, eastwards to India.

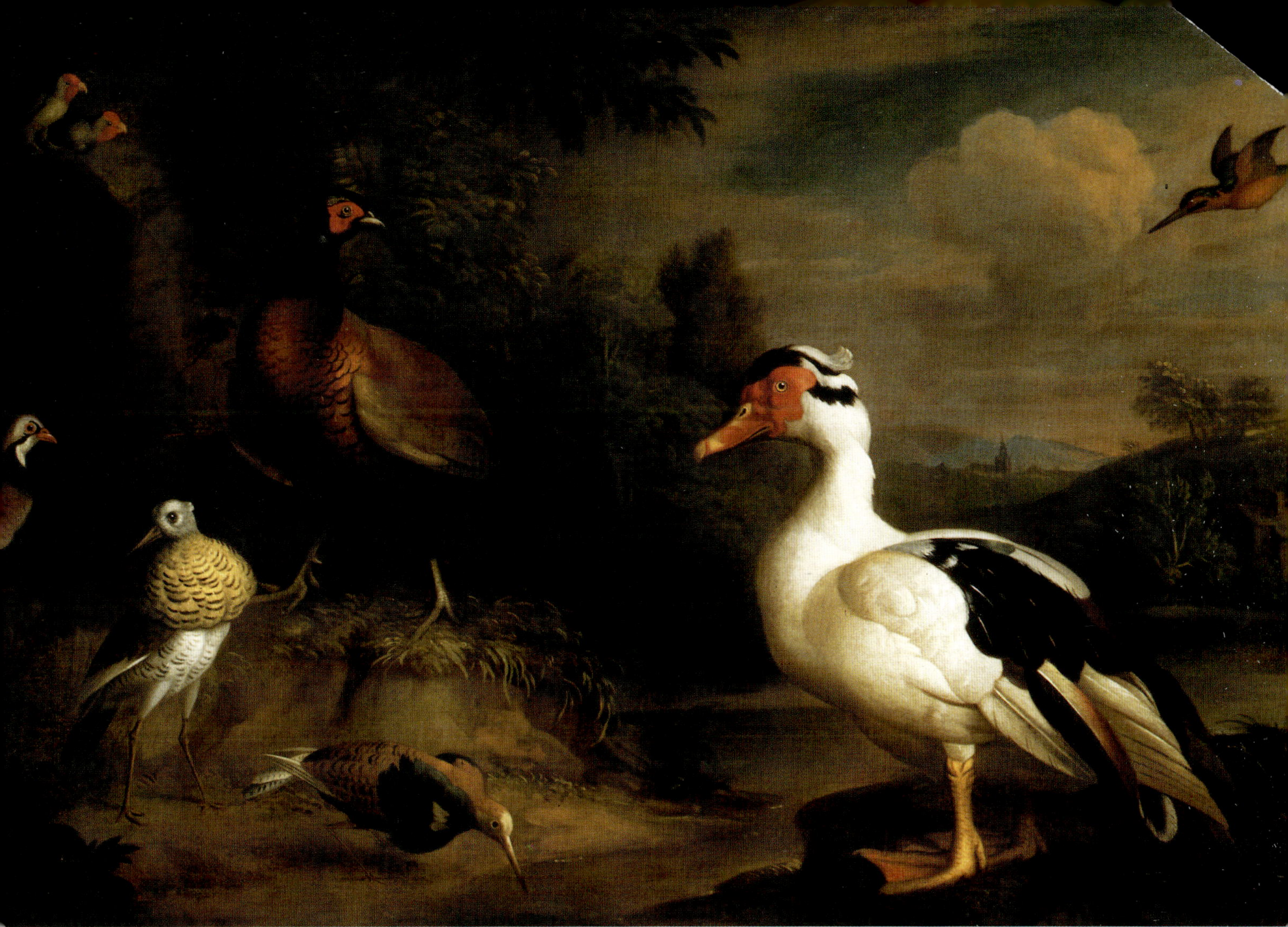

TOBIAS STRANOVER
born Sibiu, Transylvania 1684, died England post-1731

Tobias Stranover was the son-in-law of Bogdani, and the decorative fruit and bird paintings of the two men are very similar in content and design. Stranover was born in Sibiu, the capital of wine-growing country in central Romania situated in the northern foothills of the Transylvanian Alps. He travelled to Hamburg and Dresden and finally settled in England, where he married Elizabeth Bogdani. Their two children were baptised in London in 1721 and 1725. Repeated use of the same fruits and bird species in the two men's pictures suggests close collaboration on a number of occasions, or perhaps merely a shared studio. Bogdani left all his bird models, with his house and contents at Finchley, to Stranover and his wife in his will dated 18 September 1723.

BIRDS IN A LANDSCAPE
oil on canvas, 99 x 134.5 cm
Courtesy of Sotheby's, London

In this picture, Stranover painted two ruffs, the one nearest the muscovy being the more interesting because Bogdani painted exactly the same ruff. We can be so sure of this because each ruff grows the same unique combination of colours and pattern of neck frill every year. Apart from this scientific evidence, Bogdani painted a similar composition with the muscovy duck prominent on the right and a single ruff (the one with the black feathers having small white patches) on the left of the picture. They might well have got their birds from the Lincolnshire fens either direct, or from a London market stall. Ruffs were still thought to be sufficiently remarkable for the eminent zoological author Thomas Pennant to go to Lincolnshire in 1769 to see them, not long after Bogdani and Stranover had painted their pictures of these sartorially extraordinary birds. Pennant went to Lincolnshire because the phrase 'taken at Crowley in the Countie of Lyncolne' in a pamphlet of 1586 was still being quoted in all English texts referring to ruffs. It was to be repeated in nineteenth century texts until the draining of the Lincolnshire fens no longer made this true (see page 76).

Tobias Stranover

PEACOCKS, HENS AND MOUSE
signed, oil on canvas, 127.6 x 101.6 cm
Courtesy of Rafael Valls, London

Apart from similar birds in his canvases, Stranover also shared with Bogdani the manner of painting beady eyes, very clearly demonstrated in this particular picture *Peacocks, Hens and Mouse*. These two eastern European artists also brought a lightness to their work that is lacking in northern European paintings of the Dutch and German schools. In this picture, this is achieved by painting the scene in full sunlight, not at dawn or dusk, or with great shadows cast across the landscape as in so many of the Old Masters' compositions. The aggressiveness of earlier pictures where a dog is frightening the birds has also been replaced by a gentler provocation. Indeed, it can hardly be called that, for the mouse is only trying to eat its food where it happens to have found it, unaware of any commotion it might be creating. This, however, achieves the interest and provokes the reactions in the birds that give additional life and focus to the composition.

The light striking the blue and gold of the plumage of the peacock is inspired painting. The white feathers of this partial albino peacock add to the bright effect. The white feathers of the hen, the speckled hen and splendid pyle coloured cock are brilliantly executed and one could wish that the cock was fully in the picture so that his wonderful glossy tail feathers might also have been included. To have two such immensely proud and beautiful birds as the peacock and fighting cock showing signs of concern over a small mouse, adds a touch of humour rarely seen in paintings of this character and period.

Blue peacocks must have been numerous in eighteenth century Europe for so many to have been incorporated in bird pictures. They had figured in folklore and mythology for centuries, but were not often painted in the seventeenth century where macaws took pride of place and provided brilliant splashes of colour. It was not difficult to keep several blue peacocks in captivity for they associate well together, living a very orderly and routine daily life, only separating in the breeding season when the males wander off with three or four hens to an area of their own. The parks of English country houses provided plenty of space and security for these birds which quickly become tame and approachable under these conditions. Casteels, Cradock, Bogdani and Stranover all painted them repeatedly in the early years of the eighteenth century. The last documentary evidence for Stranover that has been preserved is an entry in Lord Fitzwalter's accounts for 1731 (now in the Hampshire Record Office) of payment of £10 to him for a 'fowl piece with a peacock in it'.

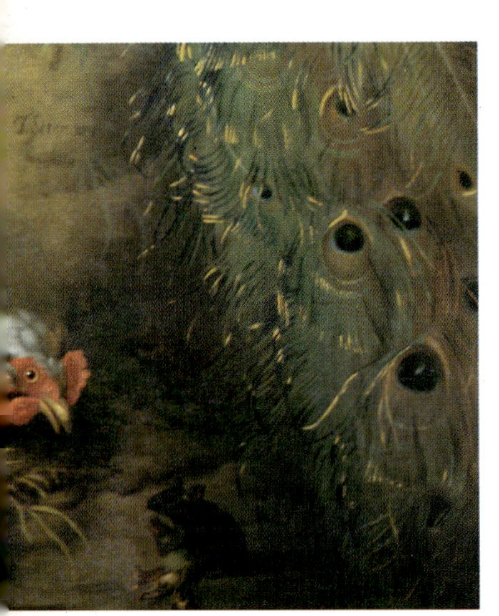

While the male birds are unsure of the mouse, the hen appears to be thinking about snatching its food.

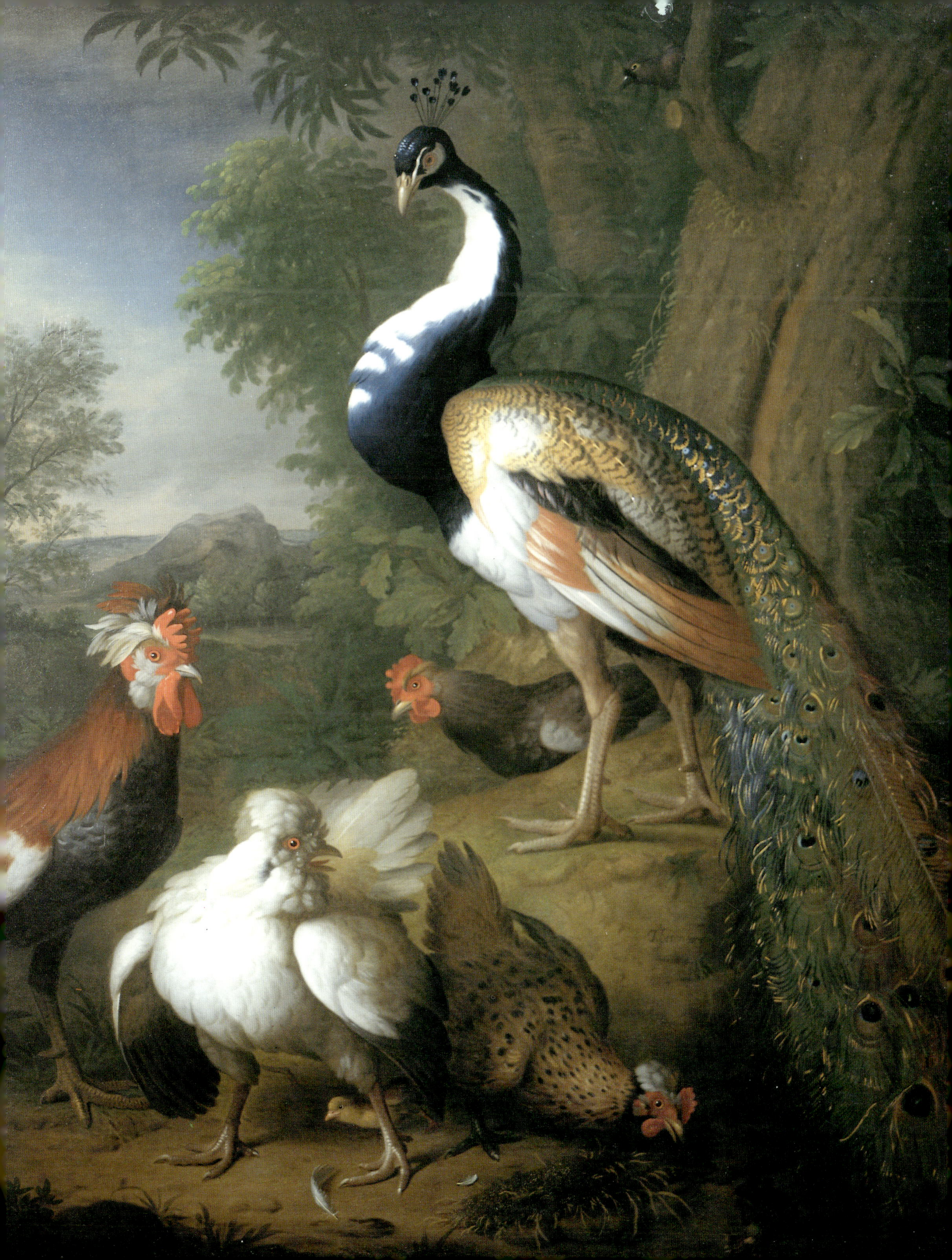

Tobias Stranover
MOBBING THE OWL
oil on canvas

Owls are special and owls are different. Unlike most other birds they are awake and hunting for their food at night, and sleep during daylight hours. They have faces more like ours – round, with eyes facing forwards and not set on the side of their heads like other birds. They turn their heads around almost 180 degrees, moving them in order to see or hear better. In short, they look, move and act more like us than any other bird species.

That they are able to accomplish all this at night leaves us lost in admiration and some envy at their heightened senses of sight and hearing. These accomplishments, combined with silent flight, appear uncanny to some people who fear and hate owls in consequence. The superstitious also thought that they foretold a human death when they hooted.

Artists have reflected these ambivalent attitudes to owls to a remarkable degree. The birds were portrayed by painters of classical scenes as symbols of wisdom when they accompanied the Greek goddess Athene (or Roman Minerva). When placed in pictures of the crucifixion, they were symbols of evil. Their close association with death was used by the Old Masters when they placed a living owl as both symbol and purveyor of death in still life pictures. In scores of early Dutch, Flemish and Italian paintings, a solitary owl presides over a hunting trophy scene, the only live bird among a mound of corpses.

Far less sinister are the owl choirmasters conducting a chorus of birds. This was a favourite theme for a picture, giving the artist the excuse to collect together a large number of birds around a tree. In nearly every case, an owl was placed at the centre of the group, sometimes with one foot raised in the act of conducting the avian choir (see Bogdani's choir). Presumably the intelligent, 'wise' owl was the one bird who could read music.

Here, in Stranover's painting of *Mobbing the Owl*, we have another example of man's keen interest in, and observation of owls. Small birds indulge in the pastime of mobbing an owl when they discover one hiding in some ivy-covered tree to sleep through the daylight hours. Owls catch and eat small birds as well as mammals, and the mobbing is sometimes relatively playful, but at other times, particularly in the nesting season, it is more in earnest. When one of these small birds first spotted this owl sitting in the hole in the tree, it would have used its special alarm call, high-pitched and very different from any other of its calls. This would have been recognised, not just by its own species, but by birds of other species who would gather round to see what was the cause for alarm, and then add their own alarm calls until there was quite a chorus. A few braver birds might then dive-bomb the owl. The owl responded in one of two ways. Either it stoically sat tight until the other birds tired of shrilling, or it flew away to find another perch. An owl may have to shift its position several times if a mob like the one in Stranover's picture gang up to make a good day's rest impossible.

In some interpretations of the scene *Mobbing the Owl*, men have made use of the birds' behaviour by turning it to their own advantage. A tethered owl is put on a stump in the open, in daylight. Around it, limed perches are set up so that when the small birds alight in order to shout their protests at the presence of the owl, their feet stick to the branches and they are then easily caught and killed prior to baking in a pie.

The eagle owl is clearly angry with the exotic birds being such a noisy nuisance in this version of *Mobbing the Owl*. The blue jay and oriole, cardinals and touracos with a mynah from India will whistle and trill and chatter sufficiently to dispel any chance of a peaceful day's rest.

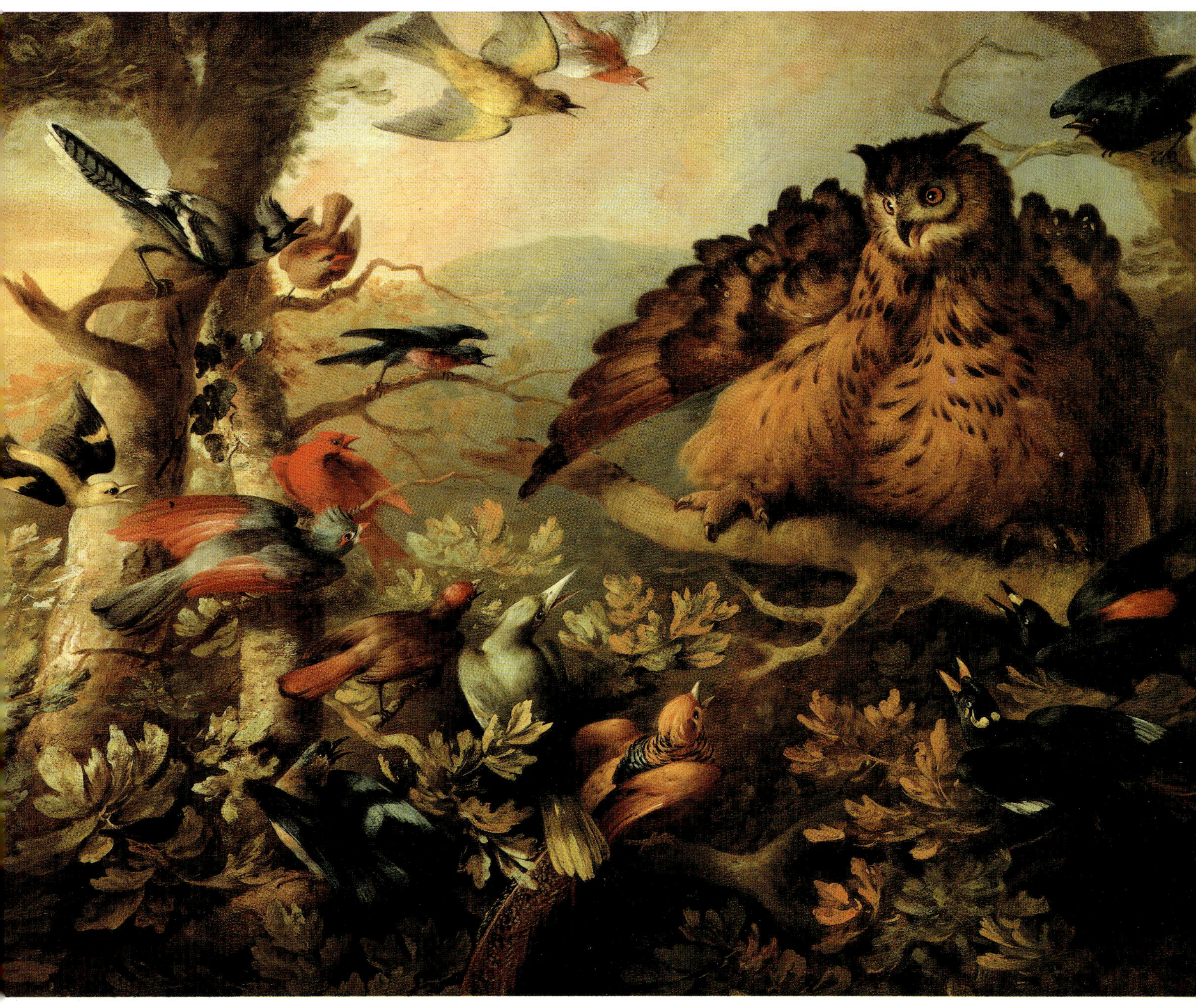

Stranover's *Mobbing the Owl* has an inscribed verse:

'Minerva's bird on wisdom ever bent
Is mock'd by those on lighter thoughts intent
The ruffled sage, his anger clearly shows
At those who gaily flit beneath his nose.'

MARK CATESBY

born Castle Hedingham, Essex 1683, died London 1749

Very few pictures of North American birds had been painted, and even fewer published, before Mark Catesby visited Carolina and took sufficient specimens and drawings back to England to write his monumental two-volume book, *Natural History of Carolina, Florida and the Bahama Islands*, 1731-43. It was to be the foundation of natural history and bird art in America and the best illustrated treatment of the flora and fauna until the time of Audubon nearly a century later. The 220 hand-coloured illustrations, etched by Catesby himself, included 109 bird plates.

Catesby was born and educated in Essex and early acquired an interest in natural history from his grandfather and from an acquaintance with the work of John Ray, perhaps with the Father of English Ornithology himself. Catesby went to America to visit his sister who was married to Dr William Cocke. The Cockes were in Virginia and Catesby spent 1712-19 with them, travelling in America and voyaging to Jamaica. He collected seeds and plants and sent them, with drawings, back to England where he acquired a reputation as a man 'pretty well skill'd in Natural History designs and paints in water colours to perfection'. He was encouraged by patrons in England to return on another collecting trip in 1722 and went to Charles Town, South Carolina. He not only collected plants this time, but mammals, reptiles, insects and birds. He preserved them either by dropping them into jars of rum or by drying skins in an oven, stuffing them with cotton and coating them with tobacco dust to ward off mites. Some of these he sent on ahead to England and a number were lost in transit so that his habit of making notes and field sketches prior to shipment was a wise precaution.

His travels across wilderness areas, with dangers from Indians and traversing unknown territory, must have been very exciting and arduous, but Catesby made light of them. He once wrote that he was 'setting out for the Cherukees a Nation of Indians 300 miles from this place and who have lately declared war with another Nation which diverts them from injuring us and gives me an opportunity of going with more safety.' On another occasion, a servant making his bed one morning discovered a rattlesnake curled up between the sheets. Catesby said, 'How long I had the company of this charming Bedfellow, I am unable to say.'

Upon his return to England he wrote the text, made finished watercolours from his sketches, etched and coloured many of the plates himself for his book which took until 1743 to complete. Catesby dedicated his book to Queen Caroline and all the original watercolours are preserved in the Royal Library at Windsor Castle.

THE BLEW JAY
watercolour
Courtesy of the Royal Collection © Her Majesty the Queen

The watercolour of the blue jay is one of the best designed of Catesby's paintings. He drew the bird in the greenbrier or bamboovine, which has berries in October particularly favoured by the blue jay. Catesby made a more animated drawing than usual, inspired by the striking colour and mischievous character of this bird. It is a wonderfully intense blue, with black barring and white patches on its blue wings and tail. The female is similarly, but not so brightly, coloured. Catesby aptly described the blue jay's peculiar jerky movements as being like the 'jetting motion of our jay' but said their 'cry is more tuneful. The bird calls its own name, repeating a piercing jay, jay'. This is not only one of Catesby's more lively paintings, it is also one of his best artistically and ornithologically.

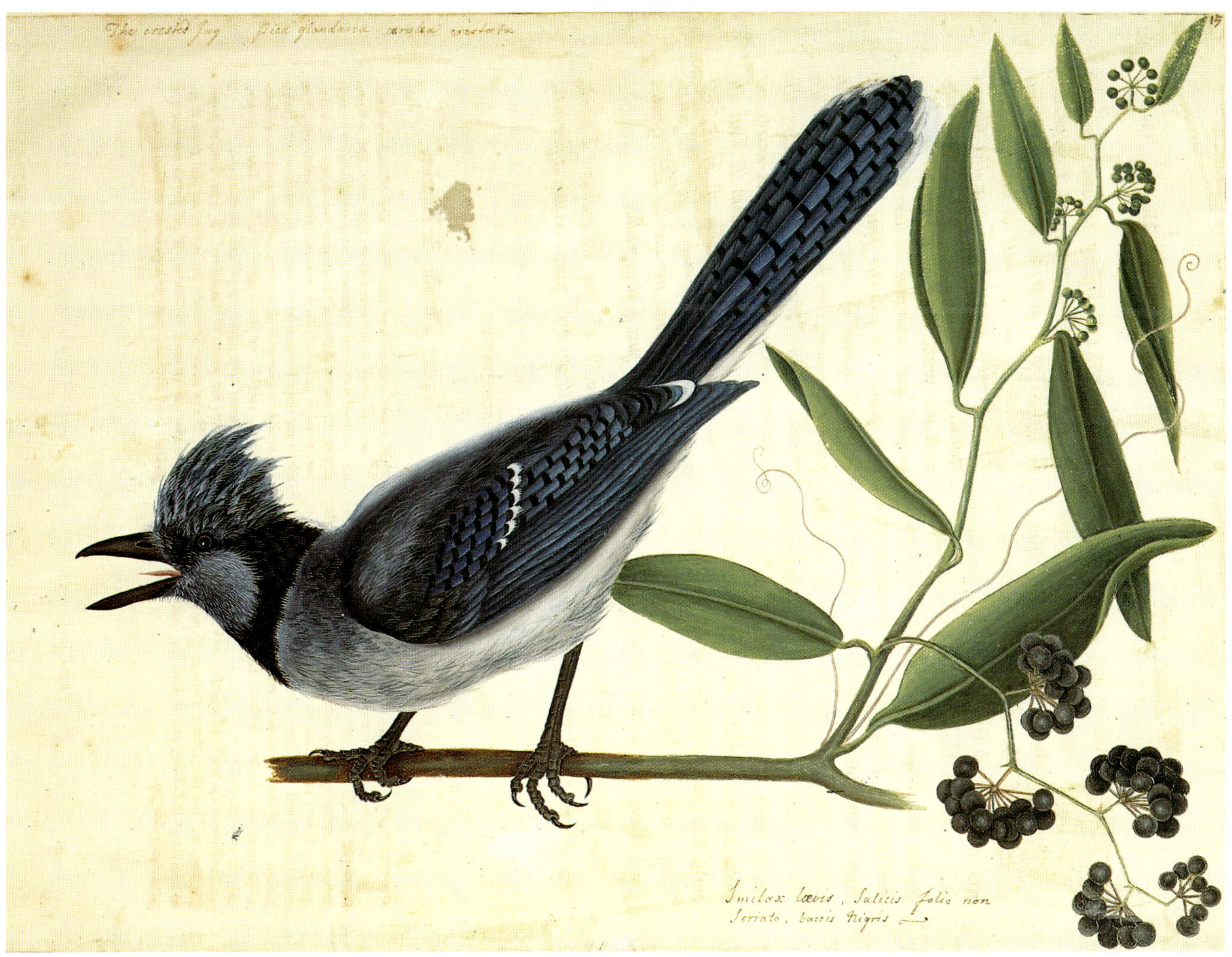

The original watercolour for Catesby's etching (which is printed facing in the opposite direction) of the 'Crested Jay' in The Natural History of Carolina, Florida and the Bahama Islands, *1731-43, Plate 68. In the text, Catesby called it 'The Blew Jay' and the plant 'The Bay-leaved Smilax'. The top inscription reads: 'The crested jay Pica glandaria cristata caerulea.' The inscription beneath the bird reads: 'Smilax laevis, Salicis folio non Serrato baccis nigris.'*

VAN HUYSUM

The founder of the artistic family, Justus van Huysum (1659-1716) was born and died in Amsterdam. He painted flowers and fruits, landscapes, portraits and battles in seascapes. His canvases were large, painted in the grand style. Jan van Huysum (1682-1749), also of Amsterdam, mainly painted flowers and fruit, but he also tried landscapes. However, he was better when he worked on smaller canvases and his lovingly detailed flower pictures are the best part of his work. No-one appears to know the connection between Justus and Jan, but the names of two of Justus' sons are known, Jacob (c.1686 who died in London 1740) and Justus (1684-1707). None of these is regarded as an animal painter.

SCARLET MACAW ON AN URN WITH FLOWERS
signed 'Huysum', oil on canvas, 118 x 107.8 cm

Scarlet Macaw on an Urn with Flowers is signed 'Huysum' only, with no initials or date which could have been of some assistance in attributing the painting. Even the signature has been 'strengthened' or otherwise tampered with at a later date, so the attribution cannot be made with any certainty from this piece of evidence.

In the history of European bird painting, the macaw is the only exotic (or foreign) bird to dominate a complete era. The image might be the scarlet macaw or the blue and gold macaw, but from the time of these birds being brought to Europe from Central and South America c.1500, for the next two hundred years they were prominent in the still life paintings and bird assemblies of the Old Masters. In still life pictures of trophies of the chase, a live macaw presided over the booty from a perch positioned to give it importance. Macaws also overlooked tables laden with gleaming metallic vessels and food. They were among the birds thought to be the most intelligent and important in the bird world and so artists placed them in the top branches of trees in pictures of the Garden of Eden, or bird choirs, and other large assemblies of birds. Close studies of macaws were not so common, and Huysum's picture, though painted on the grand scale, is a far more intimate view of a macaw than was usual. Huysum painted his scarlet macaw at the end of the Golden Era of Dutch/Flemish still life. This picture shows the changes occurring across the seventeenth-eighteenth century boundary. It has plenty of interest, but is not crowded. It is monumental in conception, but simpler in execution. It has skill in composition but the decorative arrangement has overridden naturalness, especially in the curve of the macaw's tail which is echoed by the curved iris and tall poppy.

The Huysums were predominantly flower painters and this picture is as important for its flowers as the bird. It was part of a long tradition to paint flowers and birds together, sometimes with the birds quite small, like other similar accessories, butterflies and shells. Rather less often was the bird the most important, and therefore larger, part of the composition in flower and bird oil paintings. Birds were more usually placed in landscapes. Detailed studies of single birds were made in watercolours, a branch or spray of flowers and blossom being added merely to provide a perch for the bird or add a touch of colour. In the course of the eighteenth century far fewer large oil paintings including many birds, and far more watercolour studies of single specimens, were painted than in the previous two hundred years. Huysum's oil painting, where the flowers and bird are balanced in equal importance and interest, is therefore most unusual.

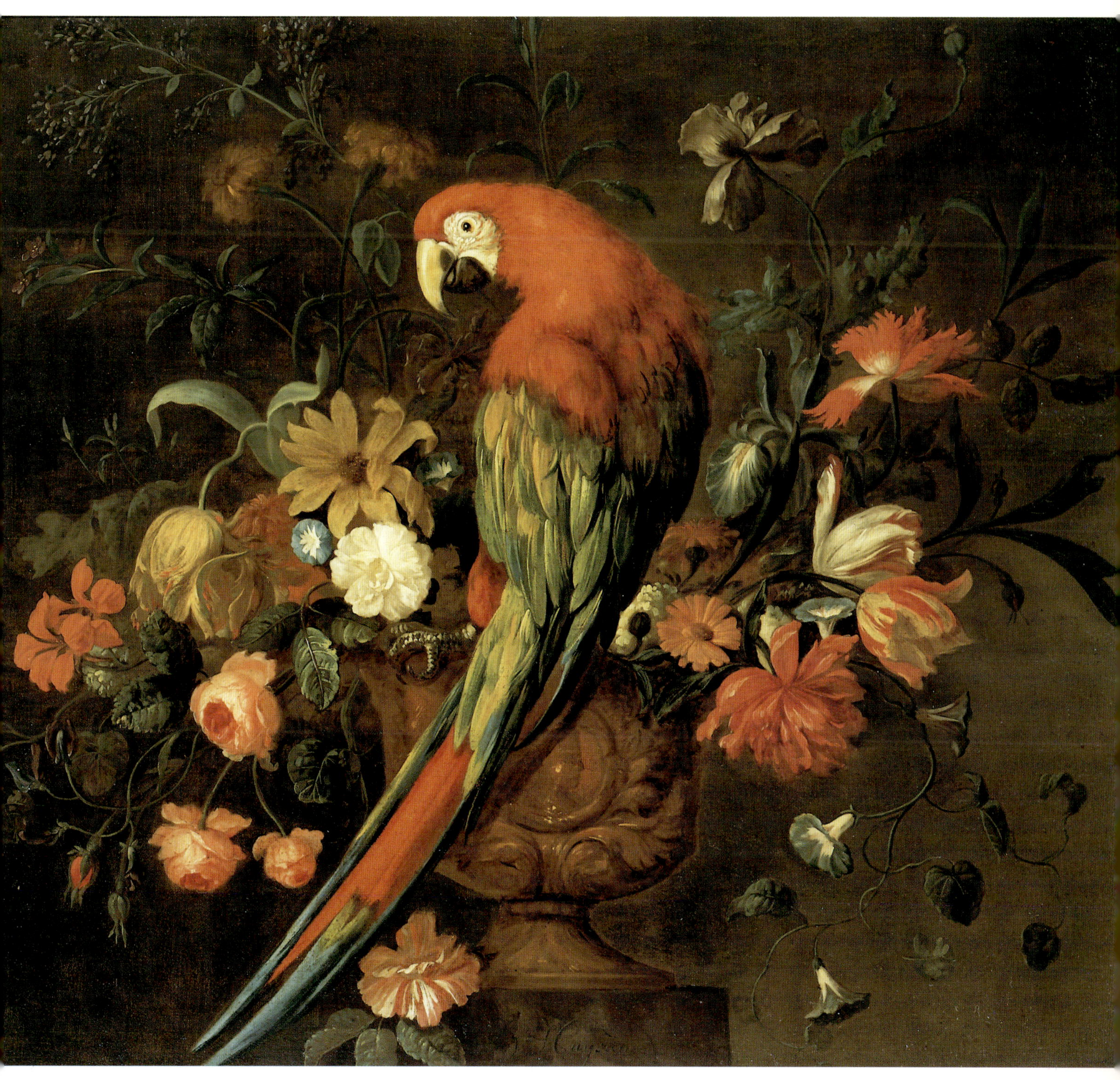

JEAN BAPTISTE OUDRY
born 1686, died Beauvais 1755

Like Desportes, he established his name as a one of the greatest French painters of still life and animals. He was born twenty-five years after Desportes, and so did not enjoy royal patronage for the painting of live animals in the royal menagerie, because Louis XV, whom he served, was interested only in hunting and let the menagerie fall into ruin. Oudry became outstandingly skilled in painting dead trophies of the chase and live hunting scenes, including the royal hounds. After studying first with his father, and then Michel Serre and Nicolas de Largillière, he was elected a master of the Academy of Saint Luke and was later to be a professor there. He received his first commission from Louis in 1724 and began his splendid career by designing twelve hunting pieces. Much of his time was spent designing for the Beauvais and Gobelins factories, and at the end of his life many of his designs were incorporated in a series of *Metamorphoses* and illustrations for *La Fontaine's Fables*.

BIRDS BY A STREAM
oil on canvas, 170.4 x 228.6 cm

Oudry made some vivid watercolour studies of birds. Though many of these were copied from the work of the Gobelins models of Pieter Boel and from a large album of birds from Chinese sources, he also painted direct from birds remaining in the menagerie. (A large collection of these watercolours is in the Fogg Art Museum of Harvard University.) He referred to these sketches when painting birds in his oil paintings. Apart from the dead birds, most of his oil paintings of birds have an element of aggression. Foxes and dogs 'surprise' or alarm ducks, fowls and partridges, and very few lack some drama or obvious incident in the lives of the birds.

The *Birds by a Stream* are all active, for Oudry has got a good deal of movement into this otherwise tranquil scene. The white goose with spread wings is vitally alive. Here the light catches the left side of the body and underwing, also the leading edge of the left wing. Oudry has painted this goose as though it were a still life study of feathers, while the other birds are treated in a less detailed manner. Oudry is too good a painter of live birds, however, to have merely animated a dead specimen for this picture. Beneath those feathers on the sinuous neck and plump but now taut body, are firm muscles. This bird could take off within seconds if it chose to fly.

The canvas is crowded, yet well composed and the activity of the live birds contrasts with the calm water which is taken out of sight round the left bank and into the reeds. The flowers and trees are lovingly painted, creating the perfect environment for water birds by an inlet giving access to the private garden where they are safe. The dovecote, with domestic pigeons, adds to the cosiness of the scene. The only false note, to modern eyes, is struck by two lapwings on top of a stone plinth. This is a most unlikely position for these grassland birds who are either seen in the air or on the ground in meadows and rarely seen perched elsewhere. The graceful shape of the lapwing and its wispy crest often proved to be irresistible to both Dutch and French bird artists who frequently included this bird in their paintings. In Oudry's picture, it is the only wild species among domestic pigeons, geese and ducks.

The increased interest in breeding doves, during the eighteenth century, to produce new colours or gradually extending the length of crests or leg feathering, is reflected in the number of Dutch/Flemish, French and English bird paintings which included domestic doves. These canvases often also provide a fascinating glimpse of the various designs of thatched, timber-framed dovecotes on wooden poles. This design of a dovehouse supported by tree branches is neater than the one Cradock painted (see page 28).

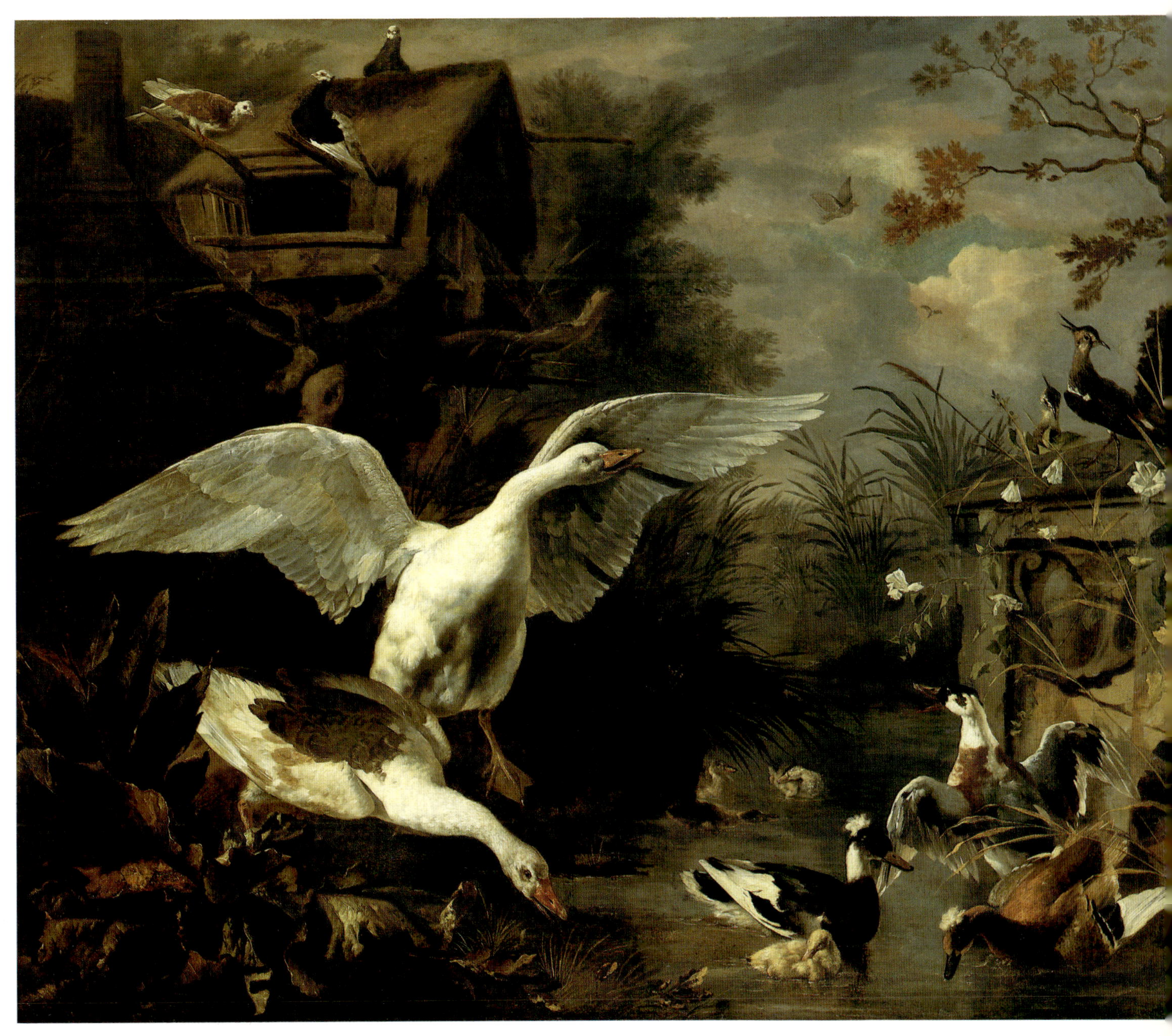

Jean Baptiste Oudry
THE WHITE DUCK
signed and dated 1753, oil on canvas, 97.7 x 63.7 cm
Private Collection

Oudry first established his name as a painter of still lifes and *The White Duck* is regarded as his still life masterpiece. Besides being a most unusual study of objects, all of them white, it is also a fine example of a pupil taking to heart the lessons of his master. Nicolas de Largillière (1656-1746) was Oudry's teacher. Largillière was born in France but received his art training in Antwerp, and practised fruit and flower painting in England under Sir Peter Lely before returning to Paris where he became director of the Academy in 1728. At the Academy, Oudry was one of his pupils and his teachings, particularly his preoccupation with the difficulties of painting white, were recalled by Oudry in 1749 when, three years after Largillière's death, Oudry lectured to the Academy and recalled having been sent by Largillière to gather a bunch of white flowers. Largillière had placed the flowers in front of a pale background to demonstrate the varying tonalities. Largillière painted flowers extremely well, and was especially skilled in the use of pastel colours in all their delicate shades. Although not a noted flower painter, Oudry also painted a few beautiful flower pictures.

Largillière told Oudry how to paint white: 'If you want to paint a silver vase coloured white, put beside it other white objects like satin, paper and china, which will help you find the exact tone wanted for your silver vase.' Oudry was a professor at the Royal Academy in 1753 when he exhibited a painting of a white duck, white tablecloth, a silver candlestick and a white bowl of cream decorated with nuts, and set all these against a white ground. The painting of the modulation of a single colour was received with acclaim and some awe at the technical mastery and innovation. Largillière's instructions on how to paint in the grand manner using the effects of light on tones, and how to show where the coloured reflections revealed closely related values, were all perfectly exploited by Oudry in this painting.

As a study in tonality, this painting is superb. It has the added dimension of *trompe-l'oeil* effects where the shadows behind the paper impaled on the wall nail and the outspread wing of the bird create an illusion of depth to the picture and three dimensional substantiality to the objects. The crumpled white cloth offered Oudry several surfaces, some in full light, others in half light, or shadow, to explore the different whites of the same material seen in varied intensity of light. The deep, thick plumage of the duck's body also afforded a wide range of cream tones. *The White Duck*, in Oudry's hands, became a painter's symphony of tonality.

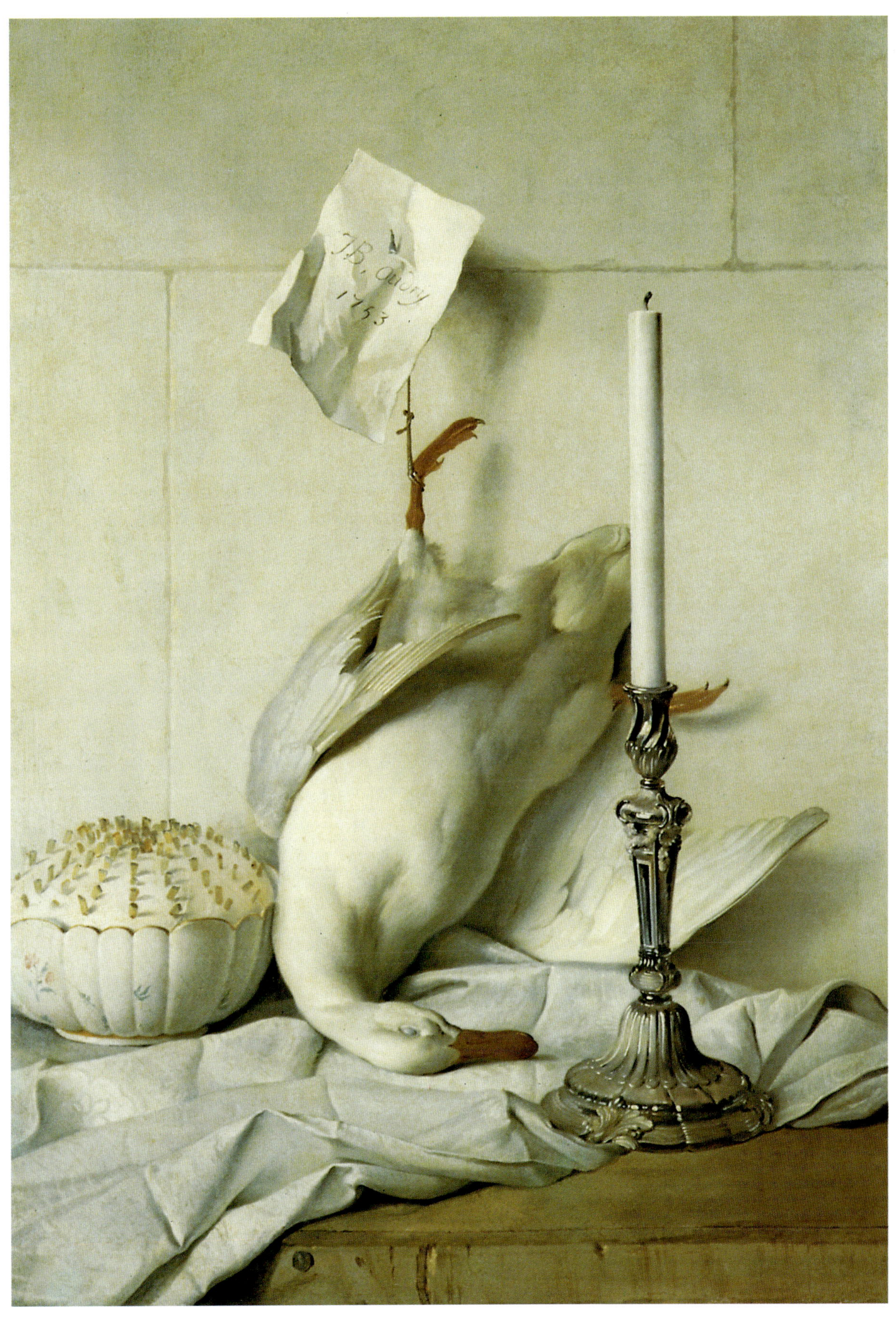
J.B. oudry
1753

ROBERT GRIFFIER
born London 1688, died London? 1750

Robert was the son of the Dutch painter Jan Griffier (born Amsterdam 1645 (or 1652), died London 1718). He was born in England, became a citizen of Amsterdam in 1716 and lived there for many years, then returned to London by 1727 and died about 1750. He painted still life pictures, birds and landscapes and copied Old Masters very accurately. He was also a picture dealer.

EGYPTIAN GOOSE AND OTHER AFRICAN BIRDS
signed, oil on canvas, 152.4 x 144 cm
Courtesy of Leger Galleries

The *Egyptian Goose and other African Birds* was owned by the Earl of Shrewsbury and Waterford before its sale. The title is not strictly accurate. This is quite usual for bird paintings. Most were hung on walls and enjoyed for their decorative and artistic qualities, and few either knew or cared which species of bird had been represented on the canvas. Work commissioned by menagerie owners was in a different class. Then the artist was not just painting a picture, but recording species present in the collection and the birds had to be correctly painted, hopefully in an attractive setting, but the landscape was of secondary consideration. This painting would appear to be a record of distinctive birds in a waterfowl collection, with a flying dove and jay added to enliven the top part of the picture. The main bird, however, is not an Egyptian goose, but a swan goose alternatively called a Chinese goose. There are two Egyptian geese on the left-hand side of the picture. The third waterfowl species, represented by the largest bird sitting on the water, is a muscovy duck. Only the Egyptian goose could be called an 'African' bird. The dove, jay and lapwing are of far wider geographical distribution. The Egyptian goose is like a large shelduck and is widespread in tropical Africa south of the Sahara. It was recorded in England in St James's Park in the mid-seventeenth century when it was called 'gambo-goose' or 'spur winged goose'. By 1785 they were not uncommon 'in gentlemen's ponds in many parts of the kingdom'. Feral birds (that is escapees living free and breeding in the wild) established themselves in England from these ponds.

Muscovy ducks, introduced into Europe by the Spanish from the South American port of Cartagena in the sixteenth century, quickly settled down to domestic life and have been familiar in Europe ever since. Their wild ancestors were birds of tropical forest lakes and rivers in Central and South America.

The keeping of geese, and experimenting with different breeds, had many advantages. Geese provided meat, eggs and feathers for bedding and quill pens. Goose grease was used for cooking and curing ailments. So important to the economy of the country was the goose that it was, until recent times, the most popular of all domestic poultry and gave its name to important fairs in England (Nottingham Goose Fair dated back to 1080) where they were traded. Wild geese also played a part in the lives of our ancestors, for the flight of wild geese heading north to their breeding grounds, was a sign of spring welcomed right across Europe.

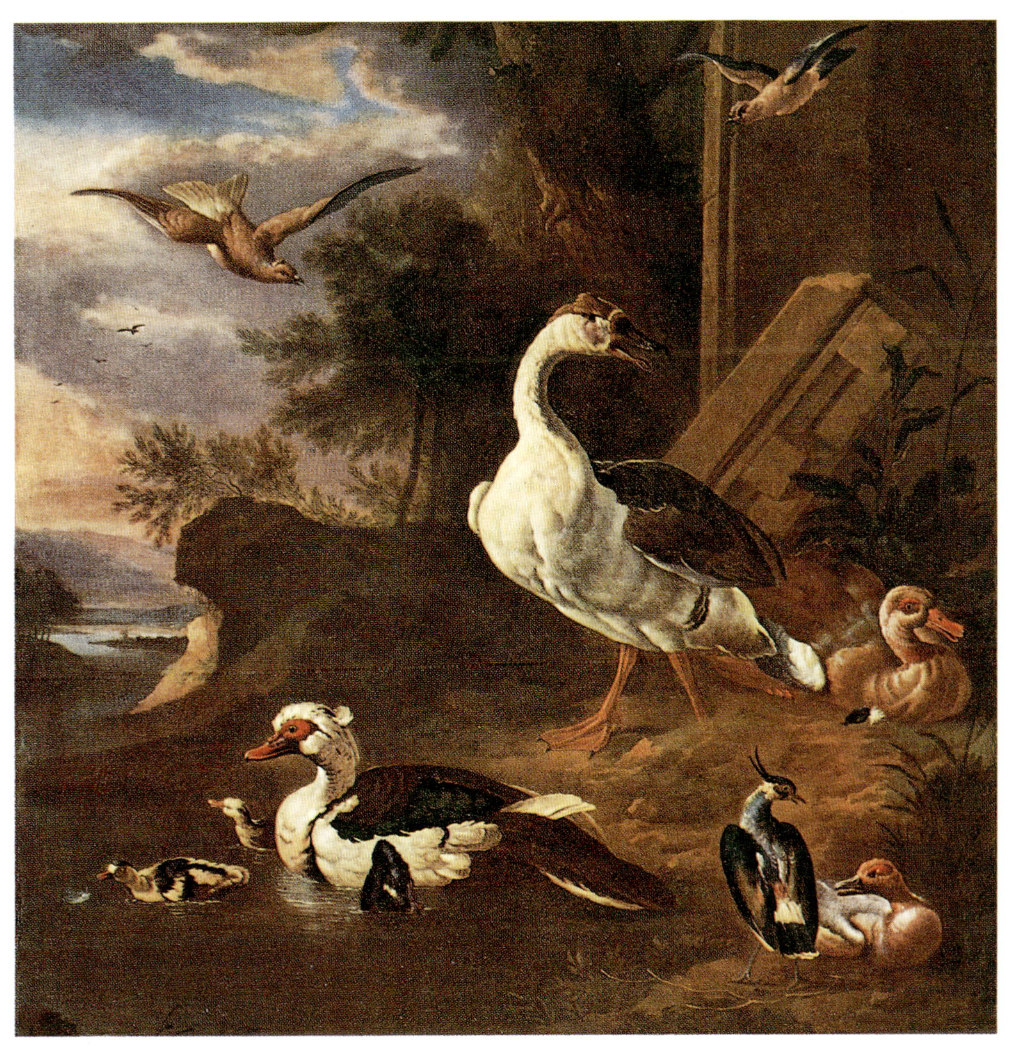

GEORGE EDWARDS

born West Ham, Essex 1694, died Plaistow, Essex 1773

Edwards was the third British bird artist, following Albin and Catesby, to paint pictures of birds and use them to illustrate a book with hand-coloured etchings. Edwards had a natural talent and inclination to draw birds and mammals, and learned to etch from Catesby. He practised his drawing for many years and gathered a large portfolio of watercolours before he decided to write and illustrate a bird book.

Edwards was born into comfortable circumstances and when his father died, he was left sufficient money not to have to work and so he travelled in Europe, modestly, and painted whenever he found something to interest him. It was not until his collection of drawings was seen by James Theobald, FRS, when Edwards was aged thirty-six, that he was commissioned by naturalists to produce bird paintings. Theobald introduced Edwards to other members of the Royal Society. Sir Hans Sloane, the president of the Royal Society and of the College of Physicians, employed Edwards for a number of years to draw mammals, fishes, reptiles and, more especially, birds. Through Sloane, Edwards was appointed as beadle, or custodian of the Royal College of Physicians' property in 1733, and moved into a house on the premises. Provided with a home, a small salary to supplement his patrimony, light duties (later expanded to include the oversight of the library), Edwards had sufficient leisure over the next thirty years to publish the books for which he is remembered today: *A Natural History of Uncommon Birds and Some Other Animals*, four volumes 1743-51 (with a frontispiece and 210 plates, 189 of which were bird plates) and the sequel, *Gleanings of Natural History*, exhibiting figures of quadrupeds, birds, insects, plants (most of which have not, till now, been either figured or described), three volumes 1758-64 with 150 plates, 128 of them with birds.

Edwards was in receipt of many foreign birds from shipments arriving in the port of London and he also went to visit aristocrats who had aviaries on their estates, or people who owned a single pet bird. He haunted pet shops, including one aptly named 'The Parrot and Cage', and saw birds which formed part of the attractions in London coffee houses and inns. Most of the birds were live. He drew the bird's outline, then painted it with watercolour, one copy being made for the owner and a second for Edwards' own use. He painted very few composite pictures, so this untitled picture, labelled *Birds in a Landscape* here, is a rare example.

BIRDS IN A LANDSCAPE
signed and dated 1732, pen and ink with gouache, 30.5 x 51.5 cm
Courtesy of William Drummond

This fanciful baroque landscape with everything hopelessly out of proportion and the birds oddly placed is a naïve but charmingly idiosyncratic composition. The birds set against the sky are ruby-throated humming-bird, waxwing, goldfinch, bullfinch, great tit and robin. The two birds on the branch beneath the robin were pictured on plate 130 of volume III of his *A Natural History of Uncommon Birds...*, where he called them 'Painted finch' and he said of the blue and black bird that it was 'not yet perfect'. The two have been identified as the painted and indigo buntings of North America. Many problems arise when identifying eighteenth century bird pictures because of the faded specimens the artists used and the limited palette they had available. The painted bunting is a much more colourful bird than Edwards has shown it to be.

The ruby-throated hummingbird was the first living hummingbird whose behaviour was described, by a visitor to America in 1632, although others had previously been sent to Europe as skins. It had been observed that they collected insects among flowers,

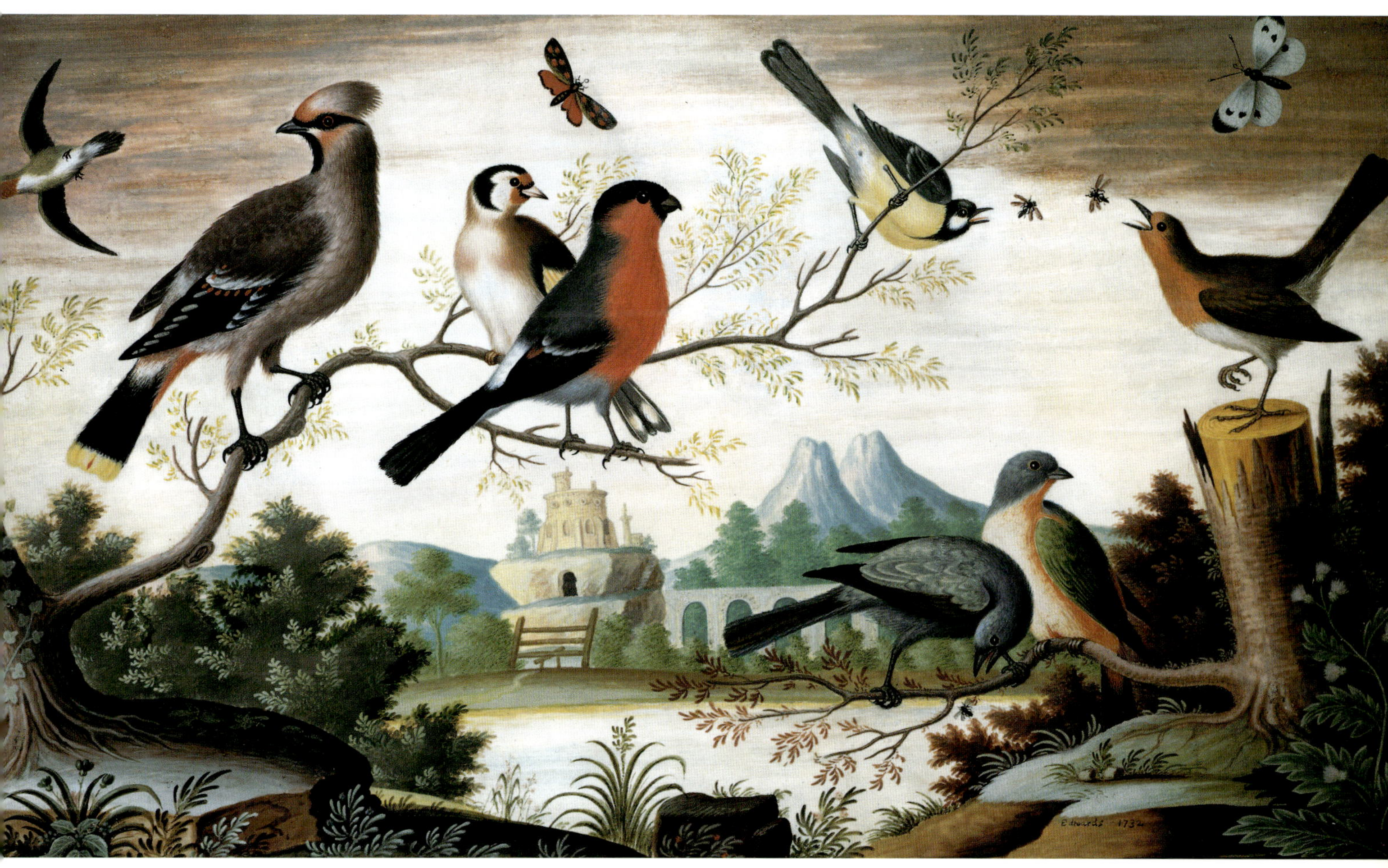

but it was not realised that they also collected nectar. For hundreds of different birds, only their physical shape and approximate colours were known for many years before any further information about them was discovered. All that we know today of the approximately 8,650 bird species has been put together painstakingly over the last three centuries and there are still some birds about whose lives we have learned very little.

The cinnabar moth and small white butterfly are present in this picture because, as Edwards explained in his book, he liked 'to fill up the naked spaces' with something colourful and interesting, whether relevant or not.

This is a picture by a bird illustrator who has little experience of painting landscapes and so has dotted some birds about in what he hoped was an attractive manner. It is quaint and it serves to show that a good landscapist is needed to make a great bird painting if the birds are to be painted in an outdoor setting or natural habitat.

CHRISTOPHER HUET
born 1694, died 1759

Christopher Huet was a charming French artist working in the period when painters were in great demand to decorate aristrocrats' new houses. He painted live macaws in fruit and flower pictures, and game pieces where the birds are both alive and dead. Huet's name, along with that of Watteau, is in the Prince de Condé's accounts in 1741 for decorative work on the family castle.

RUFFS IN A LANDSCAPE
oil on canvas, 52 x 44 cm

Huet has placed his male and female ruffs in a wet, marshy landscape with a natural sky over hills in the background, to make a pleasant, informal and intimate picture. The scale of the picture, and the simple treatment of the subject, make it suitable for a library or the house owner's study. It would have appealed either to the owner of similar land, or to a sportsman.

The ruff is a bizarre bird and the manner in which it was first brought to the notice of Englishmen is in keeping with the ruff's unique character. About the year 1586, an anonymous writer published an attack on the large frilly lace ruffs then being worn around the necks of Elizabethan men and women. In order to pour scorn on the extravagant garment and its wearers, he likened it to the ruff worn round the neck of the male birds of the species *Philomachus pugnax* when in breeding plumage.

Writing sixty years later, Walter Charleton explained both scientific and English names: 'Avis Pugnax the Ruff (because in fighting they raise up there feathers on the necke like a double Ruff).' The very beautiful elongated feathers grow thickly round the neck of the male just before the breeding season in April, and are shed again in June/July. A tuft of stiff, curled feathers sprouts from each side of the head looking like long ears, while the feathers beneath the throat grow more than two inches long to form a frill or ruff. They are so tightly layered that when the males joust and jab at one another with their long bills, the opponent's bill cannot penetrate the feathers of the breast. Perhaps the most surprising feature is that no two ruffs are exactly the same, but show a very diverse range of colours and markings. Some are barred, some plain, and the colours range from white through chestnut, brown, grey to black which is frequently glossed with purple, blue or green. The feathers may also be spangled with white or gold, haphazardly streaked or very evenly barred.

Male ruffs meet on lekking or jousting grounds and strut and fight and show off to attract the reeves. The males are polygamous and, having had a brief season of glamour, they shed their ruffs and take no further interest in the reeves, nor do they take any part in raising the young.

The ruff drawn by 'Blackborne a Paynter in Yorke', the woodcut from an eight-page pamphlet printed in London circa 1586. Known as a 'ruff' in English, and the female as a 'reeve', other Europeans call them the equivalent of 'combatants'.

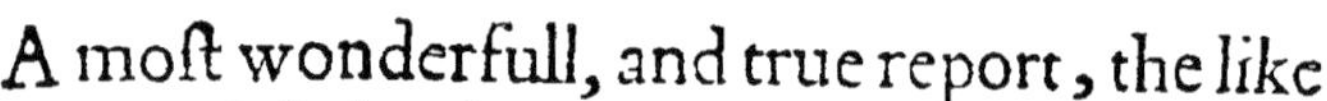

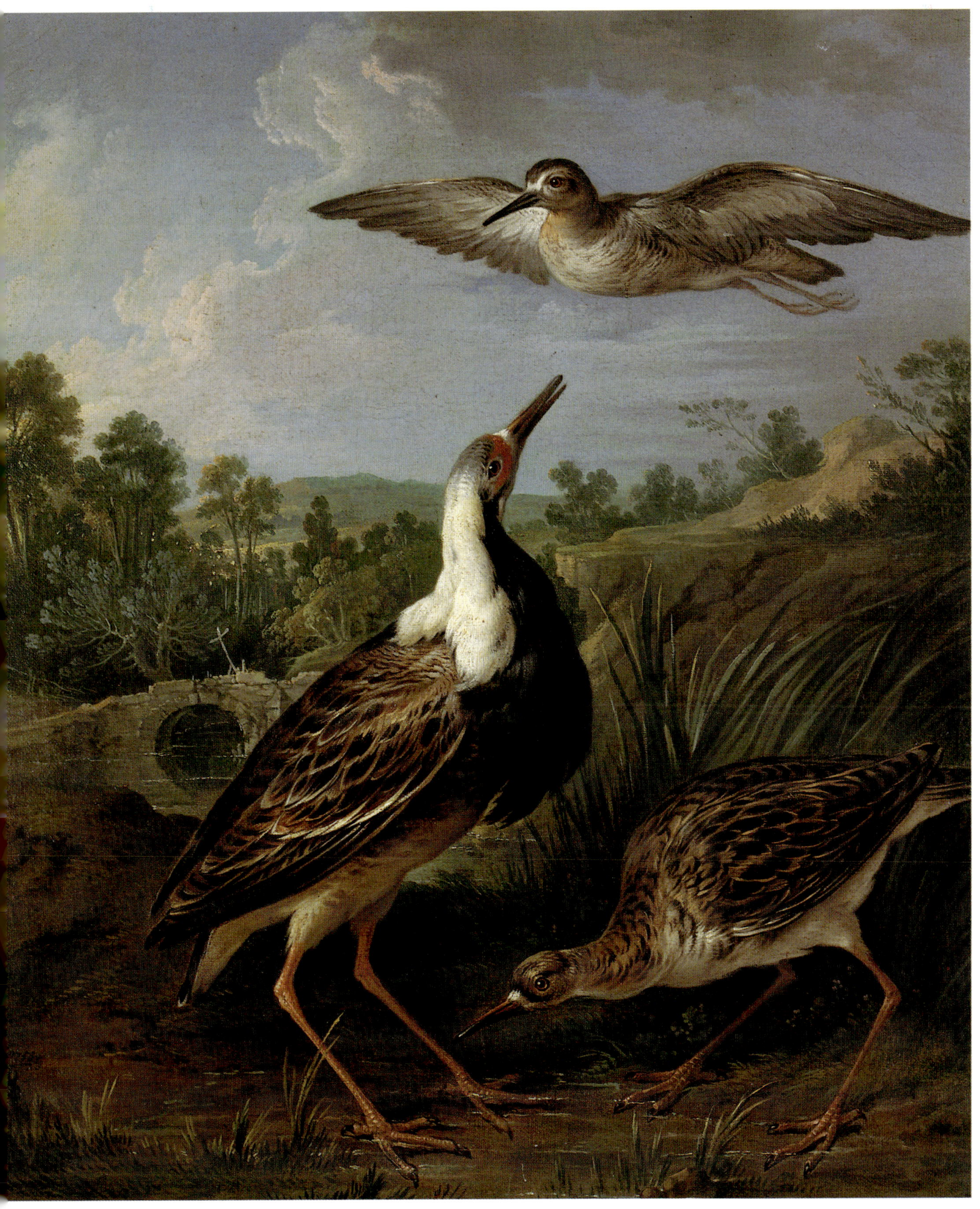

FAUSTINO DURANTE
born 1695, died Palazzolo, Brescia, 1766

Faustino Durante and his elder brother Comte Giorgio Durante (1685-1755) of Palazzolo, Brescia, Lombardy, specialised in painting realistic pictures of animals, particularly birds, for the nobility of Florence. They were highly esteemed miniaturists. Faustino first studied with Giorgio and then worked in his studio. When Giorgio died in 1755, Faustino entered the cloisters of Palazzolo.

TWO GREAT CRESTED GREBES RESTING BY A RIVERBANK
oil on canvas, 53.3 x 38.5 cm
Courtesy of Rafael Valls, London

The great crested grebe, painted by Faustino Durante, was a most unusual choice of subject. It was even more unusual to show the grebes out of water. In the water they are perfectly sleek and elegant. They only move on to land in order to build a nest and raise their young. Walking is very difficult for grebes because their legs are placed so far back on their bodies. In this position, they form powerful oars or paddles for swimming. Their feet are not webbed, like most water birds, but have lobes of stiff, horny flaps fringing their toes. Durante has painted the position and structure of the feet and legs with great fidelity, but the stance of the bird on the left is unreal.

Great crested grebes have a very distinctive courtship ceremony with bowing and head-shaking, dipping and swimming together in a water dance. When their chicks are old enough to leave the nest, the adults are solicitous parents, protecting their young chicks by giving them rides on their backs while swimming. The strongly striped downy young grebes, peering out from their parents' back feathers while taking a ride piggy-back style, is a sight well worth seeing in the spring. The parents sometimes dive while the chicks are still on board. A dislodged chick soon bounces back up to the surface, like a cork, and is retrieved and allowed to scramble back.

Durante has painted the birds in full breeding plumage, with the tippet of nuptial decorative plumes on the head in the raised and lowered positions, and has managed to convey the thick, lustrous and soft qualities of the body plumage.

The use of grebes' feathers, by the birds themselves, and by women, are both strange tales. For some reason, still not understood by scientists, grebes swallow quantities of their own body feathers. These may be found as wads in the stomachs not only of adult birds, but of small chicks. What function they perform when in the birds' stomachs has not been satisfactorily resolved.

'Tippet' was a name given to a cape of the under-feathers of grebes, worn by women in the nineteenth century (though ornithologically, the word tippet is used for the facial feathers). The use of feathers by the fashion trade for ladies' hats and decorating garments, caused a serious decline in numbers of such birds as grebes, egrets and birds of paradise. In England three women, Eliza Elder, Margaretta Louisa Smith and Winifred Dallas-Yorke, who became the Duchess of Portland, headed a crusade against this trade which led to the formation of the Society for the Protection of Birds in 1889. It took thirty years of campaigning, under the presidency of the Duchess, before the RSPB managed to get legislation passed banning the misuse of plumage.

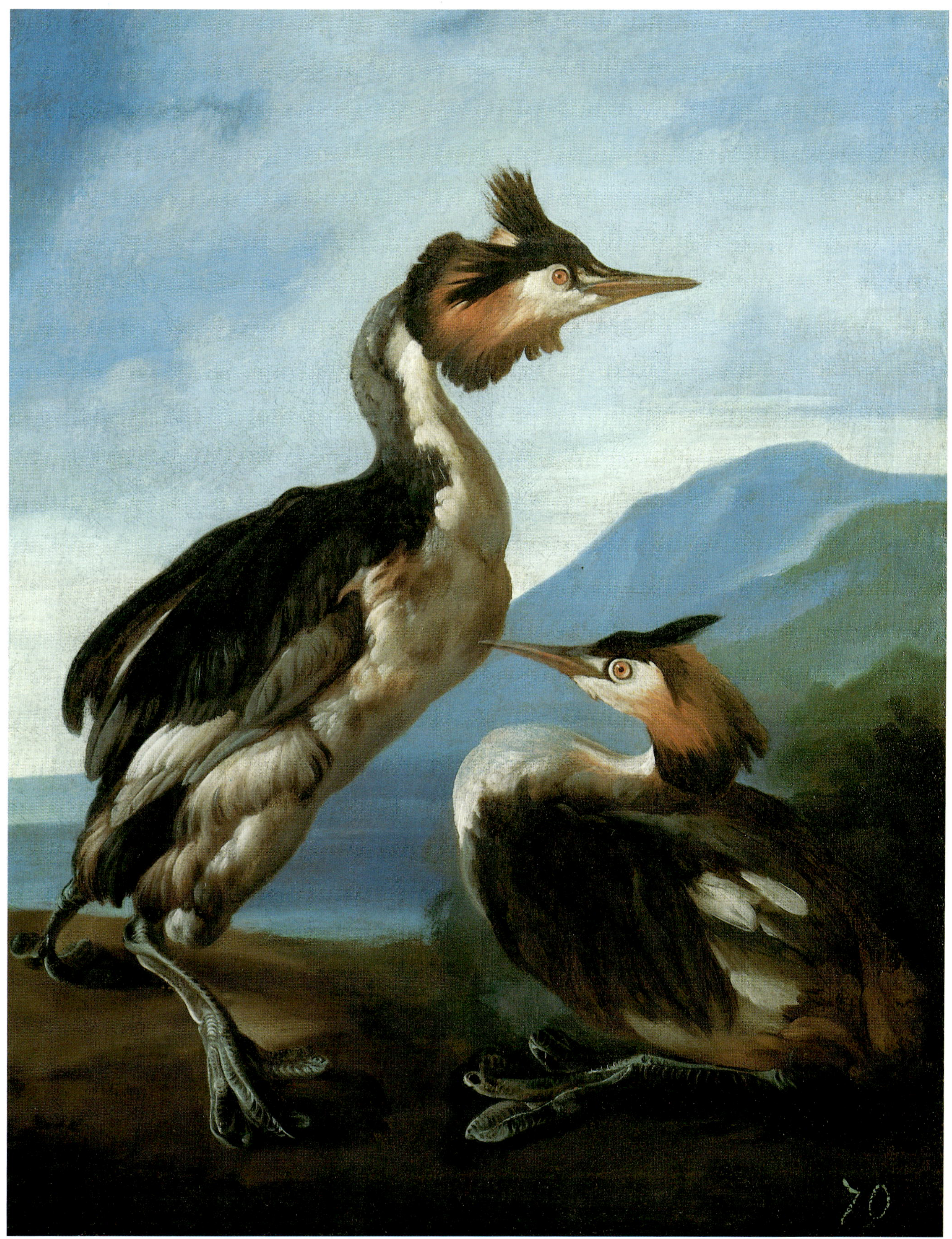

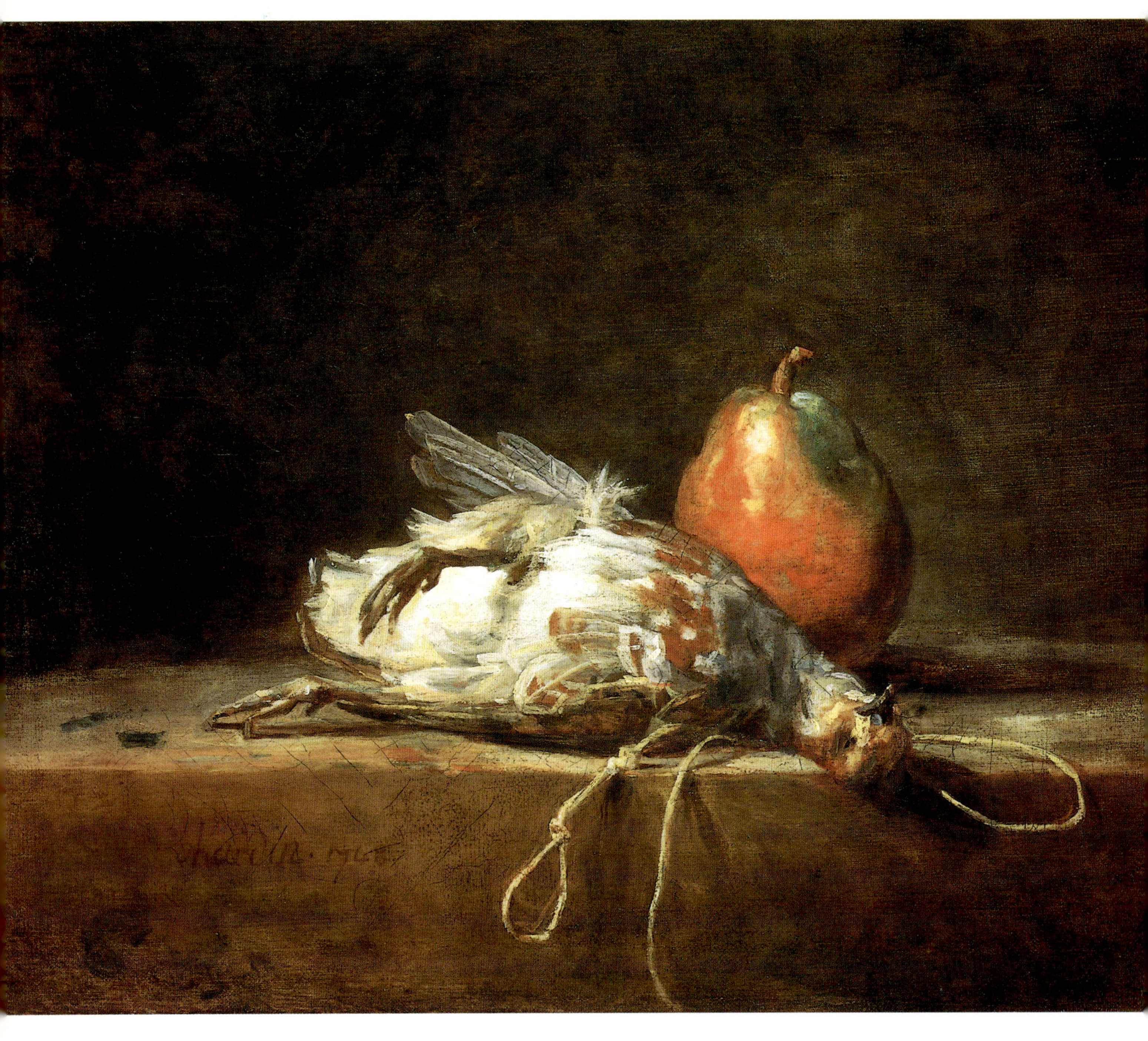

JEAN BAPTISTE SIMEON CHARDIN
born Paris 1699, died Paris 1779

Chardin is regarded as the greatest French still life painter. He painted small pictures of objects from everyday life, following the Dutch tradition, which were a commercial success in France in the mid-eighteenth century. He used Dutch themes, but adapted them to French taste and feelings. He is outstanding for his simplicity and directness of vision, but he added to his scrupulous rendering of substantial form a depth of feeling that made his pictures intimate in a way no other artist has achieved.

Chardin trained and worked in Paris, where he lived all his life. He was accepted into the Academy of St Luke in 1724 and admitted as a master painter to the Royal Academy of Painters and Sculptors four years later, on receipt of a still life picture of a ray, which was greatly praised for its realism. He became the treasurer of the Academy and hung its exhibitions for twenty years. Engravings of his work sold well to the public, and he was admired by fellow artists who were intrigued by his technique, which he developed to achieve great depth of tone by using successive applications of a loaded brush, followed by a subtle use of scumbling. This consists of working one layer of opaque oil paint over another layer of a different colour or tone so that the lower layer shows through. The effect is a broken, uneven area of colour. He was also a master of reflected light.

A PARTRIDGE AND PEAR ON A STONE TABLE
signed and dated 1748, oil on canvas, 39 x 45.5 cm
Courtesy of Städelsches Kunstinstitut, Frankfurt.

Chardin painted still life pictures in the 1720s and 1730s and then turned to small domestic scenes before returning to paint still life some fifteen years later. *A Partridge and Pear* was one of his last still life pictures. He painted some thirty bird still lifes, ranging over very few species, turkey, poultry, pheasant, lapwing, and a duck in four pictures. By far the greatest number of paintings of a single species were thirteen pictures of a partridge.

The grey partridge was increasing in numbers in European hedgerows in the second half of the eighteenth century and was by far the most regular game bird on the menu. Pheasants were much rarer at this period. The increase in partridge numbers, at the end of the century, may be attributed to the new rotation of crops when peas and beans were incorporated to return nitrogen to the soil and these plants provided a new rich source of food for partridges. Apart from domestic fowl, grey partridges had been the most frequently painted species in seventeenth century still life paintings. Not only were they the most easily available birds to paint (thousands having been snared like Chardin's partridge), their plumage is such a beautiful combination of texture, colour and markings, that artists found them a constant source of inspiration. Most frequently, the dead bird was placed on its back in order to reveal the fine vermiculation on the grey blue breast, pale brick red throat and, in adult birds, the wine-red black patch on the belly. Chardin has chosen a young bird which gives added pathos to this simple composition of a partridge with a pear. The partridge in a pear tree has its own rich traditions with a time of feasting, inferred here by association. The bird is painted with rapid, sure brush strokes, without detail but with a deep feeling for the beauty of the plumage. The feet hang limply and the broken neck is barely supported at the edge of the table, a wonderful evocation of death. The ripe fruit echoes the ruddy colours of the birds' feathers, while the whole canvas glows with autumnal warmth. This is the season when both bird and fruit have reached their peak of fitness for the table.

STEPHEN ELMER
born Farnham, died 1796

Stephen Elmer was a Farnham maltster's son and himself a maltster by trade. He continued in business while establishing a high reputation as a painter. He showed pictures of mammals and birds, rural scenes and still life paintings at the Royal Academy from 1772 and was elected an associate member. Considering his art was a part-time activity, it is ironic that he was considered at the time to be the most successful British painter of still life and dead game. Even more remarkable was the quantity of pictures that he showed at the Royal Academy (117 between 1772 and 1795, including fifty-seven bird titles), the Free Society of Artists (113 between 1764-83, of which fifty named birds in the titles), and he also exhibited four still life paintings at the British Institution gallery.

His paintings were popular because of the free, bold style in which he painted all parts of the picture. His choice of bird subjects was exactly to the taste of the purchasers. Elmer painted game birds and sporting scenes almost exclusively, so that he repeated pictures of live partridges, pheasants and grouse, set in romanticised hilly landscapes with blue skies and scudding clouds. He catered for the new gentry, men of wealth who had invested their profits in country houses and land, and who had leisure to indulge in country sports. He frequently painted spaniels in a hunting scene or with dead trophies. Occasionally, he tired of these subjects and painted a more unusual bird, such as a canary in a cage or mandarin drake with a golden pheasant. When not painting birds, he supplied equally attractive records of fishes, or hares and foxes, in rural settings. He was also capable of producing a fine picture of fruit or flowers, less often he painted figures either of gentlemen or beggars.

BLACK GAME
oil on canvas, 70 x 90 cm
Courtesy of Rafael Valls, London

Black Game is a typical Elmer composition. Most frequently, he chose a brace of birds, placed them in poses to demonstrate their main plumage colour patterns and put them in their natural habitat. He made their environment idealistically attractive, and faintly reminiscent of Scottish hillsides and moors. To give the birds some semblance of movement, he introduced an object on which they could concentrate their attention, for example the two flying swallows in this picture.

Sportsmen call the male black grouse 'black game' and the female a 'greyhen' although her plumage is brown, barred with black, rather than grey in colour. Elmer's birds are painted in spring or summer when the male has the red wattle over the eye. His tuft of longer feathers under his chin is just visible in this painting. When he throws back his head to crow or call, the feathers assume the appearance of a tooth-brush under his beak. The dramatic effect of raising the lyre-shaped tail in display is enhanced by the snowy white undertail feathers. He assumes the aggressive posture of head thrown up with wings held away from his body to make himself as large and imposing as possible when on the lekking ground in spring, where he displays in order to attract a female.

The birds mate and he then has little further to do with the female or their offspring. She does all the work of brooding and feeding the chicks, so this picture of an isolated pair, suggestive of joint parenthood and family unity, is misleading. As a reminder of a successful day on the moors, with the prospect of a good bag of grouse at the end of it, it could hardly be improved.

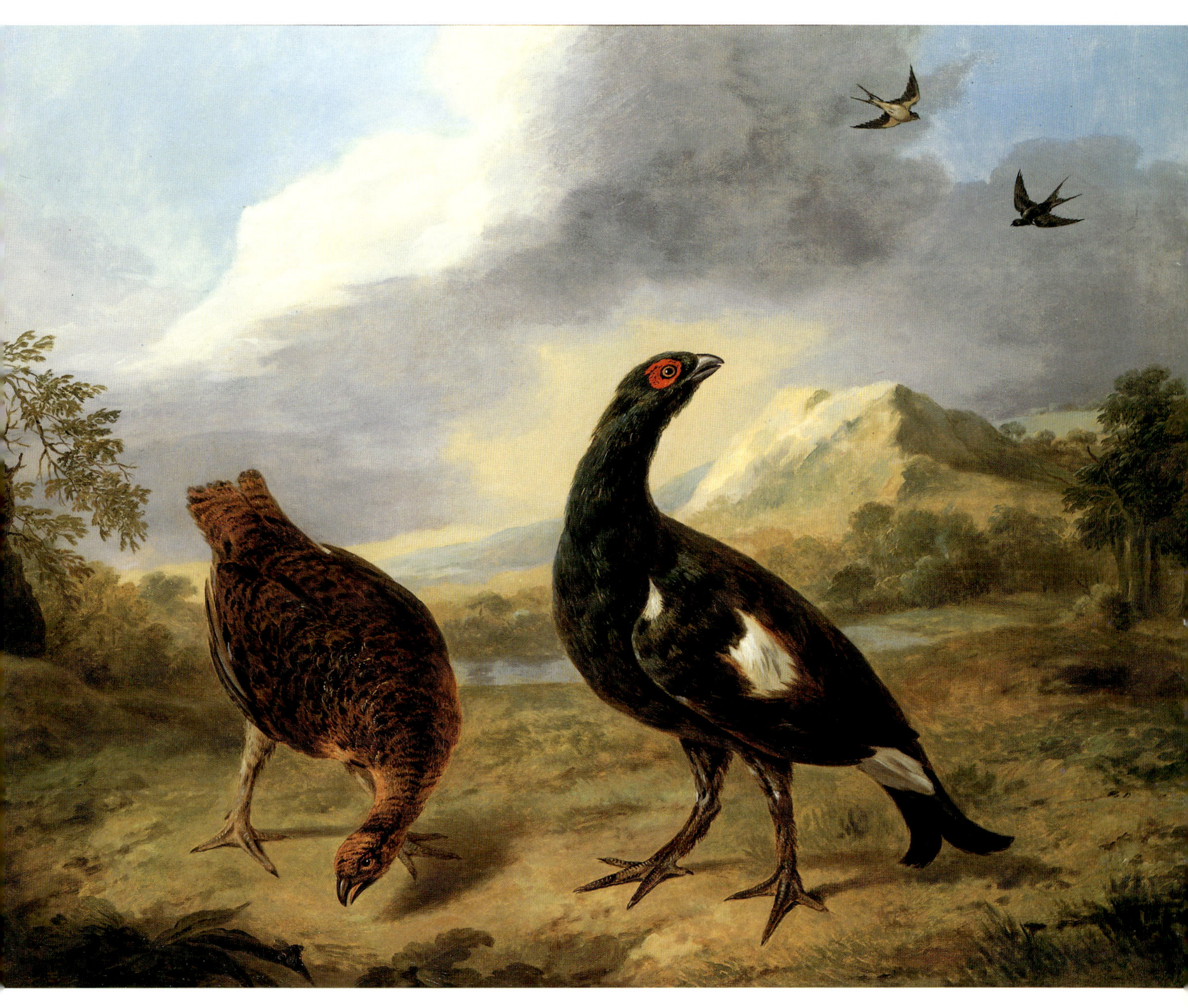

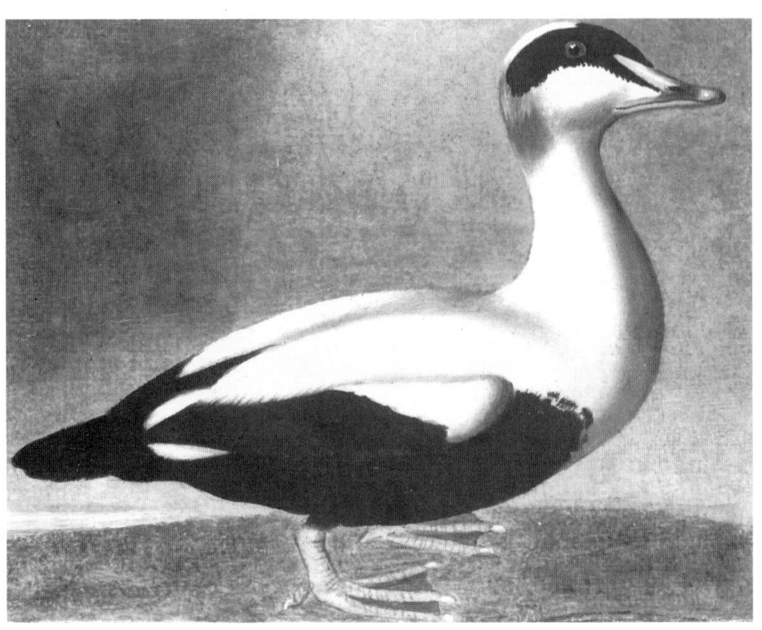

Eider Drake. *Oil on canvas*
Courtesy of Rafael Valls, London

PETER PAILLOU
born c.1712, died London, 1780

Peter Paillou's family lived in Westminster where they attended the French Huguenot church. He was apprenticed to Jacob Tribble of St Ann's, Westminster in 1724 for £8 and subsequently became a prolific artist. He painted for Thomas Pennant the zoologist, Sir Joseph Banks the explorer and President of the Royal Society, and Taylor White, a wealthy natural history collector.

Paillou was mostly employed to make watercolours of individual species, but he also painted pictures for Pennant who wrote of him being 'an excellent artist, but too fond of giving gaudy colours to his subjects. He painted for my hall, at Downing, several pictures of birds and animals, attended with suitable landscapes... all have their merit, but occasion me to lament his conviviality, which affected his circumstances and abridged his days.' Downing Hall, Pennant's house near Whitford in Flintshire, was gutted by fire in 1922 so these paintings have been lost. Nearly one hundred of Paillou's bird watercolours were reproduced as etchings, by Peter Mazell, for Pennant's *The British Zoology*, 1761-66.

Paillou's work for Taylor White (1701-1772) has been preserved in Montreal, Canada, where over 120 signed (and many more unsigned) bird paintings are housed in the McGill University Library. Taylor White, a judge, was an enthusiastic collector of animals, who had birds and mammals in dens and aviaries in London, which were recorded by artists, usually as life-size colour portraits. He also commissioned work to be done in other menageries to make his collection of paintings as complete a record as possible. Charles Collins assisted Paillou, and their watercolours, done from birds available in England and Wales between 1736 and 1780, number 659.

WATERFOWL BY A RIVER BANK
signed and dated 1774, oil on canvas, 215 x 120 cm

The bird picture *Waterfowl by a River Bank* was signed and dated 1774 and is one of a pair of large canvases. The narrowness in relation to the height suggests that this pair was painted to order to fit a specific position in a room. Though the ducks (smew, mallard and shoveller) and bittern and kingfishers may be regarded as birds of the river bank, the jay and bullfinch are woodland species. Paillou has carried the interest from the top right-hand corner of the painting down to the bottom left corner, each bird

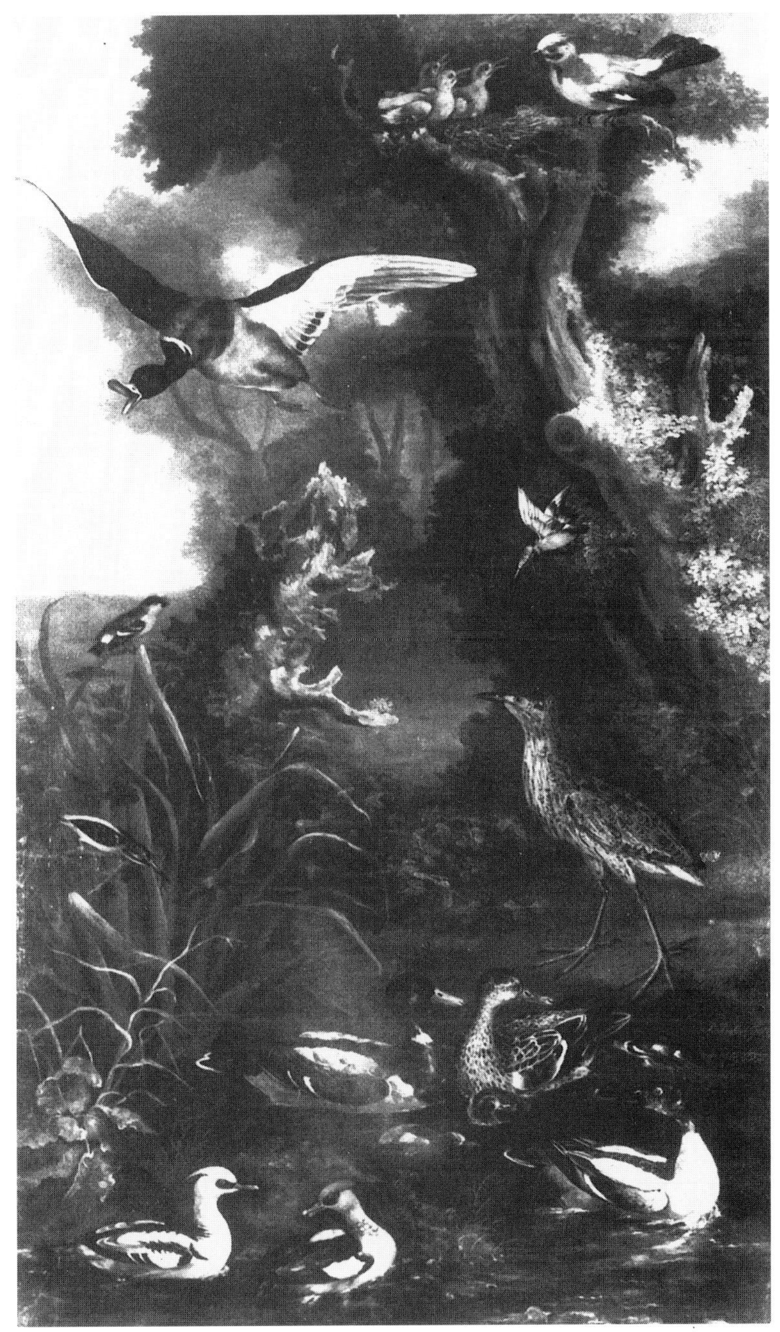

being given equal attention and importance, each being painted in its natural size with no regard for its relative distance from the viewer. The different plants and trees are carefully painted to form an integrated and intimate scene where the birds are actively pursuing their daily routine in conventional poses. There is still no original idea, no birds preening, sleeping or bathing, and the Old Masters' skill at conveying the exact time of day when the scene was captured is missing. However, this is a pleasing picture with a more natural setting. The piece of countryside is authentic and has replaced the artificial landscape garden setting with urns and fountains. This is a collection of birds that one may have been fortunate to see on a country walk in Norfolk or the fens, though not all in view at one time. So, although there is clearly a movement toward a more naturalistic background, it is still artificial in the number, and neat spacing, of the birds present.

JACOBUS VONCK
born Middelburg 1717, died Middelburg 1773

Jacobus Vonck was the last bird painter of an artistic family which had specialised in painting still life and game pictures, including exotic birds and mammals set in open country landscapes, for a hundred years. Jacobus was said to have been the pupil of the slightly younger bird artist Aert Schouman. With Schouman and Uytter-Limmege, Vonck is one of the very few Dutch bird artists who carried the traditions of the Old Masters through to the third quarter of the eighteenth century. He painted many pictures of a large ewer around which he entwined roses, convolvulus, mallows and poppies and placed a bird, such as jay, green woodpecker, hoopoe, in a prominent position in his composition. Birds are favourite motifs and occur in the majority of his paintings.

A GOLDEN PHEASANT ON A STONE PLINTH, WITH OTHER BIRDS
oil on canvas, 72.5 x 103.5 cm
Courtesy of Rafael Valls, London

In this painting, a golden pheasant with doves and a hen and her chickens, all the elements with which one has become familiar in the best of the Old Masters' bird pictures, are present. There is the careful painting of the foreground plants, in this case a fruiting bramble, birds in the distance, and an architectural feature on the horizon. Nevertheless, there is a diminution in the skill with which the birds are assembled and a loss of vitality in the birds themselves. There is still great pleasure to be derived from Vonck's skilful handling of paint, and his rendering of feathers is markedly adept.

Following the introduction of the common variety, the golden pheasant was the next species of pheasant to be introduced into Europe. It is a native of China, where it lives high in the mountains. Its scientific name is *Chrysolophos pictus*, from the Greek chrysos which means gold and lophos a crest. *Pictus* is 'painted' and this bird looks as though it has been painted from a very colourful palette. The first record (in 1735) and published picture of the golden pheasant in England occurred in *A Natural History of Birds*, by Eleazar Albin, the earliest British bird book with coloured illustrations which was published 1731-38. Albin had seen the pheasant 'in the possession of the Hon. John Spencer Esq., at his house in Windsor Park where I went by his orders to draw it.' For two centuries after Albin described it, the few specimens that were imported into Europe were highly prized as ornaments for gentlemen's country gardens. Vonck probably painted this bird in a Dutch garden about thirty years after Albin had painted his.

The brilliantly coloured cock golden pheasant has a large crest of bright yellow feathers. The feathers of his large ruff are wide, of a bright orange colour bordered by steely-blue bars. When he displays to the hen, he circles round her cautiously, then makes a sudden run to pull up short, sideways on, with his crest raised and his ruff spread widely. He peers intently over the top edge of his ruff, tilts his body towards her and lifts his wings so that the brilliant golden back and rump feathers are shown off to perfection. Just to add the finishing touch to this performance, he tilts his tail too, spreading it vertically to reveal the scarlet tail feathers. It is all extremely picturesque, especially in bright sunlight when the bird looks freshly painted in rich, glowing colours, fully deserving his name, *Chrysolophos pictus*, the golden-crested painted bird.

The distant turkey, poultry and pigeons are further evidence of increasing interest in breeding varieties. This fluffy white crested hen recurs in other paintings of the period, but the shell crest of the pigeon is a new development. The red admiral butterfly is decorative, if over-large.

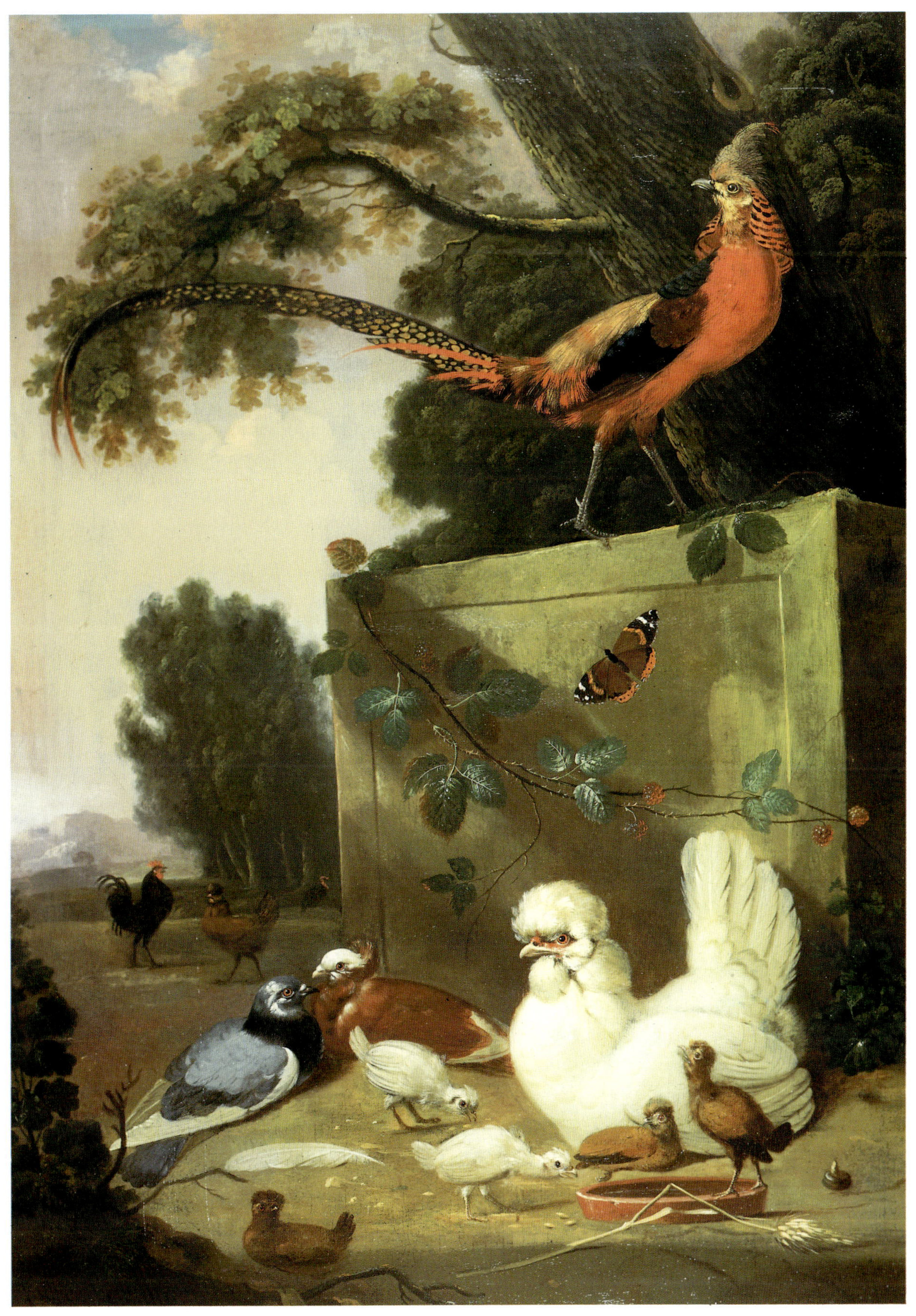

AERT SCHOUMAN
born Dordrecht 1710, died The Hague 1792

Aert Schouman is one of the last Dutch masters to have been commissioned to paint large canvases to decorate lofty rooms. Several of his pictures are very large, like the two shown here, 102 x 40 inches. His composition and the birds included in the landscape were often repeated, so that a large tree emerging from behind huge rocks was part of a standard formula.

Schouman was a prolific artist, a foremost bird painter but also a flower painter and engraver on glass. After training with F. Greenwood and Adriaen van den Burg, he became a master painter at The Hague in 1748, and three years later regent of the art academy, then the principal in 1762. At The Hague he taught van Os flower painting, and van Os became outstanding in this field, often adding birds and nests in his paintings. Schouman also painted exquisite bird watercolours (some with bodycolour) to which he added gold highlights and nearly always incorporated the rocks of which he was inordinately fond.

Prince Willem V owned a zoological cabinet and a menagerie in the grounds of the summer palace Het Loo, Apeldoorn. He had mammals, snakes and birds that came from all parts of the known world and these were painted by the artists Aert Schouman and Simon Fokke. Thirty-four treatises on foreign animals, each species with a colour picture from Schouman and Fokke's work, and accompanied by a description written by Vosmaer, were published between 1766 and 1804. However, Schouman was at his happiest when given a large space in which to paint a huge landscape and artistically dispose exotic birds within it.

The lower parts of the two large panels illustrated here include birds from North and South America, Africa, Asia, and New Guinea. Apart from predatory birds, the tolerance shown by birds to most other, different, species in the same enclosure is one of their appealing characteristics. There are exceptions, especially when feelings run high at breeding time and the space is too restricted, otherwise these toucans and pigeons, pheasants and cock of the rock, with the smaller perching birds, live together in relative peace and amity. Although this is an artificial assembly, it is also a reminder of the extraordinary way in which these several species adapted to life in a Dutch menagerie, thousands of miles from their native forests. It is also a reminder that human interference in the lives of these birds, which has taken place over three hundred years, has seriously depleted their numbers to the point where several birds in seventeenth, eighteenth and nineteenth century pictures are now the only representatives of their kind.

BIRDS IN A LANDSCAPE
two oils on panel, each 265.1 x 110.5 cm

Schouman's large paintings are not meant to be viewed closely. He painted large vistas that created an impression of a scene in which birds moved about some distance away. He did not paint in much detail, but used broad strokes for areas of colour as they would have been glimpsed in the woodland. Because he painted high, narrow pictures (often to be placed on either side of a doorway) he painted the birds from different angles, according to their place on the canvas. Those birds positioned on top of the rocks were painted as seen from below, while the viewer looks down on to the birds on the floor of the forest. A few of the birds are at eye level. This could be highly advantageous to the intelligent artist who placed the birds in a position selected to show them to their greatest advantage. Brilliant underplumage called for a high position in the scene, while crests and crowns in full display called for eye-level treatment. Subtle colouring in the plumage was best served by a near-view position. The rarest or most glamorous bird was usually placed at the centre of the group where it would arrest the eye and draw the viewer toward the picture in order to inspect it more closely. Schouman's birds are carefully and thoughtfully positioned and repay some attention to his arrangement.

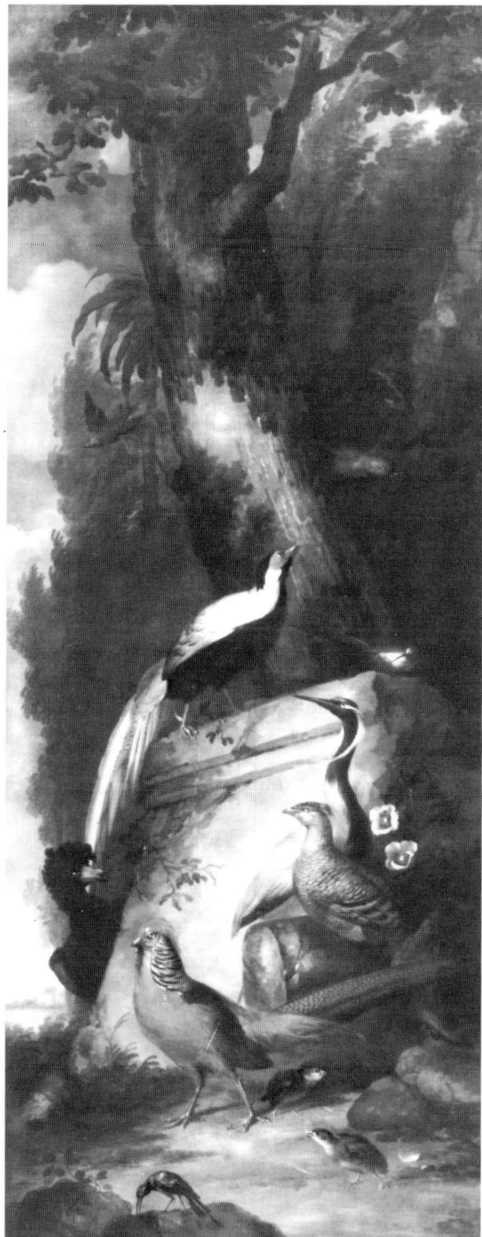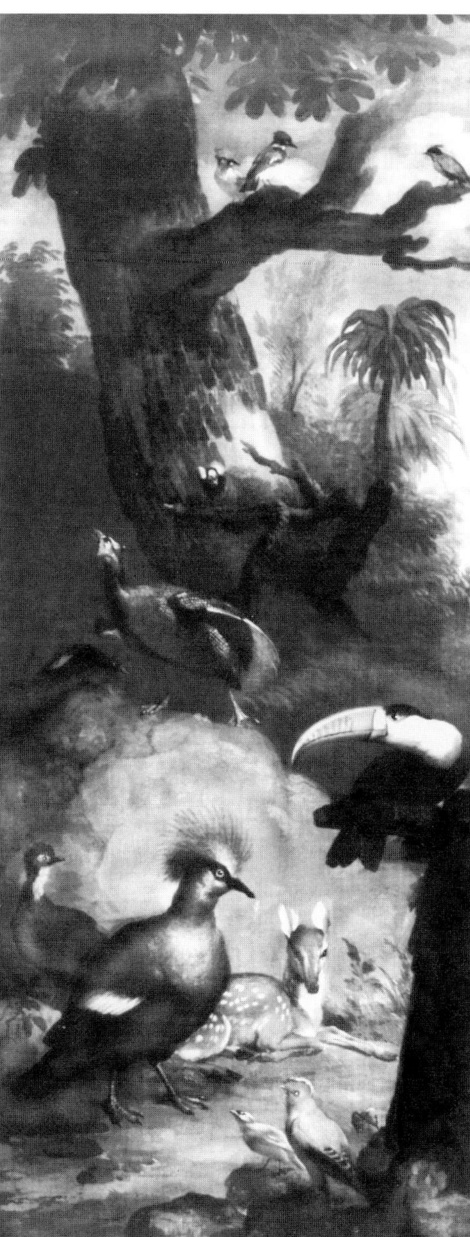

Canvases over two metres in height allow for a very large tree, and life-size demoiselle crane, silver and gold pheasants, a blue-crowned pigeon and a fawn. A red-billed toucan shows only its head and amazing bill. There are several more colourful tropical birds which Schouman has painted in the Dutch menagerie.

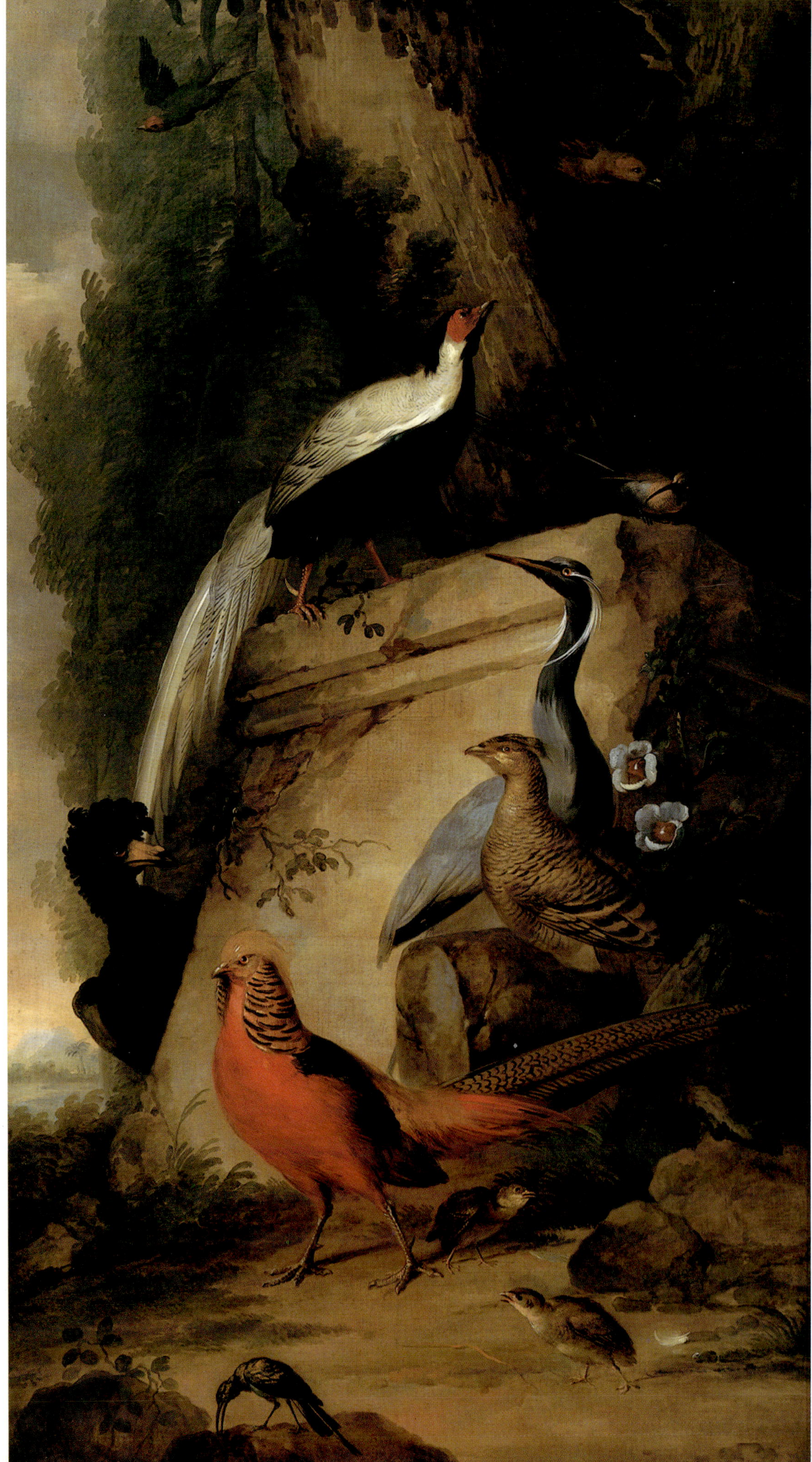

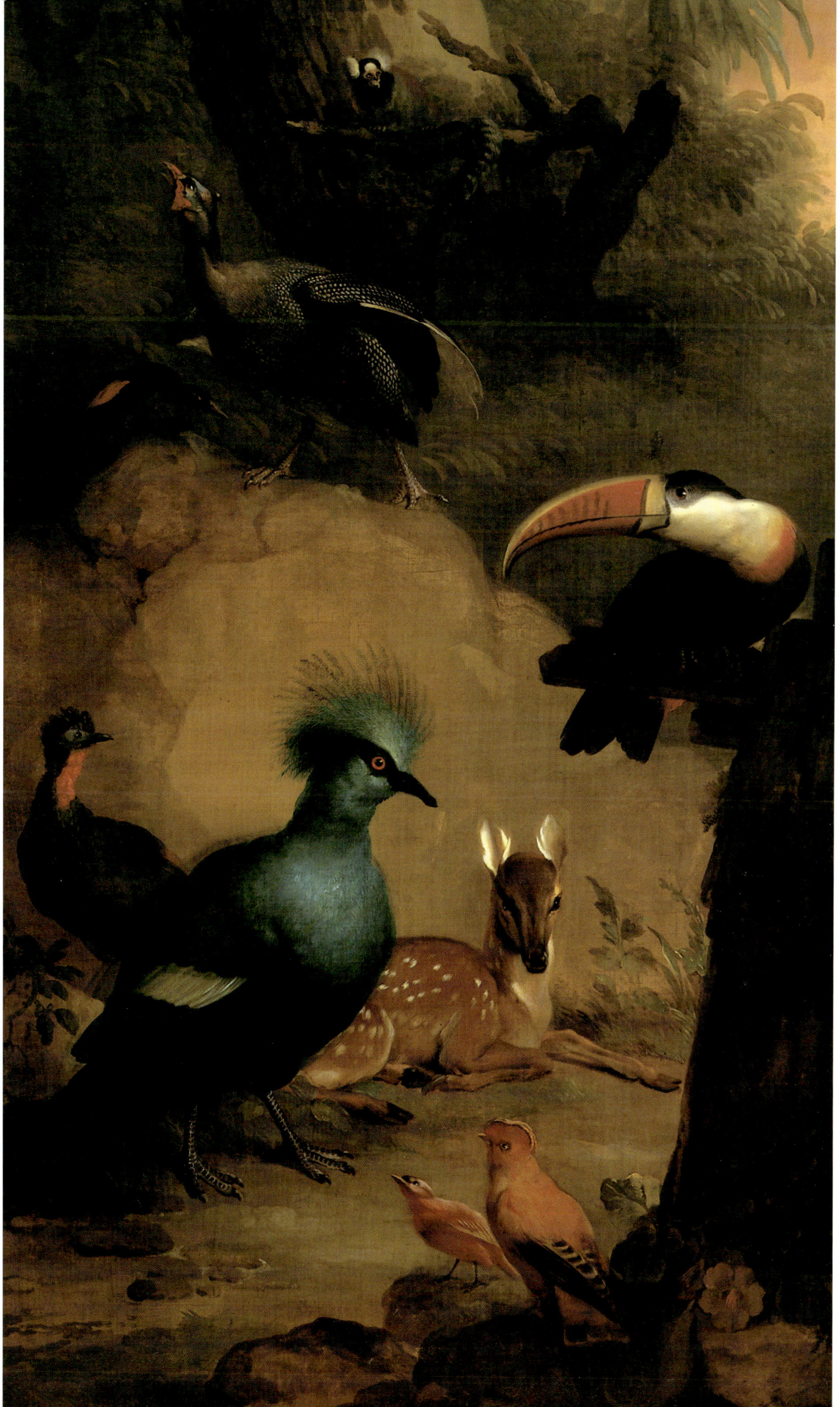

SAMUEL DIXON
born Dublin, died Dublin 1769

Samuel was the third son of a Dublin hosier. He lived most of his life in Dublin and may have studied at the Dublin Society's drawing school. By April 1748 he had opened a picture shop in Capel Street, when he advertised some flower pieces which he claimed were produced by a new invention. He sold the flower pictures in a set of twelve, each measuring about 24 x 21 cm. They were novel and sold so well that Dixon was encouraged to advertise again, stating that he was preparing 'a Sett of curious foreign Bird Pieces, in the same Stile of the former, but larger'. These were on sale mid-1750, in 'gold, peartree and japanned frames' about 30 x 24 cm.

Dixon called his invention 'Basso Relievo' which was a method of moulding the surface of a metal plate so that the bird and flower images stood out in relief. Heavy paper or card when pressed against the metal sheet was moulded into relief from the back and then the embossed surface was painted in gouache. The enterprise was so successful that Dixon employed three students from the Dublin Society's drawing school to do the painting. Most of Dixon's bird pictures were based on the plates in George Edwards' *Natural History of Uncommon Birds*, four volumes 1743-51.

TWO SETS OF TWELVE BASSO RELIEVO BIRD PICTURES
Courtesy of Christie's, London

A second set of twelve bird pictures was advertised as both 'foreign and Domestick Birds' and put on sale in September 1755. These were larger, being about 46 x 36 cm, allowing Dixon to elaborate further by adding in more insects, flowers, foliage and sometimes shells. Again, the designs were based on George Edwards' work, but Dixon copied birds from two or three plates in Edwards' books and combined them into a design of his own. Each plate, in this second set of pictures, was dedicated to a lady member of the aristocracy, thereby gaining patronage and adding 'tone' to Dixon's work. It was astute of Dixon to sell his pictures framed, for the embossed paper would need careful handling. The charming paintings in their luxurious frames made very attractive pictures and are nearly always sold today still in their original frames. The presentation was in keeping with the fashion for both rococo and chinoiserie, the pictures being light, airy and fanciful while the frames had more than a hint of the orient, with small scenes including pagoda-roofed houses and other Chinese motifs. Dixon pasted labels on the backs of the framed pictures, providing descriptions of the birds, flowers and butterflies, as well as the name of the lady to whom that picture had been dedicated.

Inevitably, such a good and successful idea was imitated. Dixon complained at first, but had to accept the fact that just as he had copied Edwards' designs, so others copied his idea. Mary Taverner, a gilder and japanner in Dublin, was quick to try to capture some of Dixon's lucrative market and Dixon complained in *Faulkner's Dublin Journal* on 27 October 1749 that 'there is a base Imitation of my foreign Bird Pieces in Basso Relievo being hawked about this city by a Woman'. Insult was added to injury when he claimed that her pictures were 'improperly painted, have faded and lost their Colours which has conduced several to bring them to me to be repaired and painted over again.'

When Dixon closed his picture business in Dublin in 1757, he tried fabric printing and when this failed in 1765, he went to London, only to find that his work was known there and his idea had already been exploited by Isaac Spackman, an Islington painter. Spackman produced a set of bird pictures in basso relievo in 1754. These also were based on George Edwards' illustrations in *Natural History of Uncommon Birds*.

Spackman produced a second series in 1764 and then a third series, all of which can be recognised as Spackman's work, rather than that of Dixon, by Spackman's less attractive, stylized backgrounds.

Embossed pictures, often attributed to Dixon, were in truth, 'Sold by Appointment of the Maker H. Baker at R. Williamson's Bookseller and Printer', near the Exchange in Liverpool, including 'The Mock Bird brought from Jamaica and in the Possession of T. White of Lincolns Inn Esq.'. Also in this collection were a 'Peacock Pheasant from China' and the peahen. McDermott of Dame Street was another imitator with a set of a dozen flower, fruit and bird pictures in 1755. A little later, in London, William Hayes produced some embossed pictures on a larger scale, but he used his own drawings.

Dixon spent three years in London selling his work in a picture shop before returning to Dublin in 1768, where he died a year later.

Blue and yellow macaw Gray finch and waxbill (3)	Red and blue macaw Indian redstart and sparrow of paradise(2)
Chaffinch, convolvulus, snowdrops, etc. butterfly (11)	Goldfinch, honeysuckle, ranunculus and others (5)
Black-billed whistling duck with a purple waterhen (1)	Indian bee-eater, black and white Indian starling, Brazilian finch (8)

Summer duck Red-billed whistling duck, shells (7)	White-headed parrot, grapes, and butterflies (9)
Canary, anemones, tulips and other flowers (4)	Cock butcherbird, poppies, and other flowers (6)
Bullfinch and blue titmouse fruit and soforth (10)	Green-winged dove, cock and hen red-throated hummingbirds with nest, butterflies (12)

Dixon's colourists have got the macaw colouring incorrect – having two macaws has confused them. The red and blue macaw is on the left, the blue and gold on the right. The names given above are those Samuel Dixon gave the bird pieces. The numbers in brackets are those he assigned to the picture in his set of twelve.

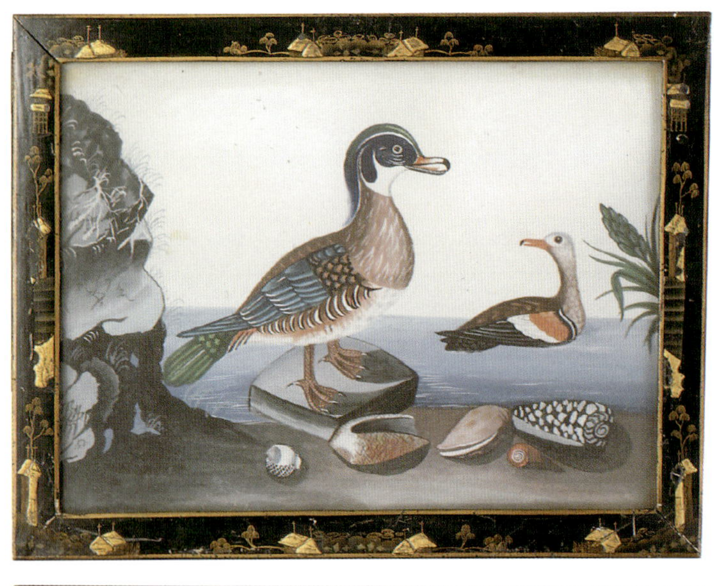
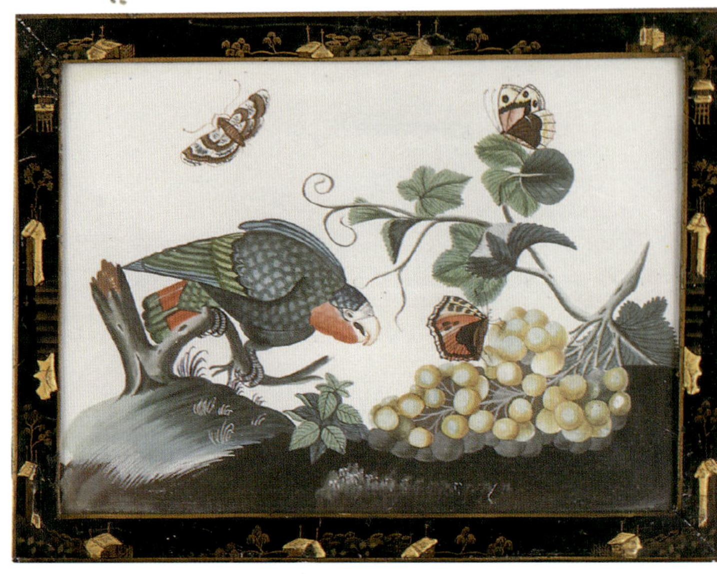
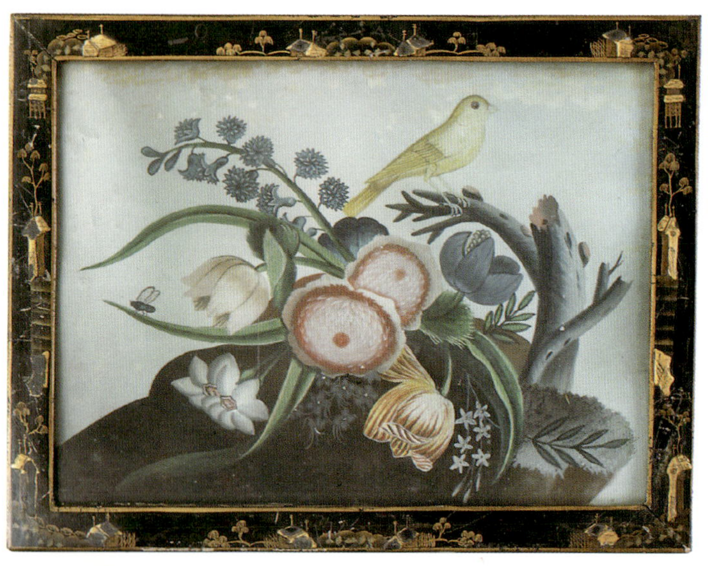
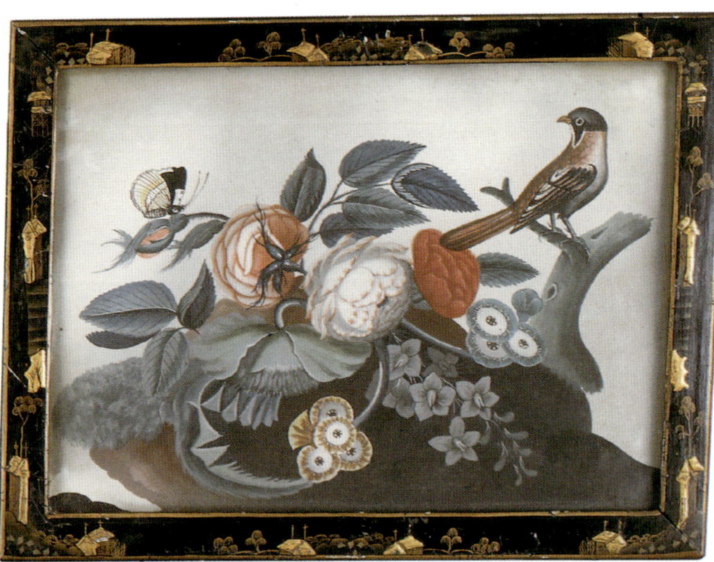
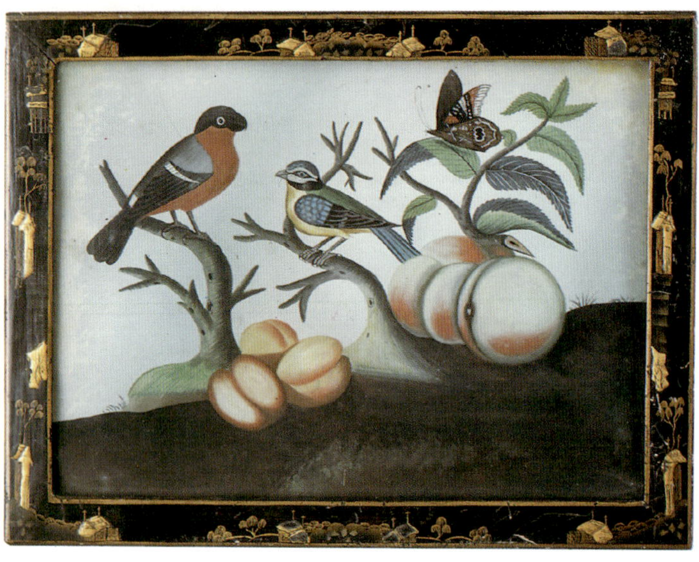
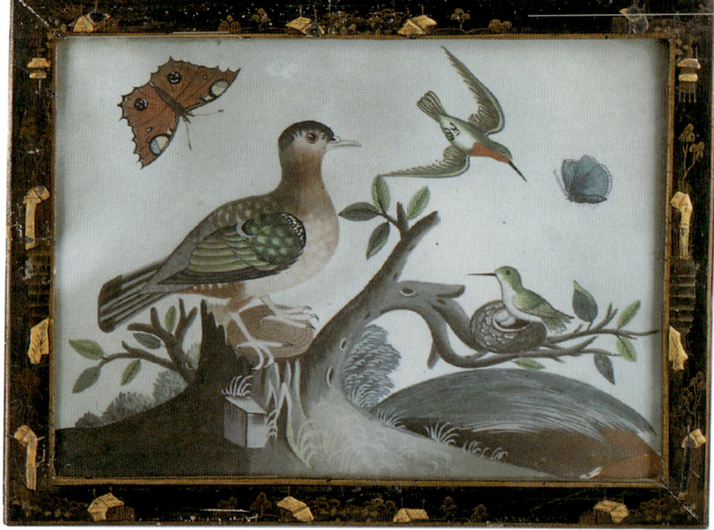

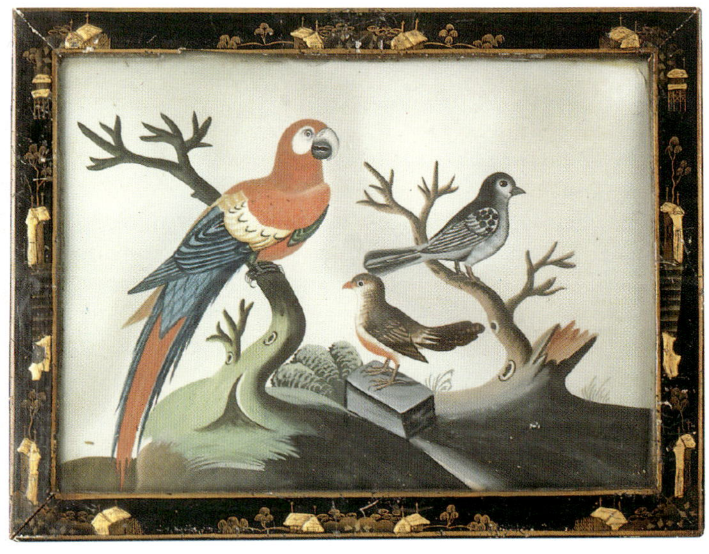
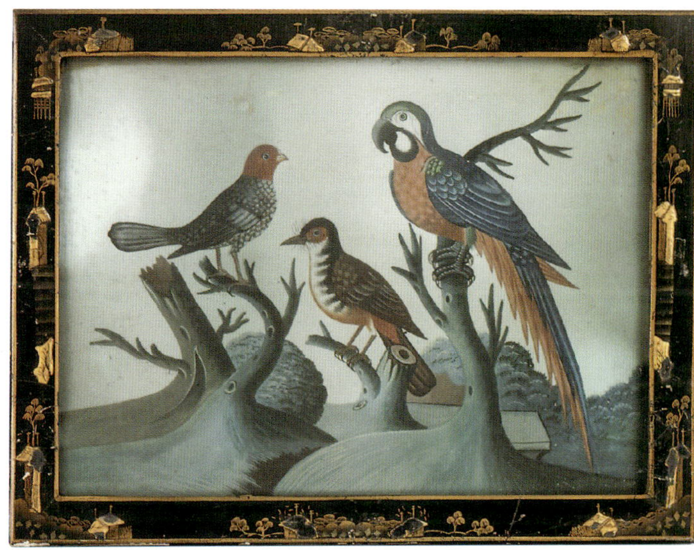
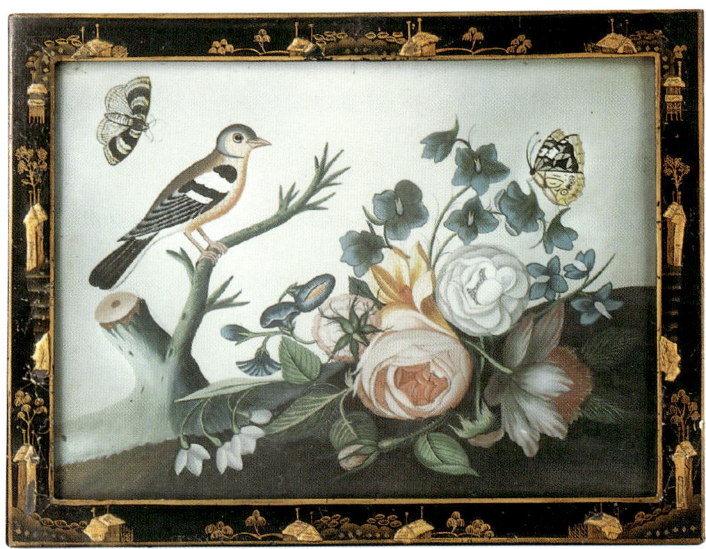
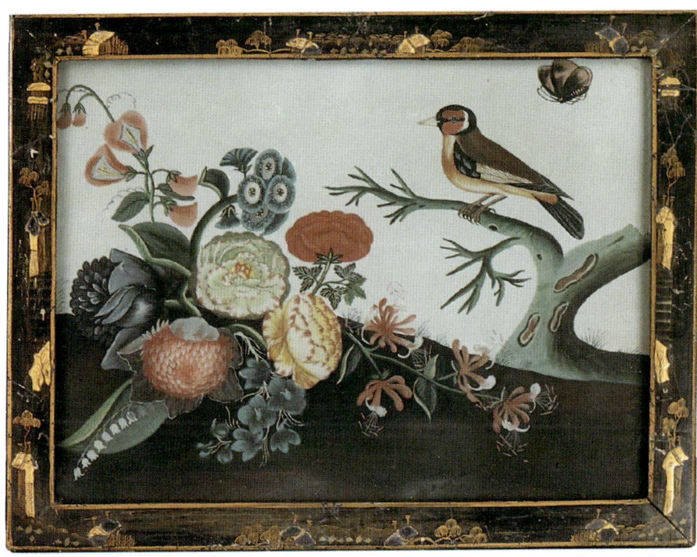
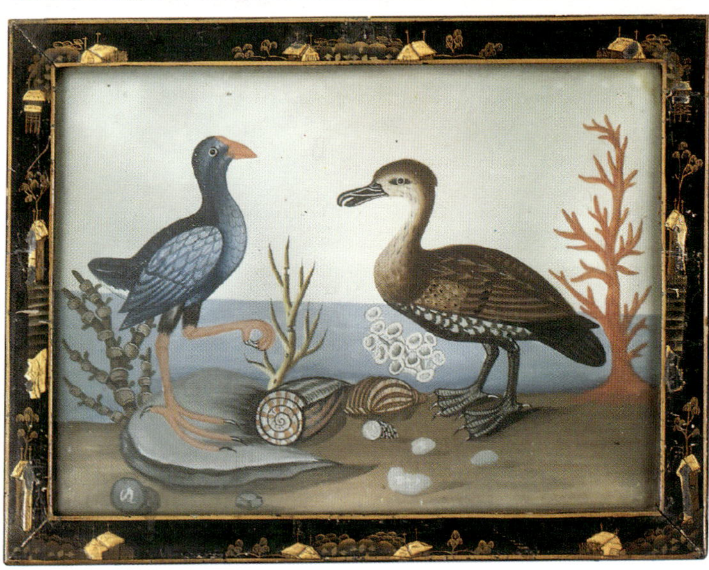
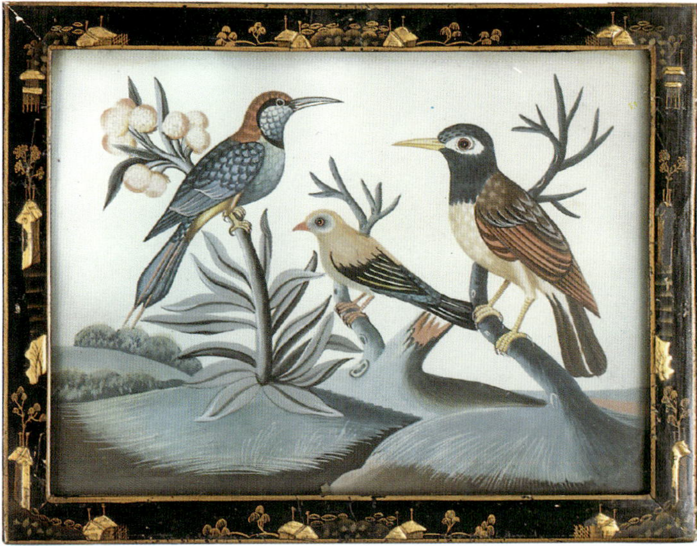

<h1 style="text-align:center">GEORGE STUBBS</h1>

born Liverpool 1724, died London 1806

George Stubbs has long been universally regarded as a masterly painter of animals, but he is far greater than that. Following recent research and the excellent exhibition of his work in London 1984-85, he is now ranked among the greatest English artists of the eighteenth century, alongside Gainsborough and Reynolds. The secret of his success was his extensive study of the anatomy of animals (including humans), for it is only possible to paint the outside of an animal correctly with an accurate knowledge of the underlying structure.

Stubbs was brought up with horses and used to handling all parts of the horse because his father was a currier and leatherseller. George learned his father's trade while teaching himself to draw and then learning anatomy with Charles Atkinson at York Hospital. He then drew portraits for a living and continued his studies by dissecting dogs and horses. When he was thirty-two years old he undertook the detailed dissection and drawing of horses which he worked on for his book *The Anatomy of the Horse*, published in 1766. This won him international fame and is still valued both for the accuracy and beauty of his own etched plates. This, with his horse pictures, secured his reputation as an animal artist but at the same time obscured his other accomplishments as a very good portraitist and conversation piece artist. In addition, his backgrounds were often interestingly unconventional.

Two of the greatest English mammal painters, Landseer and Munnings, studied Stubbs' work in detail, but although he began to publish a similar book in 1795, *Comparative Anatomical Exposition of the Structure of Human Body with that of a Tiger and a Common Fowl* (left incomplete at the time of his death on 10 July 1806, aged eighty-one), this did not make the same impact on bird art. He used a Dorking chicken and the book has etchings of his diagrams of the bird with the skin removed, then the tissue removed, and finally the skeleton. It took another fifty years before the lesson learned by the mammal painters was learned by bird artists, following Joseph Wolf who clearly demonstrated that to paint a bird accurately it was necessary to understand its anatomy. Until Wolf was active in the late 1840s, bird illustrators and artists relied on mounted specimens. A stuffed specimen did not necessarily mean that the stuffing exactly reproduced the contours of the body. Generally, it merely plumped out the skin. Neither taxidermists nor artists understood the musculature of animals, nor the importance of the manner in which the muscles lying over the skeleton mould the characteristic shape and affect the lie of the contour feathers.

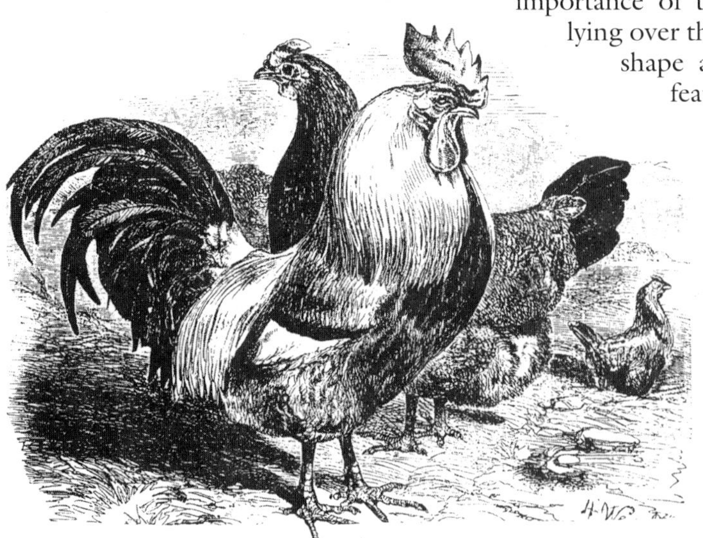

Dorking Fowl by Harrison Weir

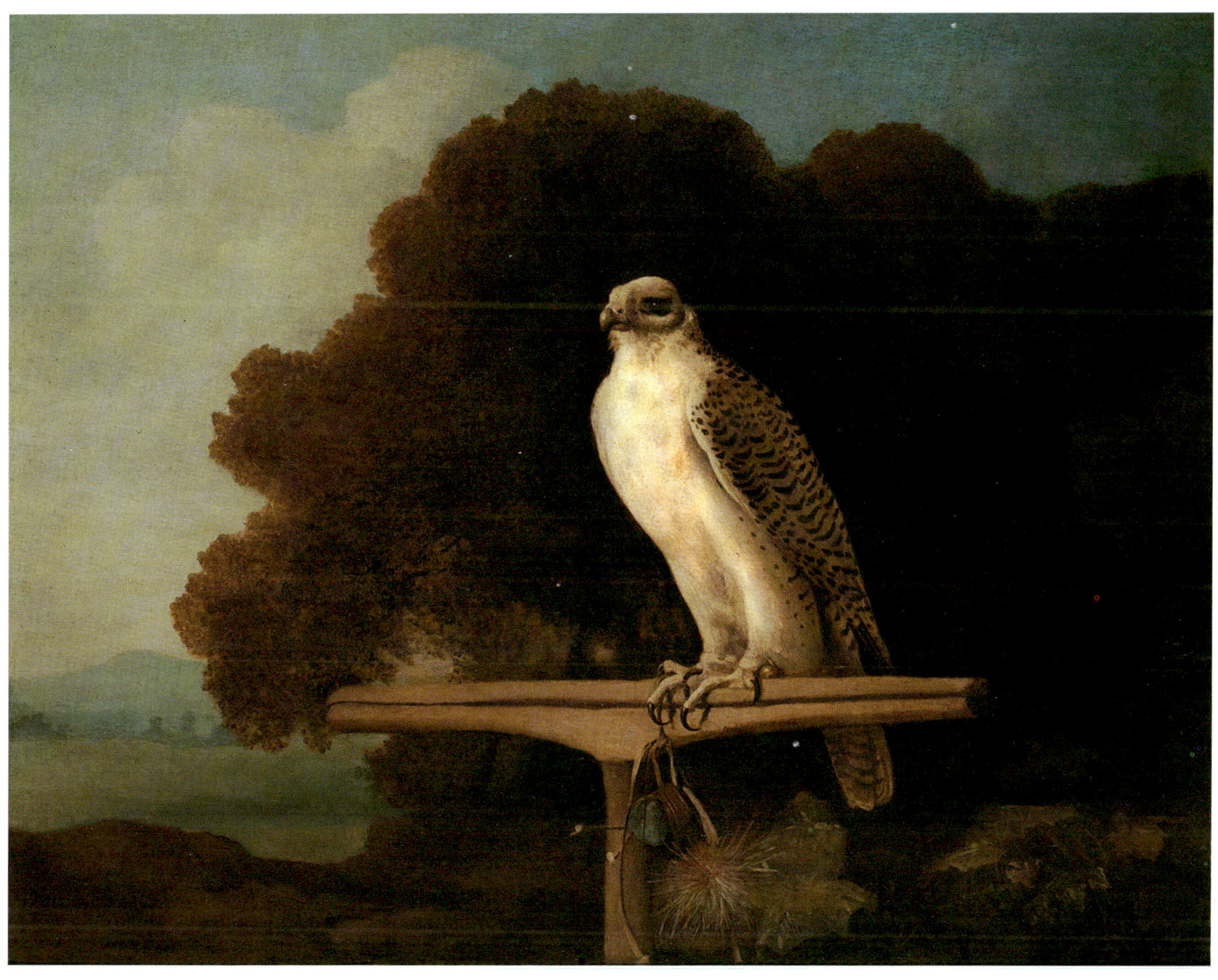

THE GREENLAND FALCON
signed and dated 1780, oil on canvas, 81.25 x 99 cm
Courtesy of Paul Mellon Collection, Upperville, Virginia

Stubbs' *Greenland Falcon* was painted in 1780 and is the only known portrait of a falcon by him. Now called the gyrfalcon, it is an arctic bird of prey found above the tree-line all round the northern hemisphere, not just in Greenland. Stubbs painted a captive live bird sitting on a perch, and signed and dated the picture underneath the perch. It is firmly and correctly resting on the pads of its feet (not clenching the perch which is how so many artists erroneously show a perched bird), and has the neck feathers ruffled from wearing the hood. The gleaming white breast feathers and beautifully barred wing and tail feathers are finely painted on this regal-looking bird. In medieval days, this falcon was reserved for the sport of a king and it was not permissible for a person of lower rank than a king to fly one. Needless to say, the anatomy is correct, and this is no flat, cardboard figure but a rounded, real-life gyrfalcon.

WOUTER UYTTER-LIMMEGE
born Dordrecht 1730, died Dordrecht 1784

Uytter-Limmege is a little known Dutch painter, one of the small group of bird painters in Dordrecht in the mid-eighteenth century. Like Vonck, he was the pupil, for a short time, of Aert Schouman. His master left to set up a studio in The Hague in 1748, and Uytter-Limmege is also recorded as having visited The Hague, in 1749. Apart from this, he and Vonck appear to have lived most of their lives in Dordrecht. Uytter-Limmege was primarily a painter of birds, but also painted portraits and was an art dealer.

A DOG CHASING DUCKS FROM THEIR NEST
signed and dated 1774, oil on canvas, 66.8 x 89.8 cm
Courtesy of Rafael Valls, London

His picture of *A Dog chasing Ducks* is unusual because of the low angle of view he has taken. The teal in the foreground is at eye-level, but the viewer looks up to the rest of the birds and the dog's head. This gave Uytter-Limmege the opportunity to paint a very beautiful portrait of a pintail duck in take-off flight. It is a remarkable study of the underwings, and the close body plumage of the underside of the pintail. The open beak and tense muscles show the bird's alarm. The pintail is a large, long-bodied dabbling duck, easily identified both on the water and in the air by the long needlepointed tail. The black central tail feathers extend far beyond the rest of the wedge-shaped tail. The male's chocolate brown head, on a long slender neck, bears another clear diagnostic mark. A white streak extending in a thin line separates the dark streak down the back of the head from the light chocolate-coloured feathers. This pintail's female is of mixed race, with white woolly topknot, a feature that occurred repeatedly in pictures of ducks in the seventeenth century. The normal colour of a female pintail is grey-brown. Unfortunately, in her haste to escape the inquisitive dog, she has trodden on one of her eggs, broken it and spilled the contents.

The Dutch love of flowers and plants, and their interest in insects, is also represented here. The small white butterfly, totally unaffected by the alarm elsewhere in the scene, creates a tiny still point in the foreground.

Using a dog to create panic among wildfowl was a very old ruse, used repeatedly by painters of live bird pictures for a century or more. A dog guarding dead birds, hares and deer was another feature of paintings in the previous century. This picture was painted in 1774, just before the emphasis shifted to sporting pictures where the interest is focused on a good sporting dog, and its master, rather than on the birds. Further into the nineteenth century, the dog became a small part of a sporting scene, where the man is shown shooting at birds, often very small birds disappearing over the horizon. There was a clearly discernible change in picture content, reflecting the attitude of the purchasing public. Art patrons, increasingly men with newly acquired wealth, wanted pictures of themselves and their possessions – their land, houses, horses and dogs. Their interest in birds, with very few exceptions, was narrowed to the gamebirds and wildfowl which they shot. The men who were interested in other species of birds, especially newly discovered species from Asia, North America and Australia, satisfied their curiosity by purchasing illustrated books and periodicals. These were hand-coloured in watercolours. There was very little demand for large oil paintings with decorative groups of unrelated species, and pictures like this *A Dog chasing Ducks* went out of fashion.

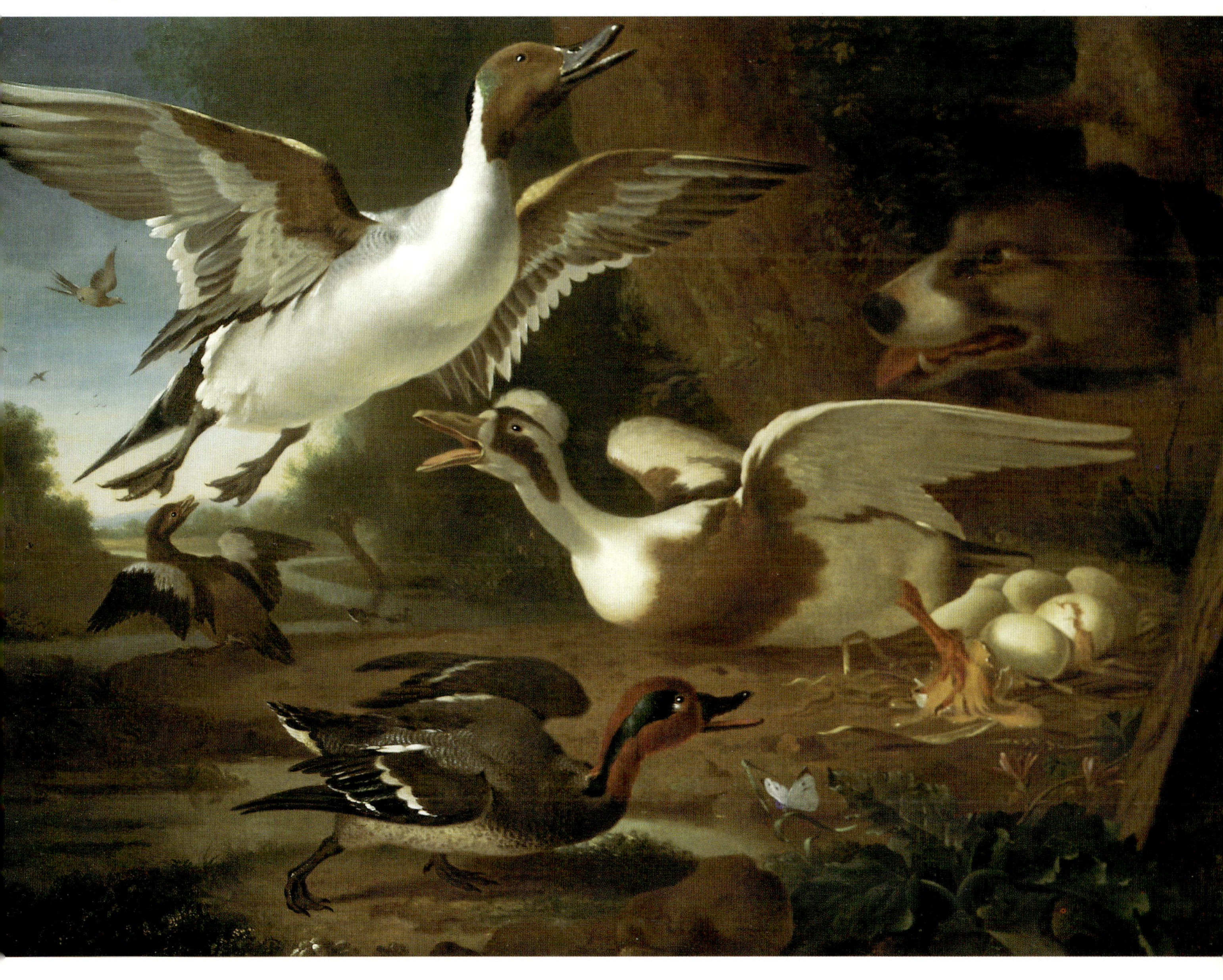

WILLIAM TOMKINS
born London c.1730, died London 1792

William Tomkins had two different painting skills. He was one of the most favoured painters of views of gentlemen's country houses and views of their parks. He showed these views, painted in southern English counties up to northern Scotland, at the Society of Artists' exhibitions 1764-68. His other ability, to paint beautiful still life pictures and paintings of live animals, was also appreciated during his life-time. The titles of the bird paintings, which he exhibited at the Royal Academy and the Society of Artists, suggest that when he travelled round the country to visit estates for the purpose of painting the houses and parks of the aristocracy, he took every opportunity to sketch wild birds and also any rarities in aviaries on the estates.

OWLS AND YOUNG ONES
signed and dated 1765, oil on canvas, 62 x 73.5 cm

In 1765 he exhibited a picture of *Owls and Young Ones* at the Society of Artists of Great Britain's exhibition in London. Also in that exhibition he showed a view of Sherborne Castle, Dorset, the seat of Lord Digby, and another painting called *Moonlight*. It is tempting to speculate whether he found the barn owls nesting on Lord Digby's estate and painted them one dark moonlit night. Since the painting reproduced here is also called *Owls and Young Ones* and no second painting of that name by Tomkins has been located, it is probably safe to assume that this is the picture exhibited in 1765.

Barn owls are easily distinguished from the other European owls by the heart-shaped white facial feathers and large black eyes. The size of the eyes and the forward-facing position enable the owl to gather as much light as possible and give it a certain degree of stereoscopic vision, enabling it to judge distance more accurately. However, hunting in almost totally black conditions is done as much by hearing as by sight and a barn owl moves its head constantly from side to side to enable it build up an audio-visual picture of its surroundings, including the prey. It is a bird of almost silent flight, but remarkably vocal for it hisses in annoyance, snores, and from the male's territorial call which shatters an otherwise peaceful night it has earned the country-name 'screech owl'. When hunting for small rodents, at dawn and dusk, it quarters fields and low plantations. Death comes swiftly and silently for its prey. The soft fluffy body feathers and lightly fringed wing feathers reduce the noise made in flight.

The barn owl female lays four to seven smooth white eggs in a cavity with no nest material though there may be some debris in the nest hollow and some owl pellets. Tomkins' wisps of grass are artistic licence to make a more attractive foreground. The eggs are laid at two-day intervals and hatch in succession. Tomkins has shown one chick smaller than the other three whose comparative age is not easy to judge because of the thick buffish-cream down. Both parents are at the nest here and both tend and feed the chicks for about sixty days before they fly, and continue with some feeding until they are independent about ten weeks after hatching.

Night scenes present an artist with many different perspectives which were explored most successfully by Wright of Derby in the next century. Tomkins is not interested in these but has painted the barn owls, almost of necessity, in the dark. His 'moonlight' looks more like a lamp introduced so suddenly as to startle the birds. It was a brave effort at painting owls at night, and made a most unusual painting in 1765.

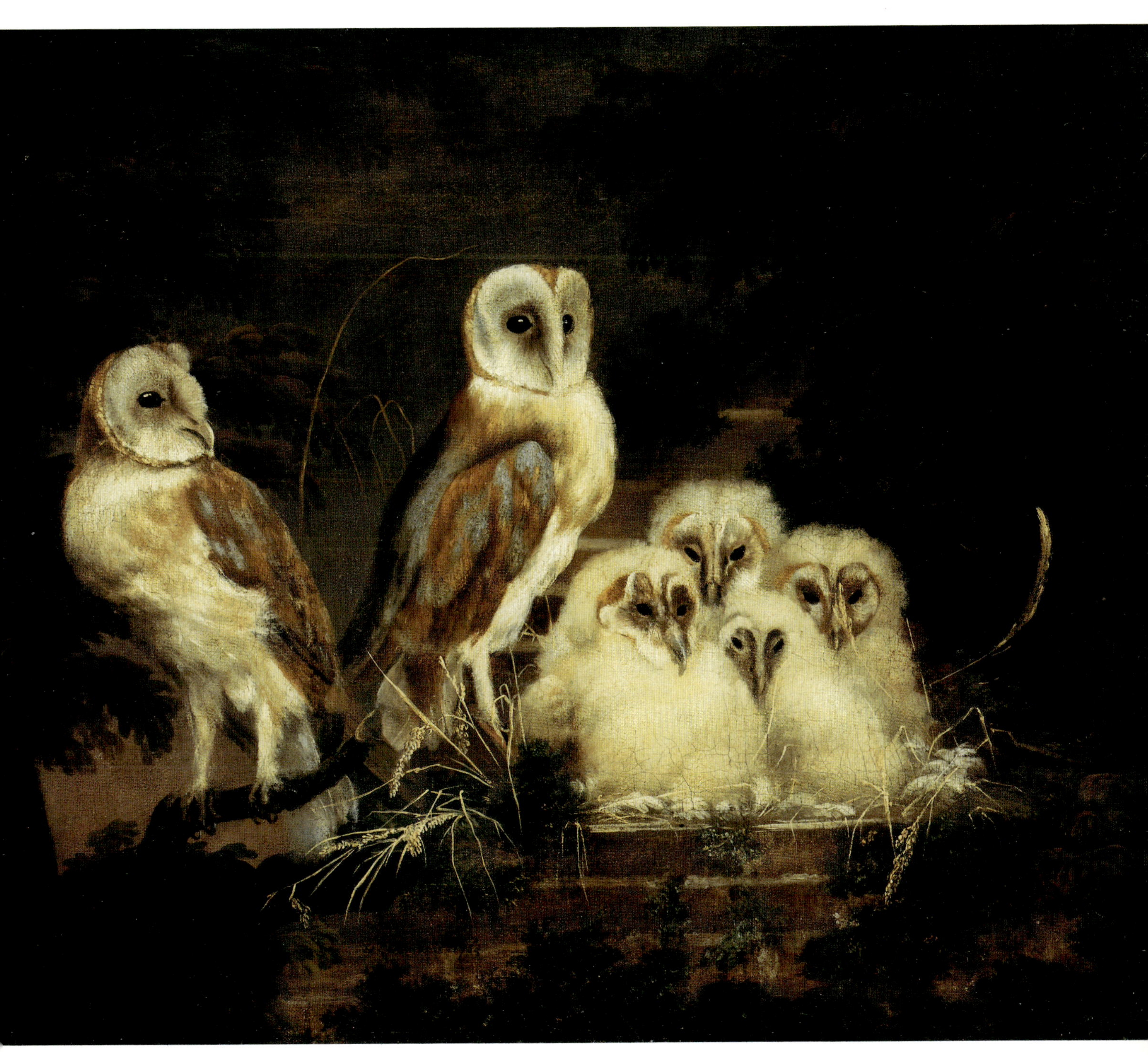

LUIS Y ALCAZAR PARET
born Madrid 1746, died Madrid 1799

Very few Spanish artists painted birds and it is fortunate that Paret, who is regarded as second only to Goya as an outstanding Spanish artist in the eighteenth century, was such a versatile artist that when he turned his attention to birds, he painted them very well.

Paret was a descendant of an old French family from the Dauphine region and he spoke French and English as well as Spanish. He received a classical education before completing his formal studies by learning oriental languages. His art education was just as thorough. He worked with Antonio Gonzalez Velasquez and was awarded several medals at the San Fernando Academy. He became a member of the Academy following study tours and received commissions from Charles III.

His career prospects were spoiled in 1774 when serving the Infante Luis. Paret was accused of assisting Luis in his illicit love affairs and was exiled to Puerto Rico for three years. On his return, following a pardon, he was forbidden to live in Madrid and spent some years in Bilbao, not returning to Madrid until the Infante died in 1785. He returned to the court but Goya's eminence and position as royal favourite were unassailable. Goya was named court painter to the new King, Charles IV in 1789 and though he was born in the same year as Paret, outlived him by twenty-eight years.

Paret painted landscapes in the rococo style in the second half of the eighteenth century when wealthy Spanish patrons favoured landscapes. In these and his genre pictures (his best being painted between 1770 and 1775 with great verve from a palette of bright colours), portraits and religious paintings, he led his contemporaries in understanding and absorbing French influences. His work had an unusual feeling for light and space, while his subjects were treated in a kindly and charming manner.

GOLDEN ORIOLES
watercolour
Courtesy of Museo Nacional del Prado, Madrid

The watercolour of *Golden Orioles* is a rare example of Paret's genre painting. He painted the birds against dense foliage of many greens and a lightly clouded sky. His birds are unusually close to the viewer. The bird with raised wings is carefully posed to show the brilliant yellow of the underwing and undertail feathers. The wonderfully rich gold of the male oriole is fully captured here and glows with reflected light from the sun. The female is a much duller, greenish bird.

Golden orioles breed widely throughout Europe and western Asia but rarely visit the colder northern European countries. They live, feed and breed in tree tops. They are shy birds and fly fast with an undulating flight from one thick canopy to another. Paret's picture is captioned 'Oropéndola, macho & hembra', the Spanish for 'golden oriole, male and female'.

When naturalists visited foreign countries and saw birds that were new to them, they frequently named them after a bird with which they were familiar in their own country. The Spaniards, seeing birds in South America that reminded them of the golden oriole back home, called them 'orioles' or, in Spanish, 'oropendola'. English-speaking scientists then adopted the name oropendola for the New World species of orioles, the *Icteridae*, in order to distinguish them from the Old World species of orioles, the *Oriolidae*. An oropendola is prominent in Reinagle's painting (page 106).

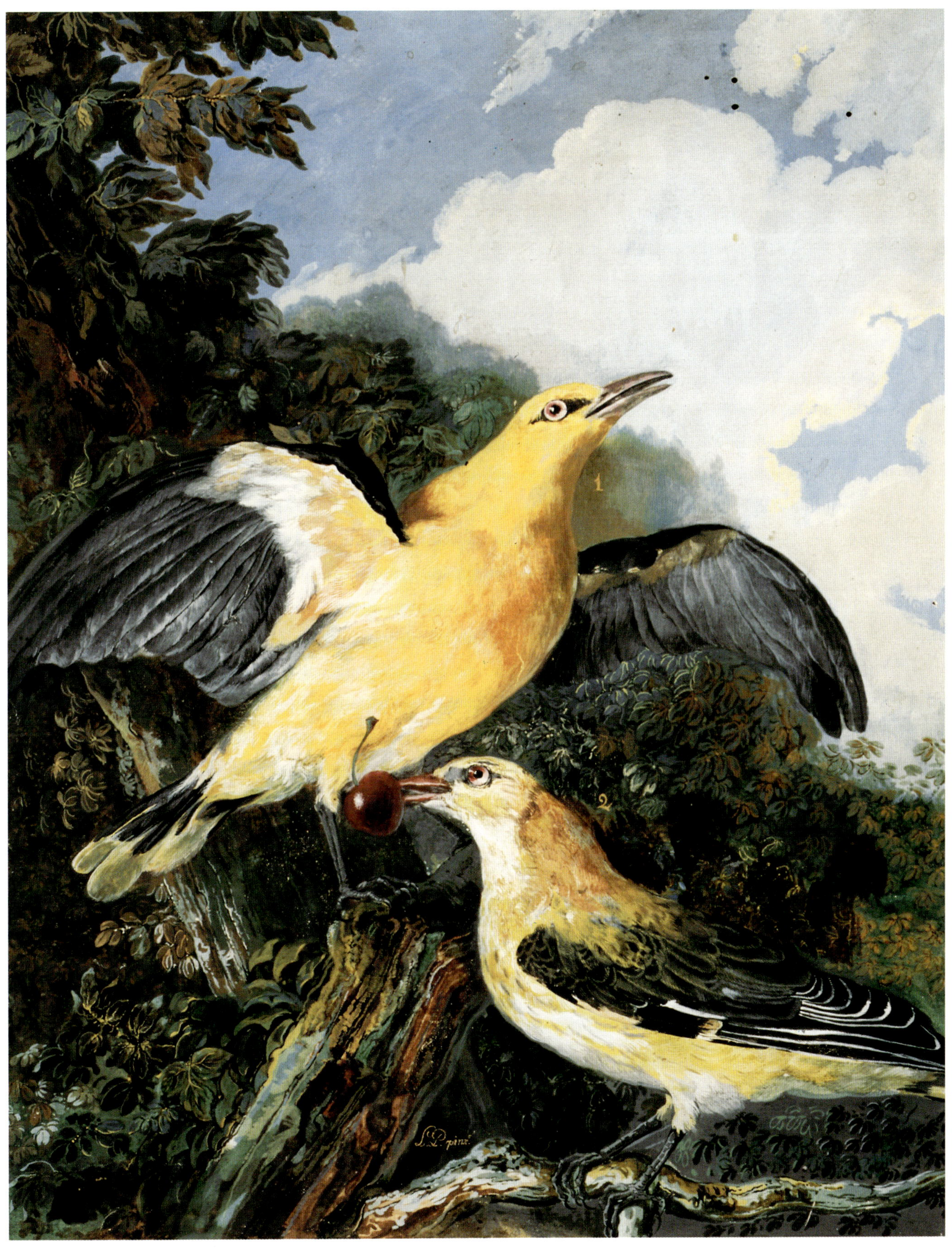

PHILIP REINAGLE
born Scotland 1749, died London 1833

Philip Reinagle was of Hungarian origin, whose family moved to Scotland in 1745, reportedly as adherents of James Stuart, the Young Pretender. Philip was trained under Allan Ramsay for whom he copied Old Masters and royal portraits. He moved to London in 1769 to enter the Royal Academy School and began to exhibit his pictures in 1773. He was a very prolific artist and showed more than two hundred and fifty paintings of birds, mammals, hunting scenes, portraits and, after 1794 when he became more interested in landscape painting, his entries were more frequently of landscapes. He excelled at painting horses and dogs and was remarkably successful at putting life into his bird paintings, which was some achievement when he painted from the mounted specimens in Sir Ashton Lever's museum.

Sir Ashton Lever's museum of shells, fossils, stuffed birds, natives' weapons and other artefacts was open to the public in London from 1774 until 1806 on payment of an entrance fee, first 5s 3d, later reduced. Lever purchased newly imported skins from ships returning to England from the colonies and often had the only example of a tropical bird known in Europe. This accounts for the truly astonishing array of species in Reinagle's painting of a *Secretary Bird, Nicobar Pigeon and other Birds* in an imaginary tropical forest landscape.

THE KING EAGLE PURSUED TO THE SUN
Oil on canvas, 277 x 416.5 cm
Private Collection

The eagle was regarded as the King of Birds in many ancient civilisations and stories in early literature describe the reasons for this exalted position. In some eastern countries it was a god, and among the Greeks and Romans the eagle was the symbolic bird of the chief of the gods, and a bearer of thunderbolts and lightning. In comparison with many other birds, the eagle was long-lived. Its great strength made it a most formidable bird, the foe of mammals up to some eleven pounds in weight, as well as of smaller birds. However, it was because of its wonderful powers of flight that the eagle was always associated in men's minds as being a bird seen high in the heavens, soaring above the tops of mountains and clouds, able to go nearer to the sun than any other living creature.

Closely associated with this idea was the belief that the eagle's eyesight was superior to that of any other bird. Its fabulous eyesight enabled it to look unblinded into the sun. It forced its young to stare at the sun, and any eaglet that turned away was instantly rejected.

In Reinagle's picture, a crowned and garlanded eagle is being pursued up into the heavens to take its rightful place. One might expect, if that were the case, that the eagle would be above all the rest of the birds in the picture. Had the painting been designed to hang on a wall, that would probably have determined such a composition, but Reinagle was commissioned to paint a picture for one of the large ceilings in Wentworth Woodhouse, the seat of William, the fourth Earl Fitzwilliam (1748-1833), in Yorkshire. The painting is unusually imaginative in concept by the gifted bird artist. It was designed so that the viewer looked directly up to it and saw the heavens spread out above him, with every bird in flight around, yet respectfully distant from, their king.

It was most unusual to paint a picture with every single bird on the wing, for this is one of the most difficult postures for a bird artist to attempt. Reinagle has had varied success in this lively scene. He has adopted a device used by Melchior d'Hondecoeter

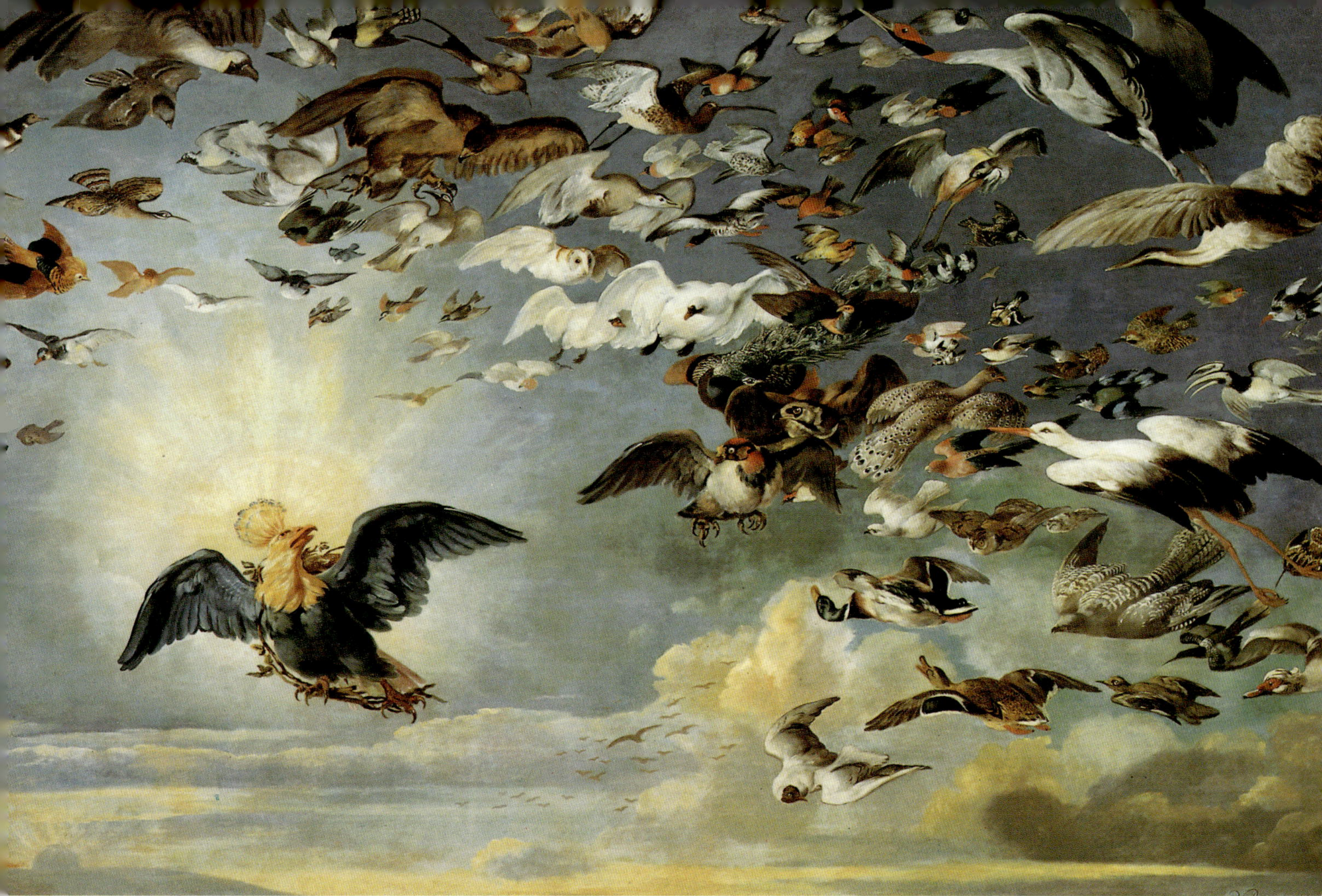

to accentuate the sense of movement in a painting by allowing some birds to be only half in the picture. He has shown birds flying in from both sides, and the top. This makes a viewer feel as though he has just chanced upon a scene and caught it at this moment in time. The fact that the birds are flying in so many different directions shows how very excited they are. Having made the eagle king, and crowned him, they are determined to make him prove, by his powers of flight, that he deserves this honour.

Once upon a time, when the birds first held a contest to see which species was most appropriate to be their king, they decided that the bird who could fly the highest would be selected. Sure enough, as they got higher and higher, the smallest, then the medium-sized, then even the larger, more powerful birds dropped away, until only an eagle continued to soar upwards. Eventually, having oustripped all the others, even his great strength began to fail. He started to drop out of the sky, returning back to earth. At this moment, out of his back feathers there appeared a tiny wren, which promptly began to fly up towards the sun. It flew higher than the eagle. When it eventually returned to earth, it was given a tiny golden crown, and the goldcrest as we in Europe know it, or the golden-crowned kinglet as the Americans call it, was acknowledged the winner of the contest.

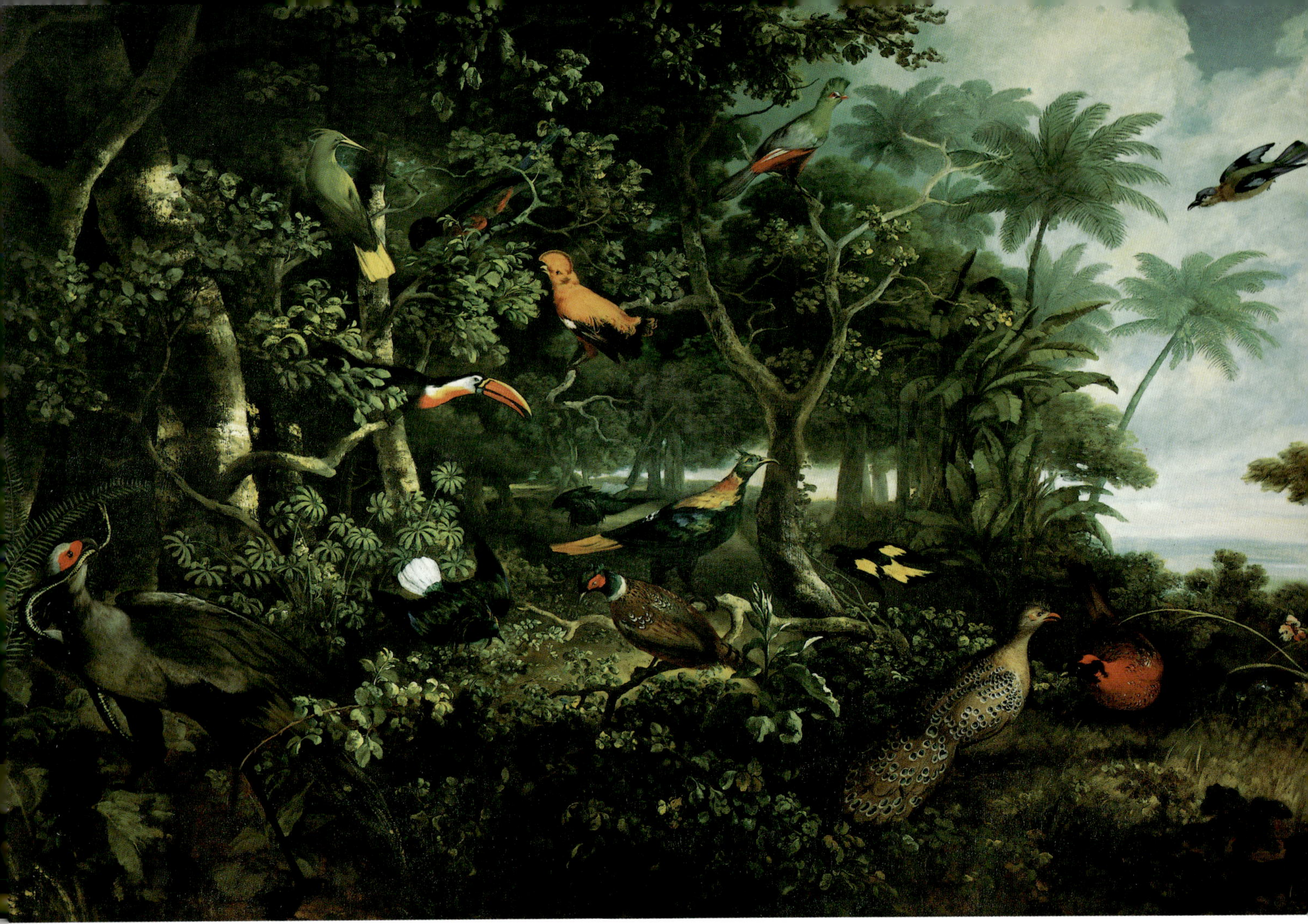

A SECRETARY BIRD, NICOBAR PIGEON AND OTHER BIRDS IN A TROPICAL FOREST

oil on canvas, 304 x 212.7 cm

Courtesy of Christopher Gibbs, London

Reinagle brought together an assembly of birds reminiscent of the Old Masters, but reflecting the changes that have occurred by the end of the eighteenth century. The importation of exotic species was now largely in the hands of British sailors, not Portuguese, Spanish and Dutch as in the previous century. The skins were bought by wealthy collectors interested in science, rather than being exclusively the property of royalty and the nobility.

In Reinagle's forest he has placed a Chinese ring-necked pheasant which was imported from about 1768, a satyr tragopan and an Impeyan pheasant from the Himalayas, and a Burmese grey peacock pheasant, all from the orient. The two Nicobar pigeons came from the Indian Ocean islands, including Nicobar. African species are represented by the secretary bird and the green crested touraco. From the opposite side of the world, the South American red-billed toucan and yellow-rumped cacique, conure, Brazilian or Guiana's cock of the rock and Central American green oropendola added vivid colour and novelty that must have given immense pleasure to Sir Ashton Lever's museum visitors. Rollers are among the most colourful of all the birds, predominantly blue.

Reinagle has painted these birds with great accuracy and colouring and shown remarkable talent in composing this most attractive scene which is a tour de force of his imagination. The picture was purchased by George, third Earl of Orford and taken to Houghton Hall near King's Lynn, where it remained until sold in 1990.

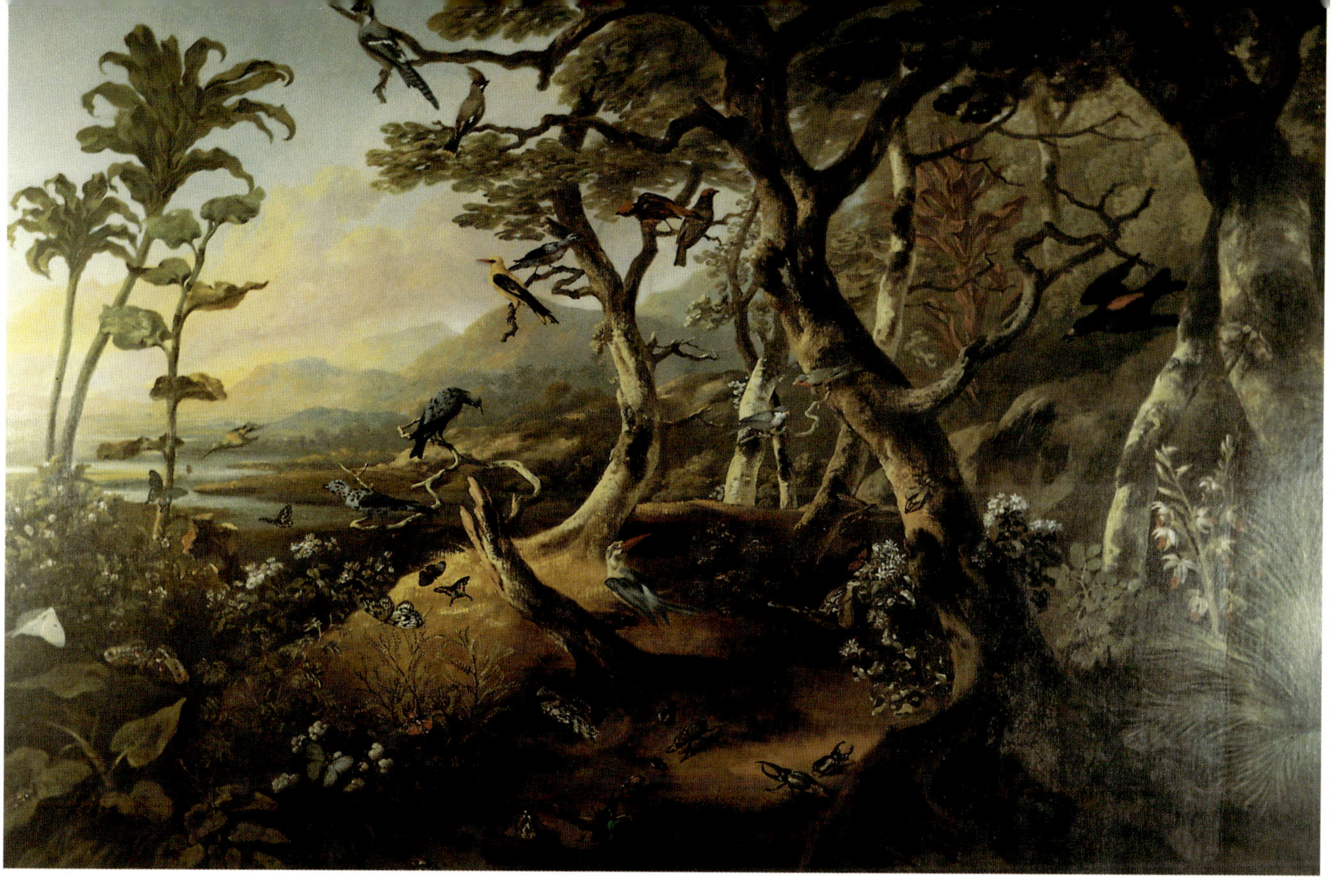

Philip Reinagle
BIRDS IN A WOODED LANDSCAPE
oil on canvas

Private collection

Reinagle has again visited Sir Ashton Lever's museum for specimens, this time choosing those of predominantly blue plumage, such as the American blue jay perched high above a waxwing. As usual, his landscape is excellent while the trees show a great love of the different shapes and characters of each plant. Reinagle also found some butterflies, moths and beetles in the museum which intrigued him, and has incorporated them in the foreground.

BIRDS ON A SEASHORE
oil on canvas.

Private collection, a pair with the above

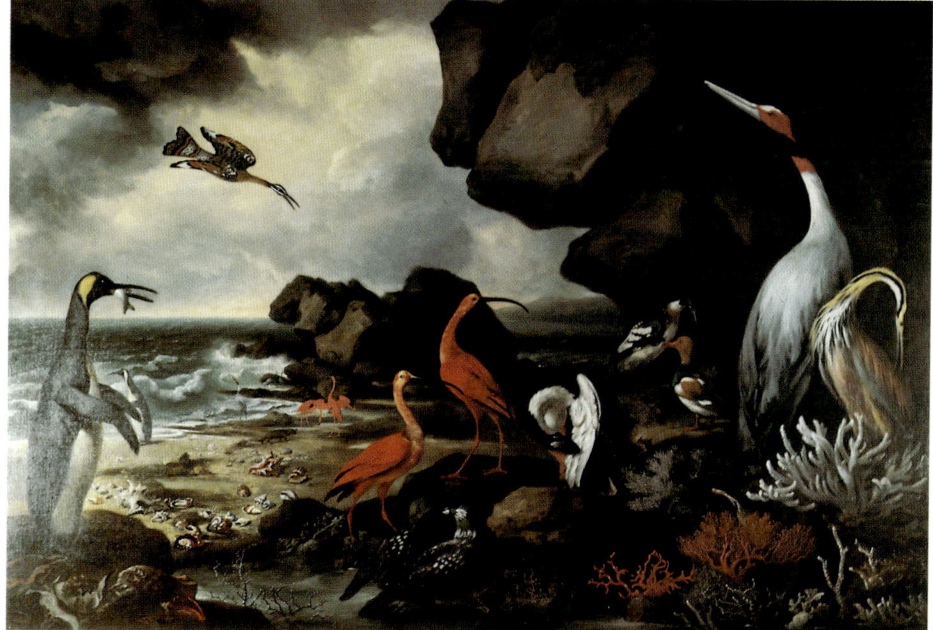

This unusual composition is painted in browns and greys, with touches of scarlet in the birds, corals and shells. A king penguin with a fish looks across to a crane and purple heron, while a preening great northern diver sits on a rock in the foreground. The two red birds in the centre of the picture are scarlet ibises, while the red birds by the water's edge are flamingos. Further touches of soft red occur in the plumage of the ducks. The bird in flight is a sun bittern, a strange addition to this even stranger assembly of birds on the seashore.

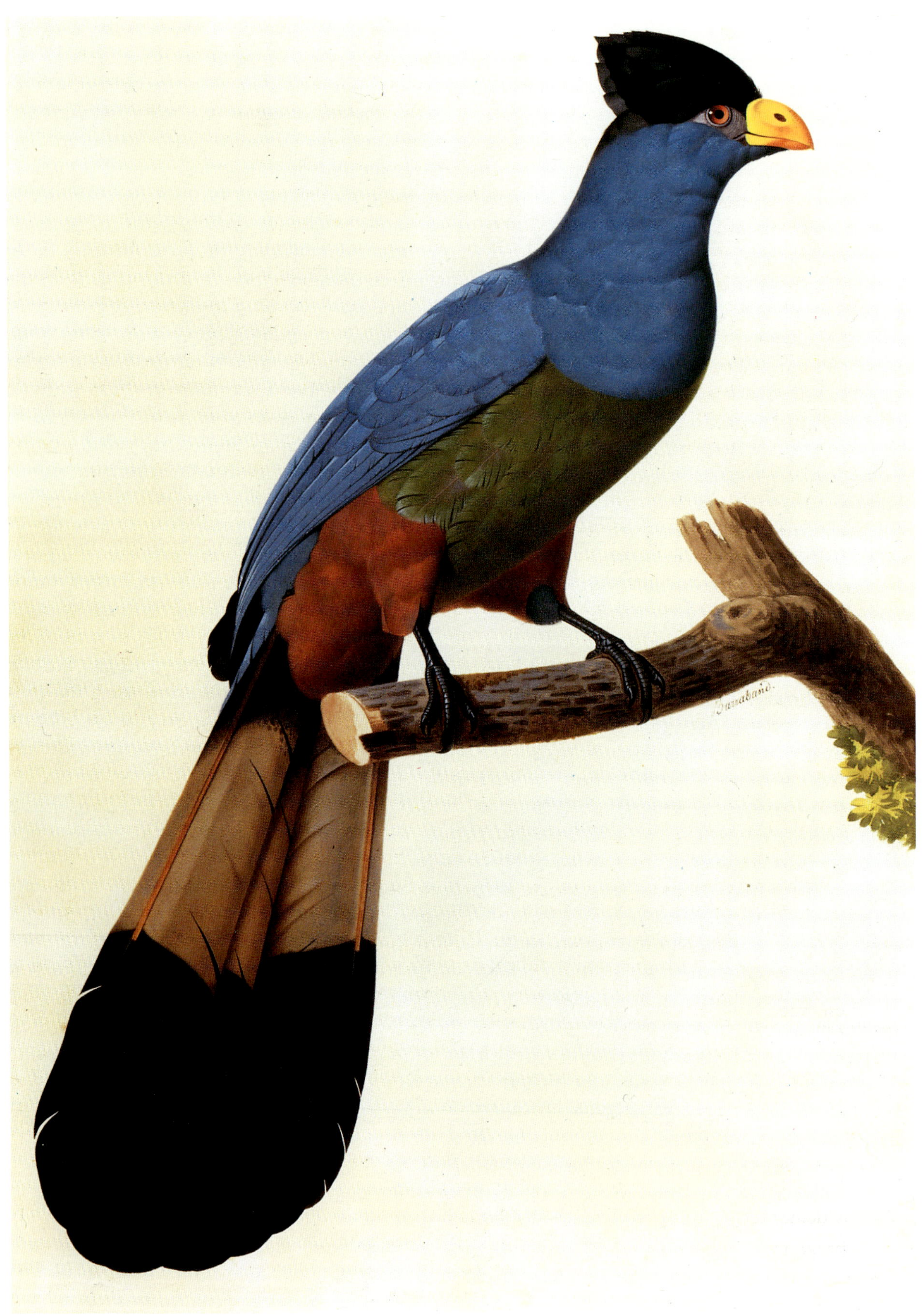

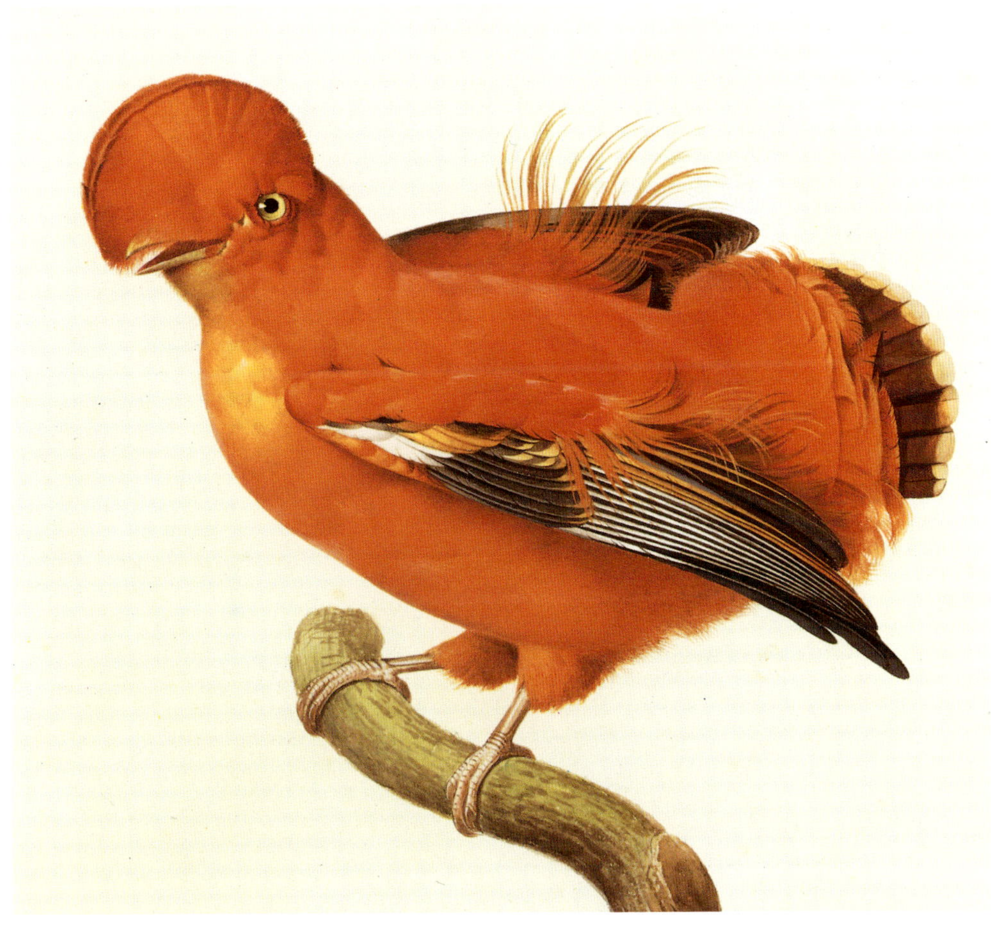

JACQUES BARRABAND
born Aubusson 1768, died Lyon 1809

Barraband was the best French bird illustrator at the end of the eighteenth and beginning of the nineteenth century. He was far more accurate ornithologically than most of his contemporaries and a superlative watercolour and gouache artist. His original paintings, on which the colour-printed and hand-finished plates for Levaillant's books about tropical birds were based, published in the first years of the nineteenth century, represent Barraband's best work. Before this, he had been a painter on porcelain at Sèvres and one of the designers for the Gobelin tapestry works. While painting beautifully coloured birds for Levaillant, he was painting porcelain which he exhibited at the Paris Salons from 1798-1806 and won a gold medal in 1804. Following these successes he was employed to decorate the dining room of the Château de St Cloud in 1804 and three years later was appointed professor of flower drawing at the fine arts school in Lyons.

Barraband's skill and versatility were recognised and his later life well documented, but all that is known of his early life is that he was a pupil of Joseph Malaine before he went to the Gobelins tapestry manufactory as a draughtsman. At Sèvres, he was particularly successful when he incorporated flowers and birds in his designs. Painting birds was but a very small part of his work, yet he excelled at it, as the brilliancy and depth of his colours and the exquisite manner of reproducing the texture of the feathers clearly demonstrates.

GREAT BLUE TOURACO and MALE COCK OF THE ROCK
watercolours for Levaillant's *Oiseaux de Paradis*

Between 1801 and 1806, 260 of Barraband's bird watercolours were reproduced by coloured-printed stipple and etched plates in François Levaillant's books and he was at work on a further set for a book about sugarbirds and bee-eaters when he died. Among his earliest watercolours were this great blue touraco and cock of the rock.

There are nineteen species of soft-feathered African touracos or 'plantain-eaters' which feed mainly on plantains and other fruits, varying their diet occasionally with insects. They have long tails and a pronounced crest which can be raised or flattened as in this picture of the great blue touraco. They are amazingly agile in trees, running along and climbing up branches, but their flight is weak and taken only for short distances. The blue touraco is the largest, measuring some 71-76 cm (28-30 inches), and most conspicuous of the group, constantly fanning open then closing its tail as it perches in the tree-tops.

If touracos are large, slender and flamboyant birds, then cocks of the rock are petite and dumpy by comparison. They are half the size of the touracos but the two species are vividly coloured and both live in the jungles of South America. The bright orange male cock of the rock which Barraband painted, is found in the Guianas and Brazil where they inhabit the undergrowth and the forest floor. The female Guianan cock of the rock is a dark olive brown. The second species is the crimson Andean or Peruvian cock of the rock which does not have the neat black edging to its crest, nor the soft filaments that overlap the wing feathers.

It was most fortunate that some of the world's most colourful and glamorous birds were painted by Barraband when at the height of his powers, for he painted out-standingly beautiful studies of these exotic species.

LUISE FRIEDRICKE AUGUSTE VAN PANHUYS
born Frankfurt 1763, died Frankfurt 1844

This talented lady was the daughter of the painter Helen Elisabeth von Barkhaus-Weisenhutten, who was her first teacher. They lived in Frankfurt, where Luise painted landscapes, flowers and insects. She married van Panhuys, who was appointed Governor of the Dutch colony of Surinam in north-east South America. They lived in Surinam from 1810 to 1816 and, while there, Luise painted the landscape, flowers and other plants, and the large and colourful butterflies, as well as making some bird studies in watercolour and gouache.

By a quite haphazard sequence of events, the birds of Surinam became well known in the seventeenth and eighteenth centuries. Maria Sybilla Merian (1647-1717) visited Surinam in 1699-1701 because she was a member of the Labadist sect and Labadists had several missions there. While in Surinam she painted the insects, flowers and birds in watercolours (see *Great Bird Paintings: the Old Masters*, p. 124). Sir Hans Sloane, President of the Royal Society and of the Royal College of Physicians in London, owned several of Merian's drawings. His protégé George Edwards was aware of these, and he also used several of the live birds and mounted birds in the extensive collection of Charles Lennox, the second Duke of Richmond (1701-1750), who had an aviary at his house in Whitehall, London and a famous menagerie at his country house Goodwood, near Chichester, Sussex. The Duke lent George Edwards some Surinam specimens which were set up and preserved 'in a glass case'. Dutch traders took specimens to Holland and it was from them that English collectors obtained a number of new species.

WHITE-TAILED TROGON AND GOLDEN PHEASANT
signed and dated 1812, watercolour and gouache, 63.5 x 78.7 cm
Courtesy of Raphael Valls, London

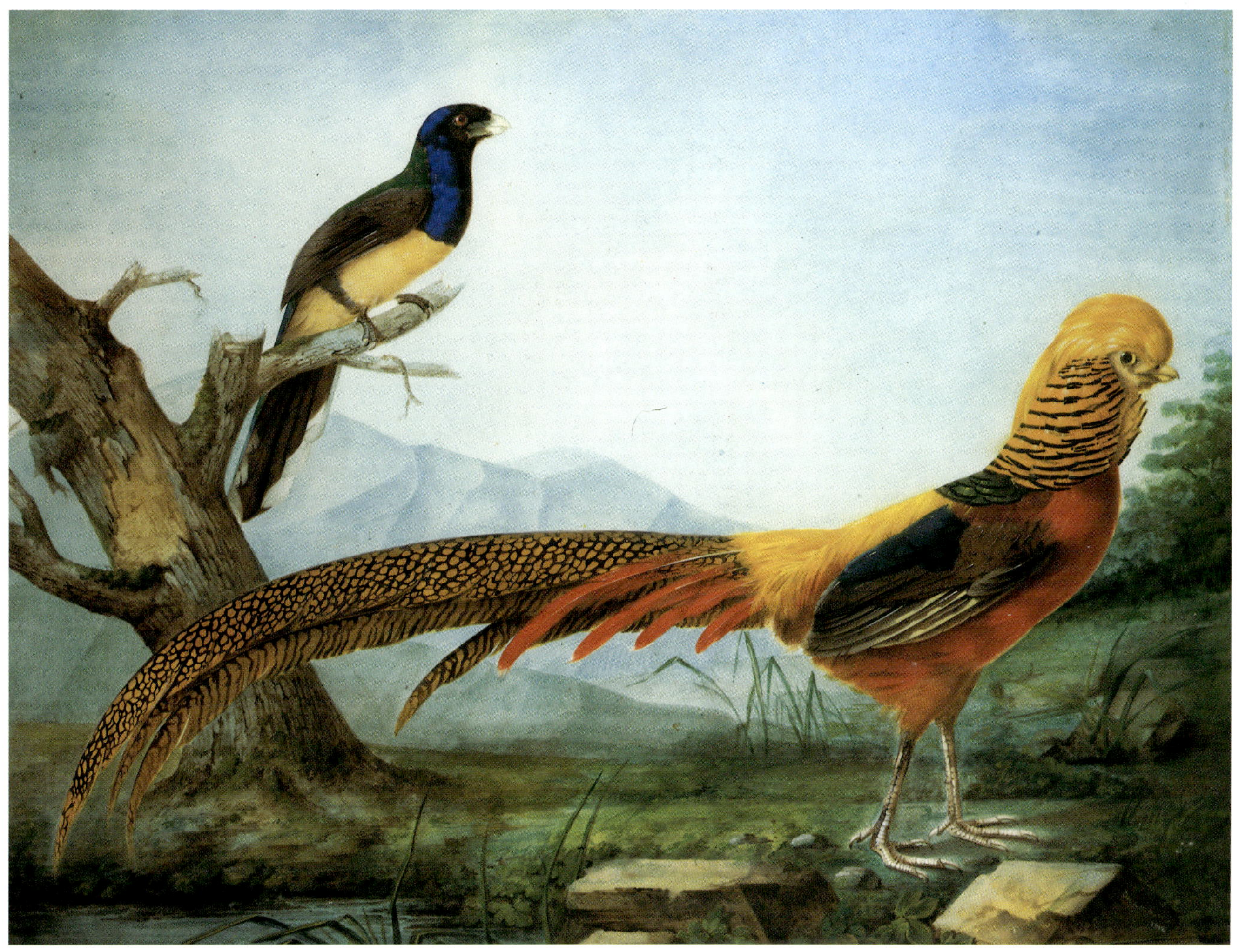

Luise Panhuys has painted a trogon native to Surinam, in a misty, warm landscape which is realistic as well as being atmospheric. One could imagine it to be a Surinam landscape, but the golden pheasant from China destroys this illusion. We strongly wish for more birds from Surinam in this composition, but the old tradition of putting a selection of colourful birds which were to hand, irrespective of their country of origin, was still too strong for Luise Panhuys to resist.

   Trogons are not only beautifully coloured, their clear colour patterns are marked off from one another in clean lines. This accentuates the sharp contrast between the brilliant yellow and blue of this species, which also has a definitive black and white pattern in the tail. The contour feathers are unusually large and have the alarming characteristic of being so soft and loosely attached to the bird that they fall out by the dozen when handled. There is no down to compensate for any loss of feathers, and the skin is tissue-paper thin. This all contributes to make trogons the taxidermist's least favourite bird subject for setting up.

   Trogons are modest in size, varying between ten and fourteen inches. They catch insects on the wing, live in thick jungles and when not feeding spend much of their time sitting motionless high up in the trees. When Luise painted her trogon, little of their natural history was known and there was much confusion in the sparse information available, owing to the male, female and young birds being so differently plumaged. It was not until John Gould published his two editions of *A Monograph of the Trogonidae or family of Trogons* in 1835-38 and 1858-75 that clarification was finally achieved. The white-tailed trogon is one of some thirty-six species in the family *Trogonidae*.

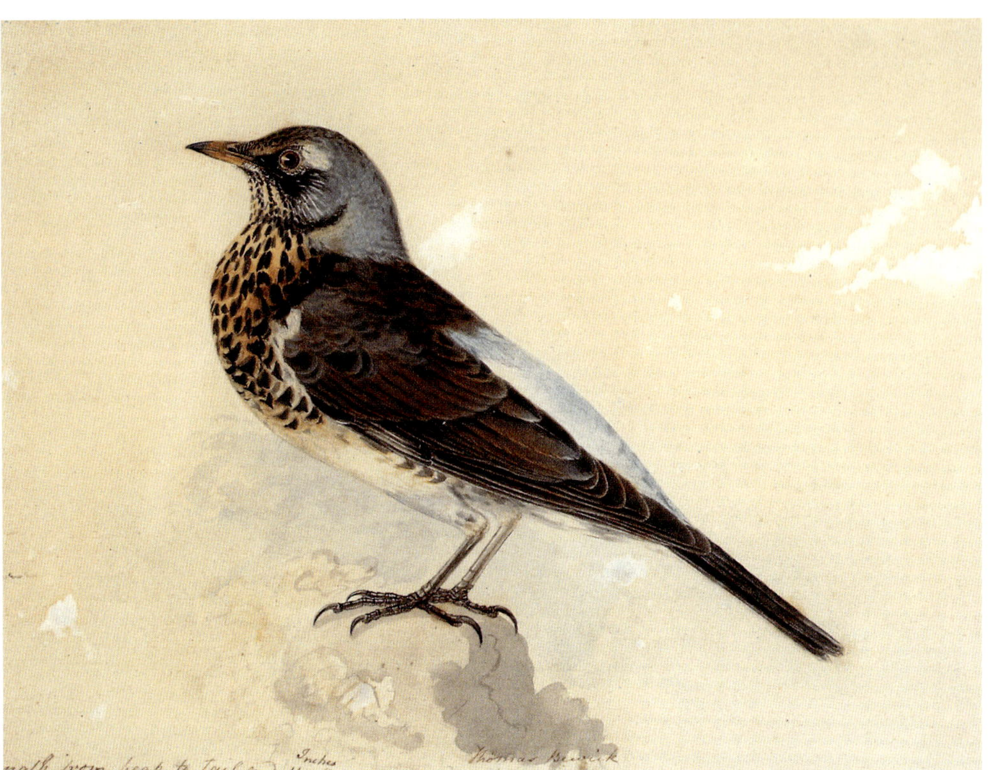

The Fieldfare, *pen and watercolour, inscribed in Bewick's handwriting, 'length from beak to Tail end 11 Inches ⅛' and signed 'Thomas Bewick' in the hand of his daughter, Jane Bewick.*

THOMAS BEWICK
born Cherryburn 1753, died Newcastle upon Tyne 1828

From being a young child, Bewick drew with a natural talent that he later carefully practised and refined by working direct from nature. He frequently drew from living mammals and birds, having early discovered this to be a far better way to get a true likeness than copying stuffed and mounted models. His training was as a metal and wood engraver in Newcastle where he later had his own workshop in St Nicholas' churchyard.

Thomas Bewick's wood engravings of birds are universally recognised and admired as small masterpieces of combined art and craft that have not been surpassed. In the field of bird book illustration, when fine art combines with first class craftsmanship, the result is outstanding. The most famous bird artist of all time is Bewick's contemporary, the American John James Audubon. However, although he was an excellent artist, he had his paintings translated into book prints by the very skilled aquatinter Robert Havell. Bewick, probably the best known and loved British illustrator of birds, was both artist and craftsman. Yet while his wood engravings of birds and the small tail-pieces that decorated his *History of British Birds* are familiar to many, the fact that Bewick painted over three hundred studies of British and foreign birds in watercolours is less well known. About two hundred and forty of these preparatory drawings were used for his wood engravings, the remainder were not published.

Bewick first inked in his outline and then used delicate tints to colour the figures. He mostly worked to the same size as his engraved figure, but the fieldfare depicted here is on a much larger scale and lacks the background that he devised for his engraved figure.

The unusually large and more finished watercolour of the fieldfare is one of the best examples of Bewick's use of subtle tones which were ideally suited to the plumage of this blue-grey and brown bird. He knew it as a winter visitor to Northumberland, where it occurred in flocks, along with redwings, from October to March. He had observed that it fed on berries, and in the engraving has placed it on a branch bearing hips. It is most often seen in fields, as its name implies, where it locates worms by listening before extracting them from the turf.

THE RING-NECK PHEASANT
Pen and watercolour transfer drawing
Wood engraving in *A History of British Birds*, Vol. 1, 1797: 282

The pheasant was the least common game bird when Bewick made this watercolour study of a ring-necked bird in 1797 from a bird sent to him by his friend the Revd William Turner of Newcastle, and then engraved it on wood. In the course of the next century the pheasant would become increasingly more prominent in rural life and in the pictures painted to record country scenes and the trophies of shooting parties. At the time Bewick painted this watercolour, pheasants were unusual but decorative elements in the parks of country residences, and they did not have the wide variety of plumage that we see nowadays.

Before man interfered with their distribution, the common pheasant ranged from Asia Minor across southern and central Asia to eastern China and Korea. The exact origin of our British common pheasant is lost in the mists of time, but it was believed to have come from Phasis, an old name for a river in a land once known as Colchis, hence the species' name *Phasianus colchicus*. Colchis, a province of Asia, is the famous scene of the Greek Argonauts' expedition about 1200 years before Christ. The Argonauts may have brought the original stock home with them to Europe, or this may be just a legend.

It is generally agreed that our feral pheasant was a medieval introduction, just pre-Norman times. This would tally with the first record of the pheasant being mentioned in English literature in 1059. Since then, few if any of our bird species have had such a history of privileged preservation, or been the subject of so many laws to prevent them appearing on the tables of any but the wealthy. The fact that the pheasant is so exotically plumaged has always been secondary to its value as a delectable source of food.

In the eleventh century, pheasants were tame birds, fattened in cages. By the sixteenth century they were established in the wild, but did not succeed in colonising the whole of Britain until late in the eighteenth century. Its sudden success is thought to have arisen from new importations of the Chinese ring-necked pheasant about 1768. This

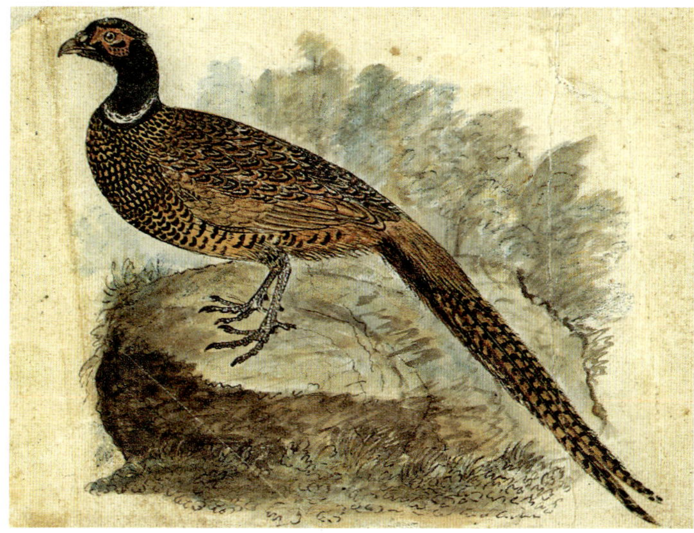

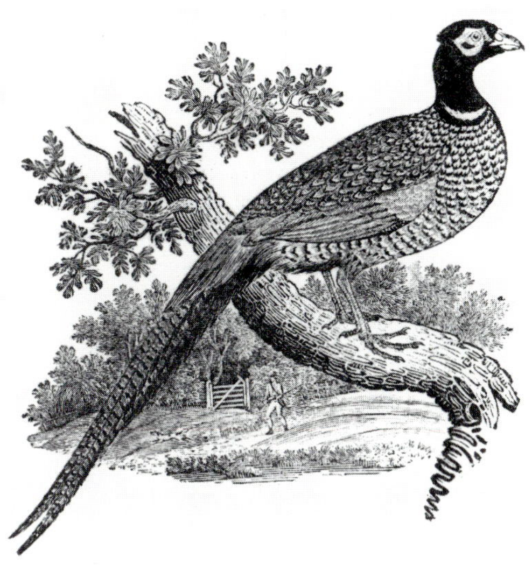

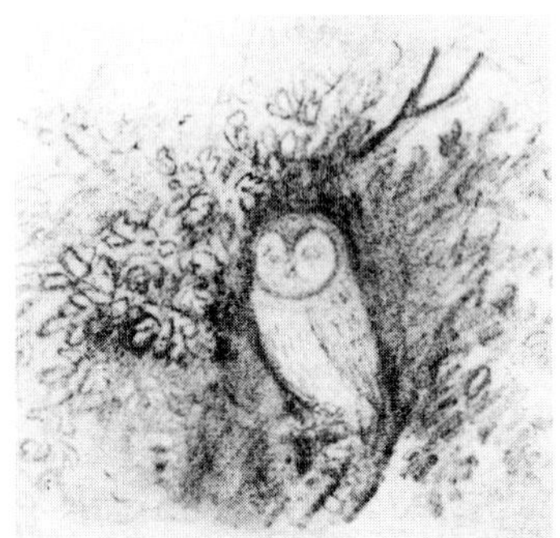

The Barn Owl, *a pencil transfer drawing (in the British Museum) for his tail-piece wood engraving in* A History of British Birds, *Volume 1, 1797: 55.*
Courtesy of the British Museum

is the bird Bewick painted thirty years later. The southern green pheasant from Japan was brought in by Lord Derby of Knowsley in 1840, and lastly the Mongolian pheasant was introduced by Lord Rothschild about 1900. These forms have interbred, so that we have many mutations stalking our fields and hedgerows. Some are greener, others are more coppery in colour; some have white collars, others not; some have grey rumps, others brown; some have white over the eye while it is lacking in most. Whatever the variation, our 'common' pheasant is a very aristocratic bird.

Bewick's *Phasianus colchicus* is an example of the copper-coloured ring-necked bird, whose markings are more exquisitely delineated in his fine black and white wood engraving than in his watercolour version. This is because the coloured drawing was used as an outline only. Bewick drew the preliminary study on thin paper and then blackened the back before wrapping it round the wooden block. Having got the main part of the design in position, he then engraved the bird, adding in the fine details, and completed the picture by engraving a background. It was not necessary for him to colour the original transfer drawing. However, he delighted in the use of colour and these drawings, so delicately painted from a very restrained palette, give us an unprecedented insight into his methods of working.

Bewick's small tail-pieces are among the most finished and detailed of his water-colours. Many of them were painted from his memory of village scenes during his youth. His skills in composition and handling of the landscape, with innumerable small details, all captured within the space of about 6.5 x 9.5 cm (2½ x 3½ ins) is without parallel. The scenes of rural life often reveal a good deal about the prevailing attitudes to birds in Georgian England. But it is Bewick's own keen observation and love of birds that enabled him first to draw them with such fidelity and realism, and then engrave them in wood, which has delighted every generation since his *History of British Birds* was first published, 1791-1804. It was Bewick who put ornithology at the forefront of scientific pursuits and captured the imagination of the general public.

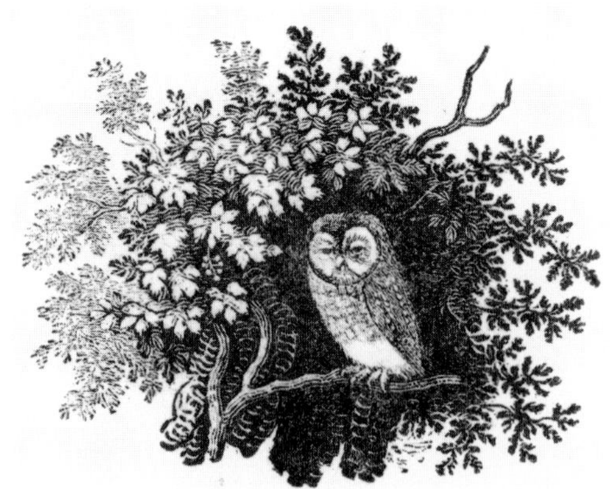

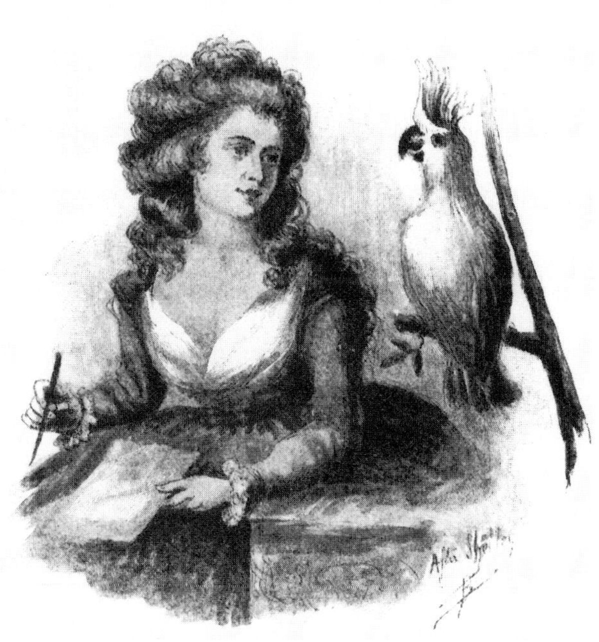

This portrait of Sarah Stone was published in Universal Review *1890, reproduced from a portrait of her by Samuel Shelley. She is accompanied by a crested cockatoo which she is painting.*

SARAH STONE/SMITH
born London 1761/2, died London 1844

Sarah Stone was a very talented lady who painted birds, insects, shells, and still life pictures in watercolours which were exhibited in London at the Royal Academy and other art shows in the years 1781 to 1802. She was careful to sign her work, and often also dated it. A *Parrots and butterfly* watercolour was signed and dated 'February 24th 1779' and, despite being early work, is already a most accomplished piece of painting. Her exhibited watercolours attracted the attention of authors of natural history books who commissioned her to paint the specimens in Sir Ashton Lever's museum in London to illustrate some of the first books about species taken to England from Australia. The editor of John White's *Journal of a Voyage to New South Wales,* 1789/90 assured his readers that they could 'rely with the most perfect confidence on the care and accuracy with which the Drawings had been copied from nature by Miss Stone...' Her contribution to this work was extensive. Of the sixty-five plates she made the original watercolours for twenty-nine birds, ten reptiles, six fishes, two insects and two mammals.

Sarah was the daughter of a fan-painter and showed an interest in painting natural history subjects early in life. Family legend relates that the Stone children, unable to afford or obtain paints easily, substituted brick dust and concoctions from the juice of leaves and petals of flowers. She married John Langdale Smith (1787-1827), R.N. about 1790. He was said to be exceedingly handsome and she 'had all the best parts of beauty, a fine countenance, a good figure, and a pleasing address'. They lived in Cowley Street, Westminster, London, the address they both gave when exhibiting their pictures at the Royal Academy in 1791. The following year they had a daughter, Eliza Frances, and in 1795 a son, Henry Stone Smith, who was to become the Chief Clerk at the House of Lords where he was employed for many years. It would appear that Sarah stopped painting pictures for exhibition and illustration work when her children became more demanding about 1803, but a reference to her as 'a fine painter' in 1822 suggests she still enjoyed painting. Sarah lived with her son, at the end of her long life, in Smith Square, Westminster.

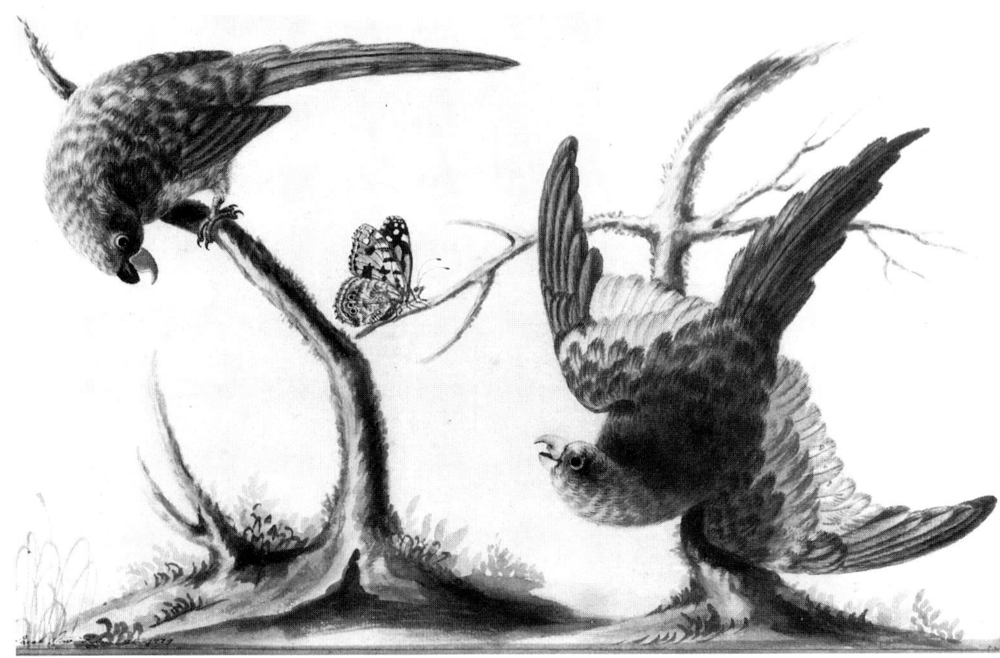

Parrots and a Butterfly, *signed and dated February 24th 1779, watercolour, 24 x 37cm.*
Courtesy of Sotheby's, London.

TAWNY OWLS IN A TREE
Signed and dated 1788, watercolour
Courtesy of Natural History Museum, London

Miss Stone more usually painted a single bird in watercolours for identification purposes and for reproduction as a book illustration. The tawny owls were painted as a picture, composed to show the birds in a typical habitat. The close view of the tree and birds demanded very detailed painting of the texture of the bark and lichen, as well as the feathers of the owls. Sarah's skill in perspective, textural painting, capturing the character of the owls, as well as devising an attractive composition, is demonstrated here.

The tawny owl is probably the best known owl in Europe, where its uninhibited hooting at night draws attention to its presence. Its call is familiar even to town-dwellers, and Shakespeare wrote circa 1598, 'Then nightly sings the staring owl, Tu-who: Tu-whit, tu-who – a merry note'. The plumage is beautifully, if subtly, coloured, varying from greyish to reddish brown and buff with black markings. The large black eyes facing forwards in the round face give the bird some degree of stereoscopic vision which assists in judging distance. An ability to twist its head round to look behind enables it to remain otherwise motionless while it listens intently for any rustling that might give away the presence of a small rodent, a frog, worm or other creature. Once located, the owl silently leaves its perch, glides on slightly arched wings, drops its legs and picks up the prey.

Tawny owls nest in the tops of pollarded trees or hollows in large trees. This hollow tree is perfect for their nesting requirements.

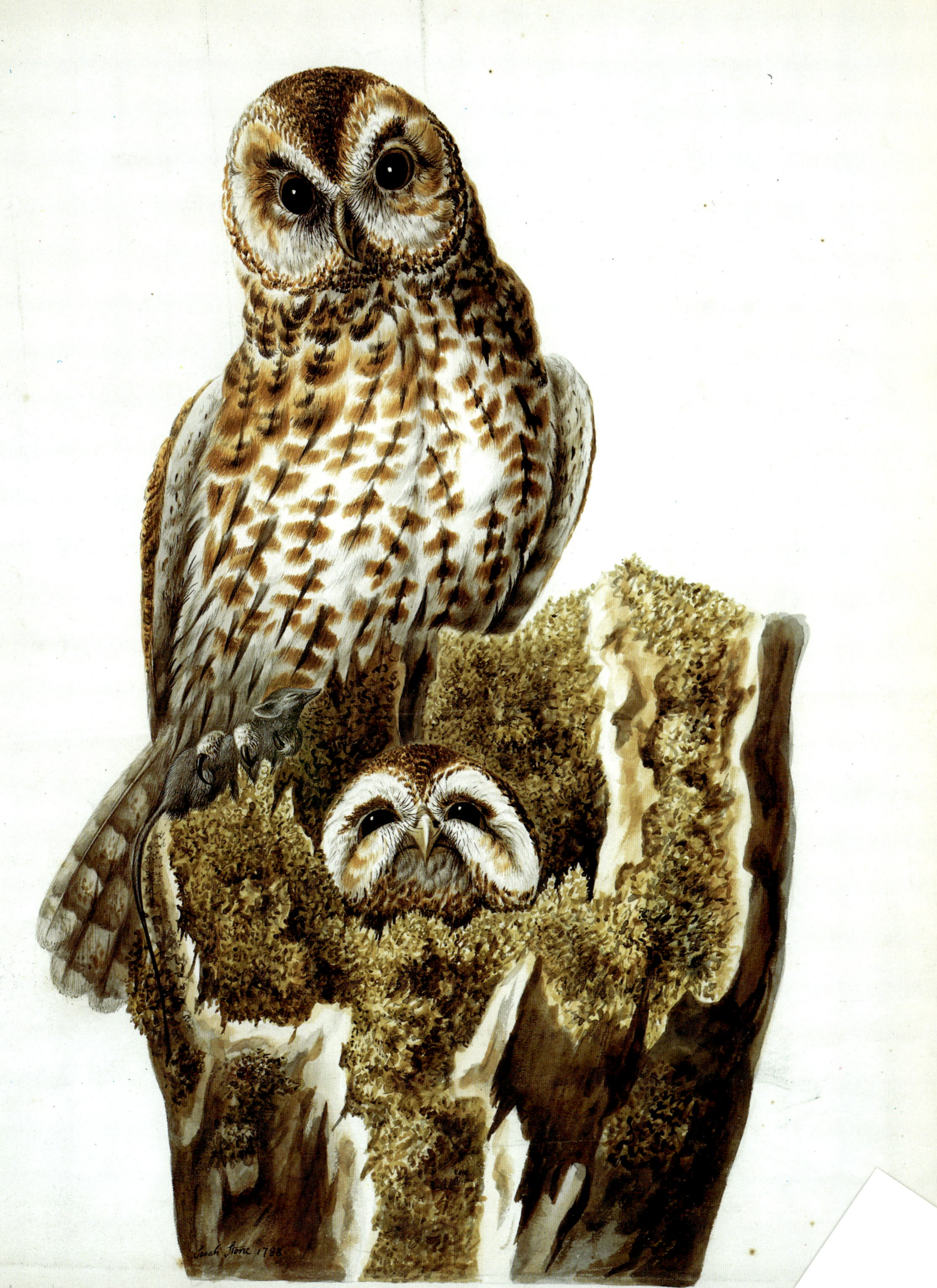
Tawny Owls
Sarah Stone 1788
Tawny Owls

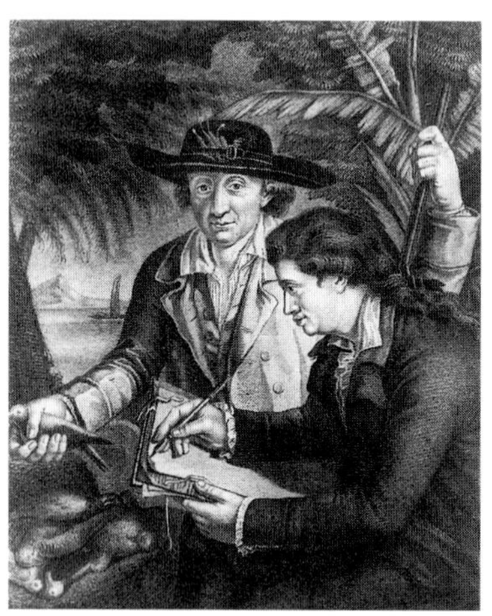

Portrait of Johann Reinhold Forster with his son Johann Georg Adam Forster, in Tahiti. Georg is drawing a live bird held by his father. Courtesy of Osterreichischen Nationalbibliothek, Vienna.

JOHANN GEORG ADAM FORSTER
born near Danzig 1754, died Paris 1794

Georg Forster accompanied his father Johann Reinhold Forster (1729-1798) on Captain Cook's second voyage round the world on the sloop *HMS Resolution*, from July 1772 to 1775. For a seventeen-year old this was a tremendous adventure and opportunity, perhaps spoilt a little by having an irascible and irritating father sharing a very cramped cabin.

Georg's father, Johann, had been recommended for the expedition following his publications on North American zoology. Georg went with him as a botanist and natural history draughtsman, having shown a modest talent in drawing. During the voyage Johann described the zoological specimens which they collected and Georg made 168 drawings of them. They visited South Africa and many islands including Tonga, Tahiti and New Zealand, then explored further south into Antarctica than any previous ship. On the way home they visited the Falkland Islands and South Georgia.

While it is generally known that the Cook expeditions discovered Australia and brought its avifauna to the notice of the world, it was, in fact, New Zealand that provided the greatest number of new species from Australasia until Governor Arthur Phillip took the First Fleet of convicts to colonise Australia (see George Raper). Georg Forster and his colleagues observed thirty-six species of birds at Dusky Bay, South Island, New Zealand, nineteen of which were drawn by Georg. More birds were noted and described while they were in Queen Charlotte Sound. Some of the beautiful New Zealand birds discovered were the blue duck, grey duck, paradise duck and scaup; the tui or parsonbird, New Zealand bellbird, South Island weka, rifleman; green kaka and red-fronted parakeet with the Pacific parrot. Georg's drawings of some of these were single studies without backgrounds and not of great artistic merit. One of his more attractive paintings was of a penguin and he placed it as he probably saw it, on an ice floe.

PENGUIN
watercolour
Courtesy of Natural History Museum, London

Georg drew this chinstrap, one of the newly-discovered penguins, taken in December 1772 or January 1773 in the Indian Ocean south of Kerguelens Land. Penguins are flightless birds of the southern hemisphere and better adapted for their life, spent mostly at sea, than any other aquatic birds. To keep them warm and waterproof, their feathers are very dense. They have several unique characteristics which are not shared with other birds. Their wings are reduced to flippers with which they propel themselves through the water at great speed. They can travel at ten knots and 'porpoise' by swimming under water for several yards and then jumping clear of the water in a graceful curve, returning again to swim underwater. While in the air, they breathe. When they wish to go ashore, they leap several feet into the air to land on the top of a rock. Penguins run, waddle or hop but when on snow they also flop on to their bellies and toboggan down slopes. A further unusual feature is the method of brooding the single egg on top of their feet in order to keep it off the ice. A special flap of skin covers the egg and keeps it warm. The male and female take it in turns to brood the egg. This involves periods of fasting that they sustain longer than any other bird, sometimes up to three months, while the partner is at sea. Little of the penguins' remarkable natural history was known when Johann Reinhold Forster first recorded them and Georg painted them.

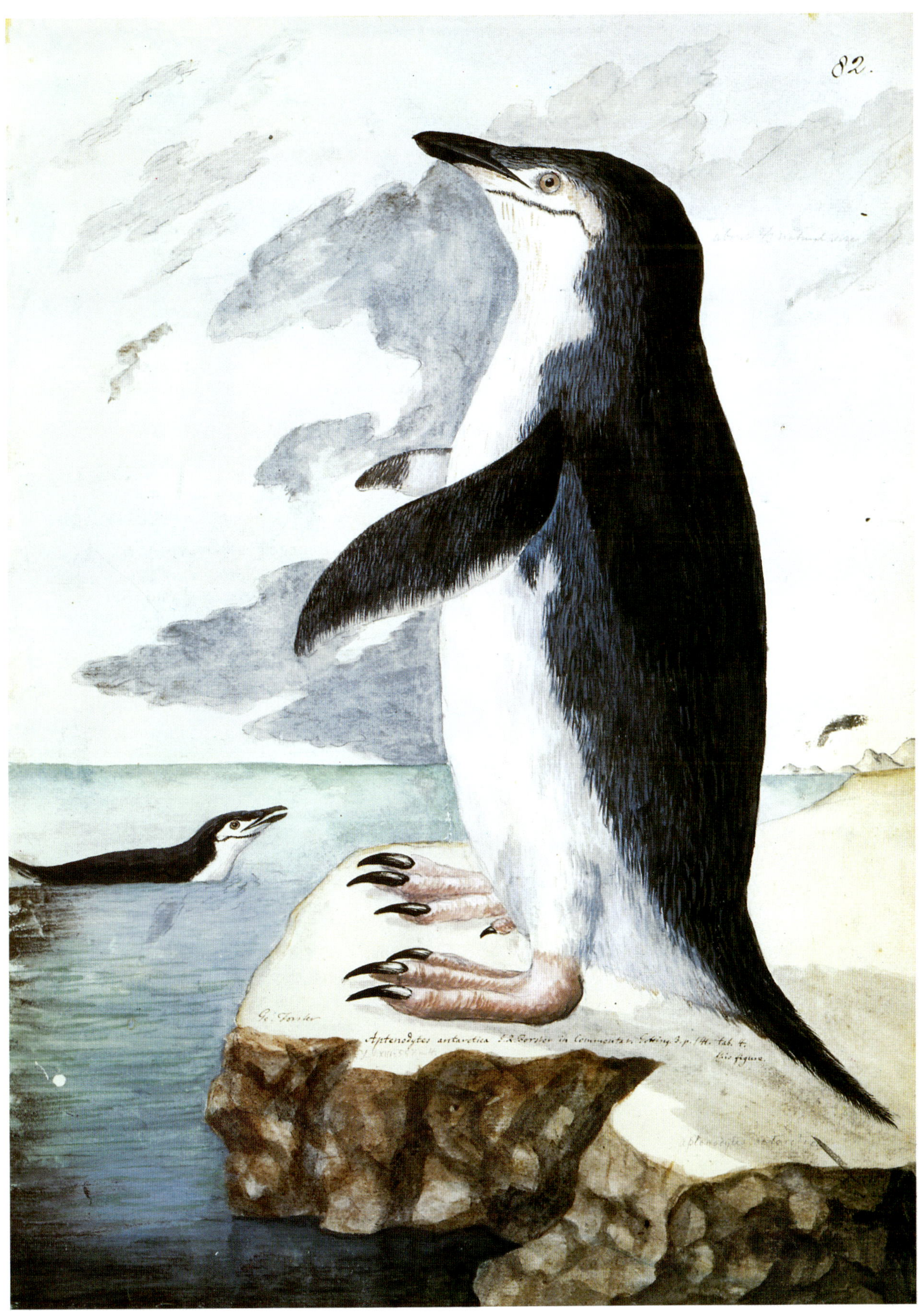

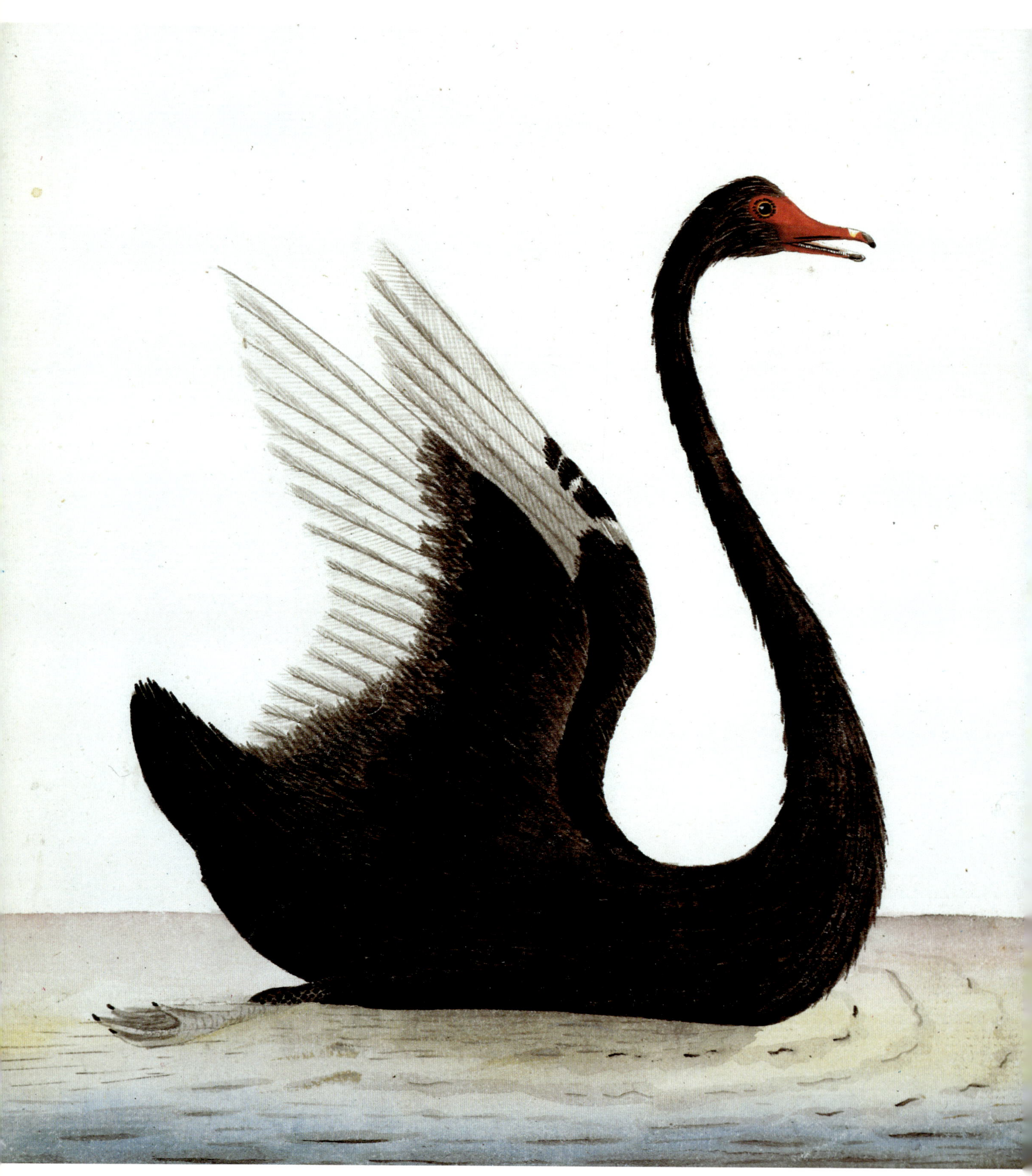

THE PORT JACKSON PAINTER
flourishing in New South Wales 1788-1792

The Port Jackson painter is known to have painted over 250 watercolours of birds, snakes, insects, fishes and mammals that were collected in the neighbourhood of Port Jackson and in Norfolk Island between 1788 and 1792. He still remains unidentified, despite a good deal of research over the last few years on the first artists in Australia. He worked in New Holland following the arrival of the First Fleet at Sydney Cove, Port Jackson in January 1788. The paintings attributed to this artist are often superior to those of his contemporary, named artists. Many of the birds which he painted were being portrayed for the first time, giving added importance to his contribution to the pictorial record of this newly-discovered part of the world.

One of the most disconcerting things about the Australian birds taken back by Captain Cook's ships and later visitors to New Holland and New Zealand was the manner in which they were just the opposite to the birds with which everyone was familiar. This was particularly true of the swans and cockatoos which were black instead of the 'proper' white. For years, salmon-crested and sulphur-crested white cockatoos had been imported from the east, so that black cockatoos, coming from an area farther east, created great excitement, even incredulity.

THE BLACK SWAN
watercolour, 24.1 x 19.1 cm
Courtesy of Natural History Museum, London, Watling 351

Europeans had been aware that black swans existed for about a century, before this painting was done, so it was less of a surprise. We know exactly the day and year when the black swan was first seen by a European explorer. The Dutch navigator Willem de Vlamingh, when off the coast of Western Australia, sent two small boats to explore an estuary on 6 January 1697. The crew saw black swans, managed to collect four, and the river in whose waters they had been found was named Swan River. Unbelievable as they may have seemed, they were just the first among Australia's extraordinary fauna to be discovered. The swan's sooty black plumage is set off when flying by white flight feathers, and its coral red bill banded with ivory adds a finishing touch of colour.

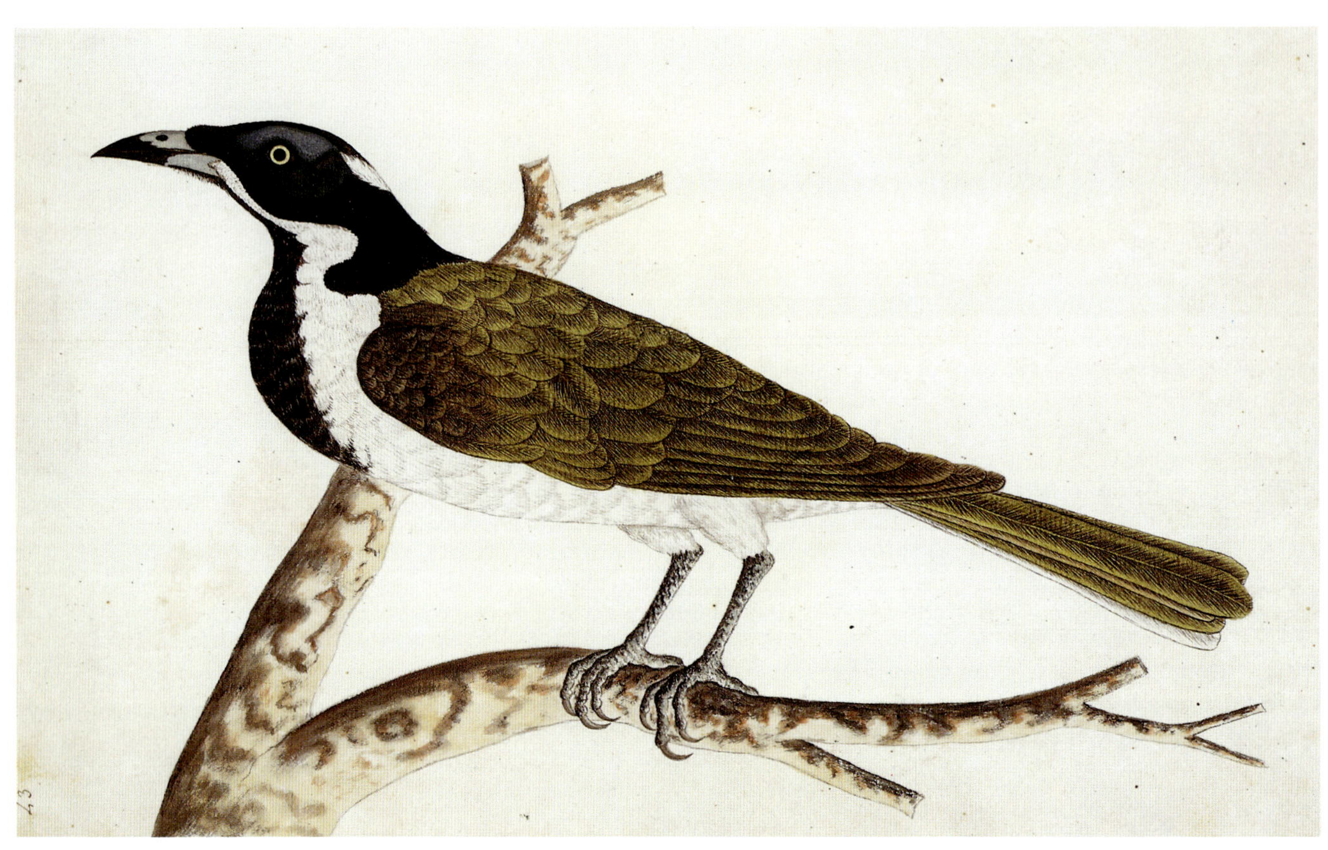

BLUE-FACED HONEYEATER
Courtesy of Natural History Museum, London, Banks MS 34:60

Honeyeaters gather flowers, nectar and small insects from plants in the forest and brushland, using their slender, down-curved bills and long tongues which have a brush-tip and sides. They curl the tongue round to form a tube through which they suck the nectar. The blue-faced honeyeater was common in the first areas of Australia to be explored, and was drawn by George Raper as well as by the Port Jackson Painter, and first described in 1801 by John Latham. The blue patch on the face makes it one of the most easily recognised among the 160 species of honeyeaters.

EASTERN SPINEBILL
Courtesy of Natural History Museum, London, Watling 181

The eastern spinebill is also in the family of honeyeaters, but with a more slender, pointed bill which earns it the nickname 'Cobbler's awl'. It feeds on insects, pollen and nectar in gardens, as well as the forests, of eastern Australia. Spinebills are capable of sucking up the nectar through their brush tongues and long bills.

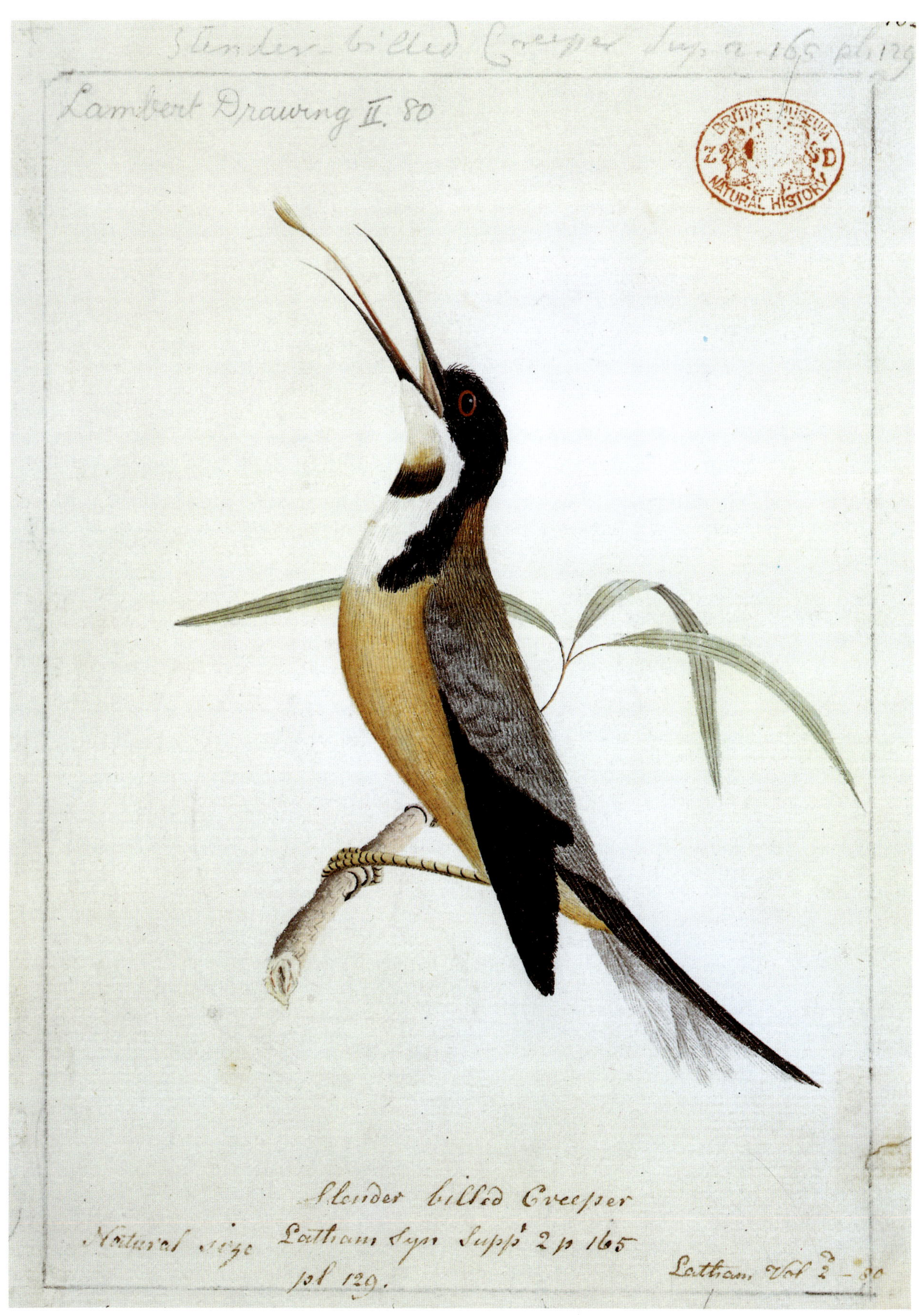
Slender billed Creeper Sup. a. 165 pl. 129
Lambert Drawing II. 80
Slender billed Creeper
Natural size   Latham Syn Supp 2 p 165
pl 129.
Latham Vol 2 - 80

GEORGE RAPER
born c.1769, died 1797/8

Following Captain Cook's three voyages, a ship set sail for Australia in May 1787 with 736 convicts and a large number of soldiers and sailors on board. With these, and supplies carried in *HMS Sirius*, the intention was to found a new British colony on the other side of the world. George Raper was a naval officer aboard the *Sirius* and he remained in the colony for five years. He had entered the navy in 1783 as a servant to the captain and risen to able seaman by the time he joined the *Sirius* at the end of 1786.

On the way to New South Wales he was promoted to midshipman. His first love, however, was drawing and painting, while the sea came second. His sensitive and careful paintings of birds, fishes, flowers and coastal profiles are now preserved in three collections. The most extensive is in the Natural History Museum, London and includes thirty-three birds. Some were drawn at Port Jackson (the bay of the city later called Sydney), where the colony was settled, including an emu with its egg and a body feather of natural size, a blue-faced honeyeater and a noisy friarbird, both of which he drew with flowers. Raper also painted some species from Lord Howe and Norfolk Islands. One was the newly discovered Providence petrel, a species which saved the new colony established on Norfolk Island in 1788 from starvation but which was over-exploited as a food source and was exterminated by 1800.

Of all the new birds which were sent back to London, as skins, none had the same impact on the public imagination as the mammals. The kangaroos, koalas and duck-billed platypus caused the sensations.

Several magnificent, brilliantly-plumaged parrots became known, but it was not until Gould took home live budgerigars half a century later that an Australian bird finally took the home country by storm. The strangest birds were black swans, and perhaps also black cockatoos. For two centuries Europeans had been used to white cockatoos with sulphur or salmon-coloured crests. Now black cockatoos arrived. Nothing, however, quite first caught and then held the public imagination as the live macaws had done, following their importation circa 1500 from South America. Black was hardly a colour to inspire great admiration in contrast with the scarlet or brilliant blue and gold feathers of macaws, but even the rainbow lorikeet, the wonderful rosellas or brilliant red-shouldered (now swift) parrot failed consistently to find their way into the bird paintings of the late eighteenth and then nineteenth centuries as the macaws had been incorporated in sixteenth, seventeenth and early eighteenth century pictures. One reason would be that the Australian birds were imported as skins; very few live specimens reached these shores for many years after their discovery. To see these birds, it was necessary to have access to private museums (particularly that of Sir Joseph Banks until his death in 1820), or pay to see Sir Ashton Lever's museum in London which had a number of Australian birds, stuffed and mounted, until it was disbanded in 1806. The British Museum was opened to the public on 15 January 1759, but only for three hours a day and to a very limited number of people who were obliged to apply in writing, and the zoological collection at the British Museum was poor.

GLOSSY COCKATOO
watercolour, 48.8 x 31.4 cm
Courtesy of Natural History Museum, London

This female glossy cockatoo was painted by Raper in 1789 and inscribed in his hand 'Cockatoo of Port Jackson. Natural size'. The male has a black head, and his lateral (not central) black tail feathers have a subterminal band of bright red.

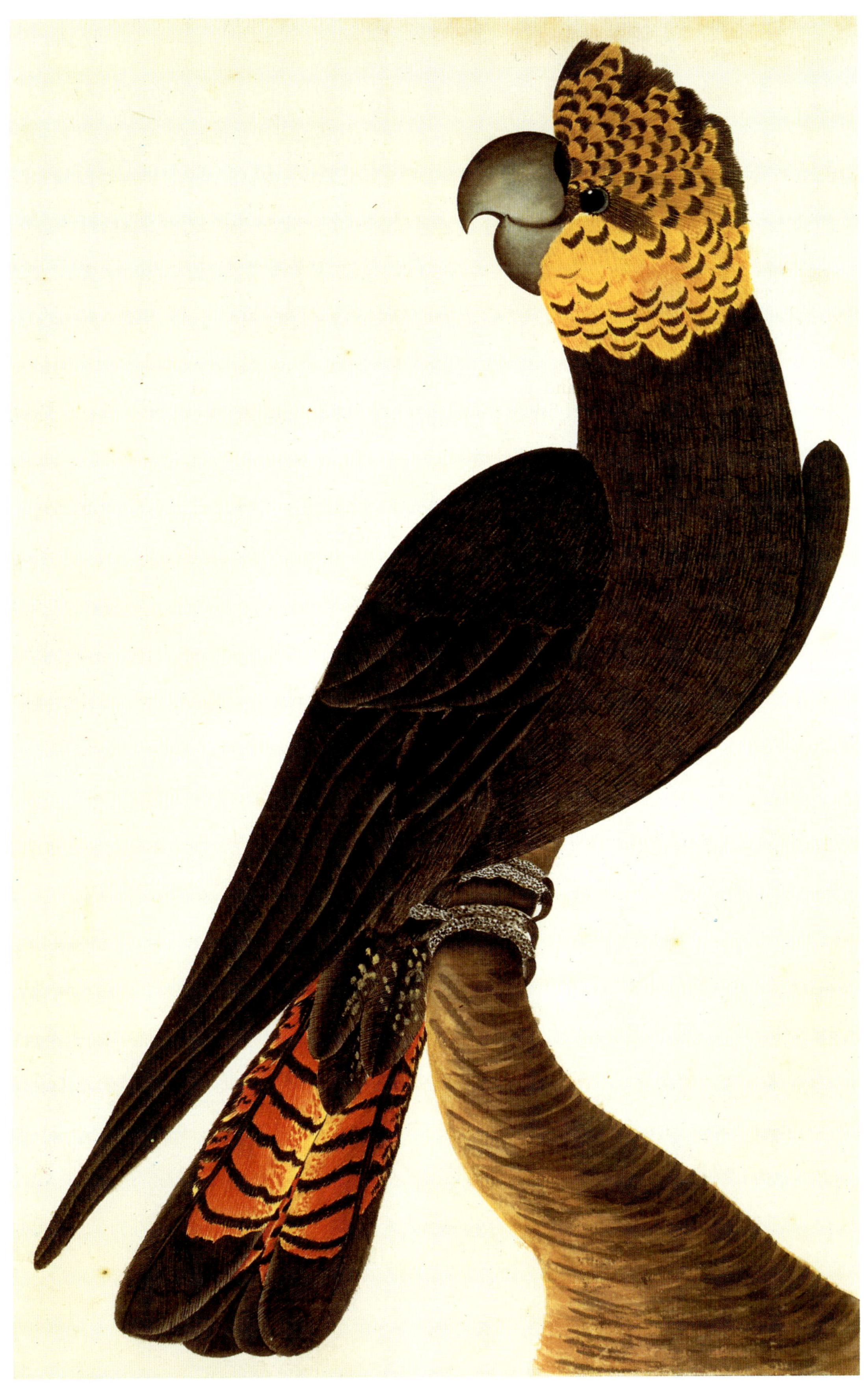

ALEXANDRE ISIDORE LEROY DE BARDE

born Montreuil-sur-mer 1777, died Paris 1828

COLLECTION OF FOREIGN BIRDS
dated 1810, watercolour and gouache, 126 x 90 cm
Cabinet des Dessins, Louvre, Paris

This remarkable *trompe l'oeil* painting of mounted birds in a cabinet was painted by Viscomte de Barde or Birde, who specialised in painting natural history subjects. It is a clear demonstration of how collections of birds, made at great expense, were carefully housed and maintained, behind glass, to preserve them in mint condition. It was necessary to keep them away from dust in the atmosphere, but above all to make certain no insects such as moths, beetles and mites could nibble away at the feathers and destroy them. Crowding a number into a small space was one reason for the unnatural posture of some of the birds. The head turned back over the shoulder, a favourite space-saving pose with taxidermists, is much in evidence here. The glass eye-makers favoured brown irises and these have been used indiscriminately, despite birds' having a wide range of eye colour.

Trompe-l'oeil painting has had periods when it was in favour, and then times when artists lost interest in it. When practised by an expert, shelves laden with precious objects were favourite subjects, exotic birds also making periodic appearances. Leroy de Barde certainly has a cabinet with some great rarities on which to practise his skill in painting them so realistically that the viewer feels he can reach out and take a bird off the shelf in order to inspect it more closely. The cabinet itself takes on a physical presence, with the space within the shelves clearly defined. The secret of effective *trompe-l'oeil* painting lies in totally accurate painting of the object in every detail combined with the placing of the deep shadows to throw the object forwards visually, so creating a three-dimensional illusion. The space within the cabinet is used to maximum capacity without an appearance of over-crowding, which is a pre-determined compositional asset for the artist. In this particular cabinet, some very choice specimens have been preserved. Of all the macaws, the hyacinthine was probably one of the rarest and most costly. It is the largest (100cm), probably the most spectacular and gloriously coloured with rich many-shaded cobalt-blue feathers. It deserves its dominant position. Above the macaw, a nighthawk in flight shows the intricate brown, cream and black plumage far more effectively than had it been perched. The aracari, Guianan cock of the rock and lily trotter are carefully assembled so as to avoid the long tail of the golden pheasant which has been very cleverly positioned in this confined space.

The second largest compartment houses a spectacular Papuan lory with a sun bittern, and some delicately coloured, smooth-shelled eggs. The puffin is accompanied by the head only of a skimmer, a bird which literally skims the surface of the water as it flies over it. This is the only bird species with a beak whose lower mandible is markedly longer. The lower mandible is dipped in the water while the bird flies over the surface. The shorter upper mandible snaps shut on any small fish or shrimp. The skimmer then lifts its head, swallows the food and inserts its lower mandible back in the water, without even missing a wingbeat.

Leroy de Barde has vividly portrayed these remarkable species in a cabinet of truly outstanding quality.

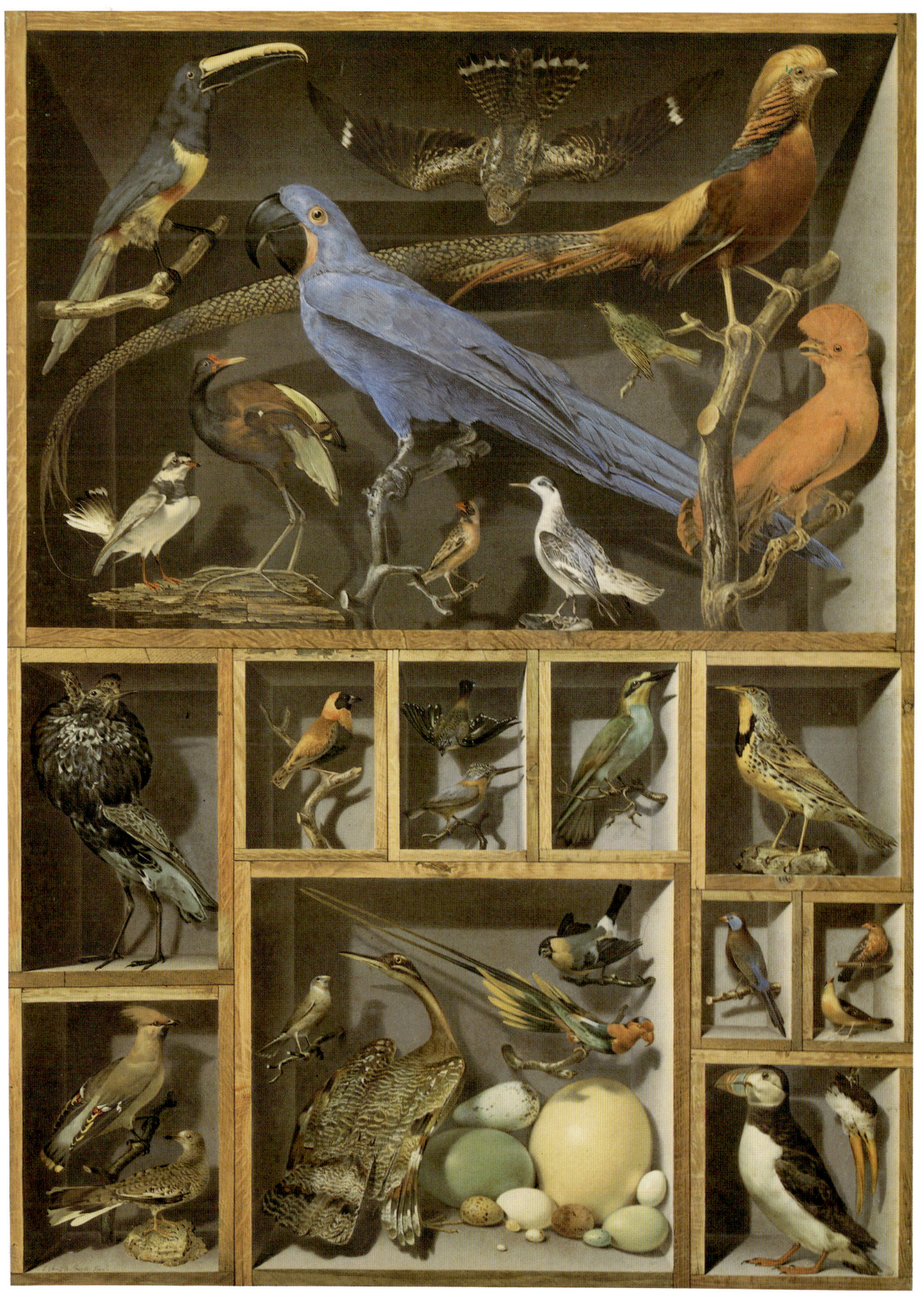

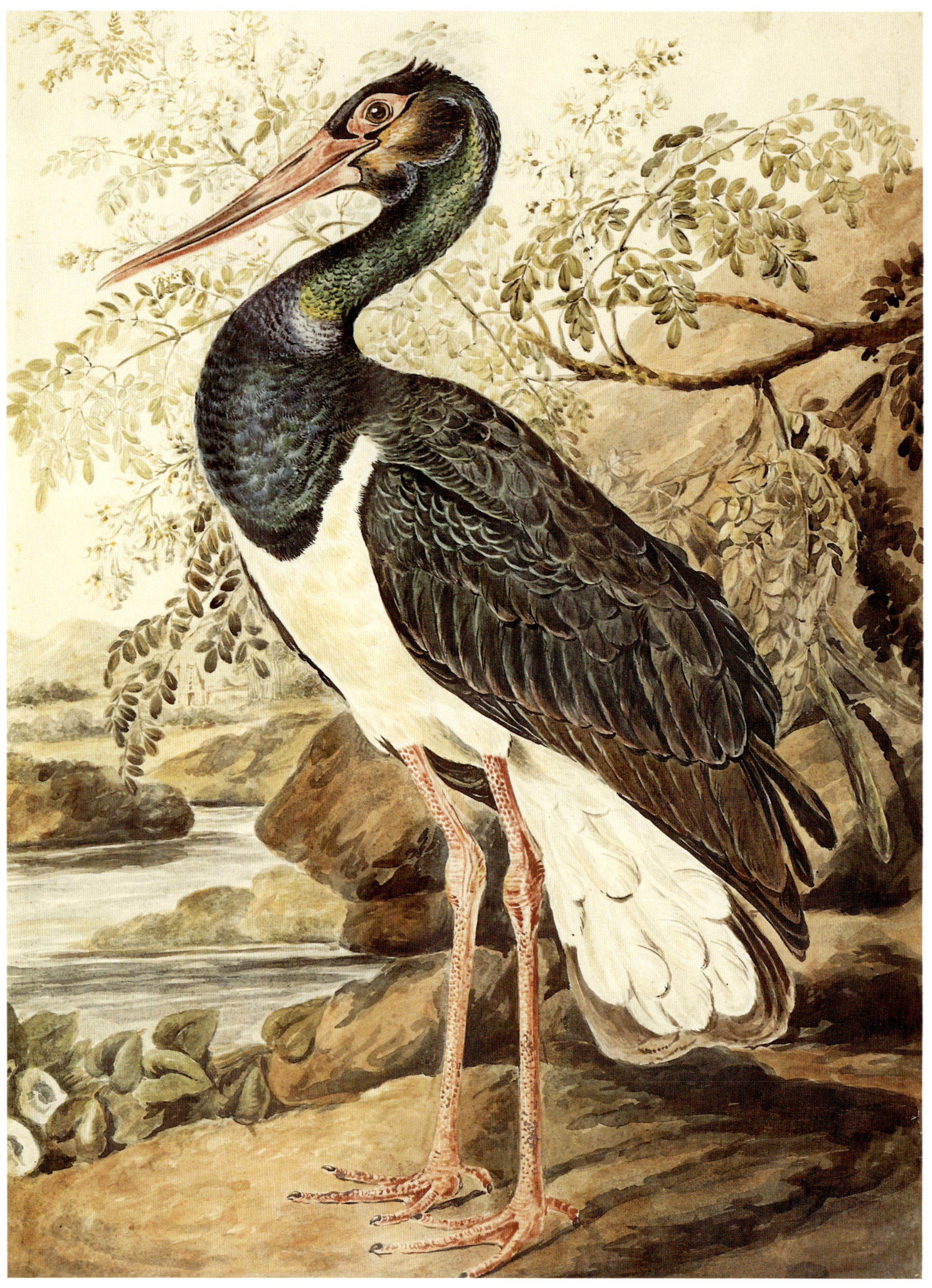

ELIZABETH, LADY GWILLIM
born c.1763, died Madras, India 1807

Lady Gwillim's achievements in painting life-size pictures of Indian birds are quite outstanding and difficult to explain. She painted a series of over two hundred beautiful portraits of birds while she was resident in Madras, 1801-07, as the wife of one of His Majesty King George III's Puisne (i.e. junior) Justices of the newly-formed Supreme Court of Judicature. Elizabeth married Henry Gwillim (1760-1837) of Hereford about 1788 and their son, Henry, was baptised at Sarnesfield, near Leominster, Herefordshire, on 11 October 1789. Her husband had been educated at Christ Church Oxford and was called to the bar, Middle Temple, in 1787. He was knighted on 16 July 1801.

Her paintings are remarkable, not just for their size, but their excellence artistically and ornithologically. She superimposed her life-sized subjects over very detailed and completely natural settings — Indian landscapes, backgrounds with trees, shrubs on which the bird either roosted or nested, with flowers, fruit and berries, small mammals and insects on which it fed. She achieved all this, and was able to paint their beaks, legs, feet and eyes, in their correct colours as seen on the live birds. In order to do this, she must have worked either from living, or freshly-killed examples, because the colours of the flesh on these parts fades soon after the birds have died. We are familiar with all of these factors in the work of artists from J. J. Audubon onwards, but Lady Gwillim's paintings pre-date those of Audubon by twenty years. Her paintings rival Audubon's and in some respects occasionally excel them, and are to be rated among the most accurate and well-presented bird portraits up to that time. Some life-size portraits of British birds had been painted by Peter Paillou for Thomas Pennant in the early 1760s and William Hayes also drew some species life-size in the 1770s. They did not, however, work consistently in a format large enough to accommodate life-size portraits of all species and incorporate landscape backgrounds. She may have seen the two books by Pennant and Hayes, containing some life-size portraits, before leaving for India. However, Pennant's and Hayes' published bird pictures did not include correct ecological settings. Lady Gwillim's large bird study, superimposed on a landscape background, was novel. Audubon was the first to publish life-size birds in their proper habitats. Had Lady Gwillim published her work she would have been credited with several innovations now attributed to Audubon.

THE BLACK STORK
Watercolour, 91.5 x 66 cm
Courtesy of Blacker-Wood Library of Zoology and Ornithology,
McGill University, Montreal

The black stork is a slightly smaller bird than the white, and very much more difficult to observe because it is shyer. Whereas the white stork nests on chimneys and close to man, the black stork prefers undisturbed forests for its nesting sites, and wet meadows where it searches for fish and insects in shallow water. This Eurasian species nests from central Europe east to China and Korea.

Lady Gwillim has painted a stately black stork with its glossy black plumage showing purple and green sheens. She has placed it in a wild open setting with forest trees and a water landscape which the bird would naturally favour in India. She painted her bird studies life-size and this bird is 96.5 cm (38 ins) in length including the long red bill and red legs, both of which are held in an extended position when the bird is in flight. Only the lower breast, belly and undertail coverts are white, and these form a very distinctive pattern to help in the recognition of this stork among sixteen other species.

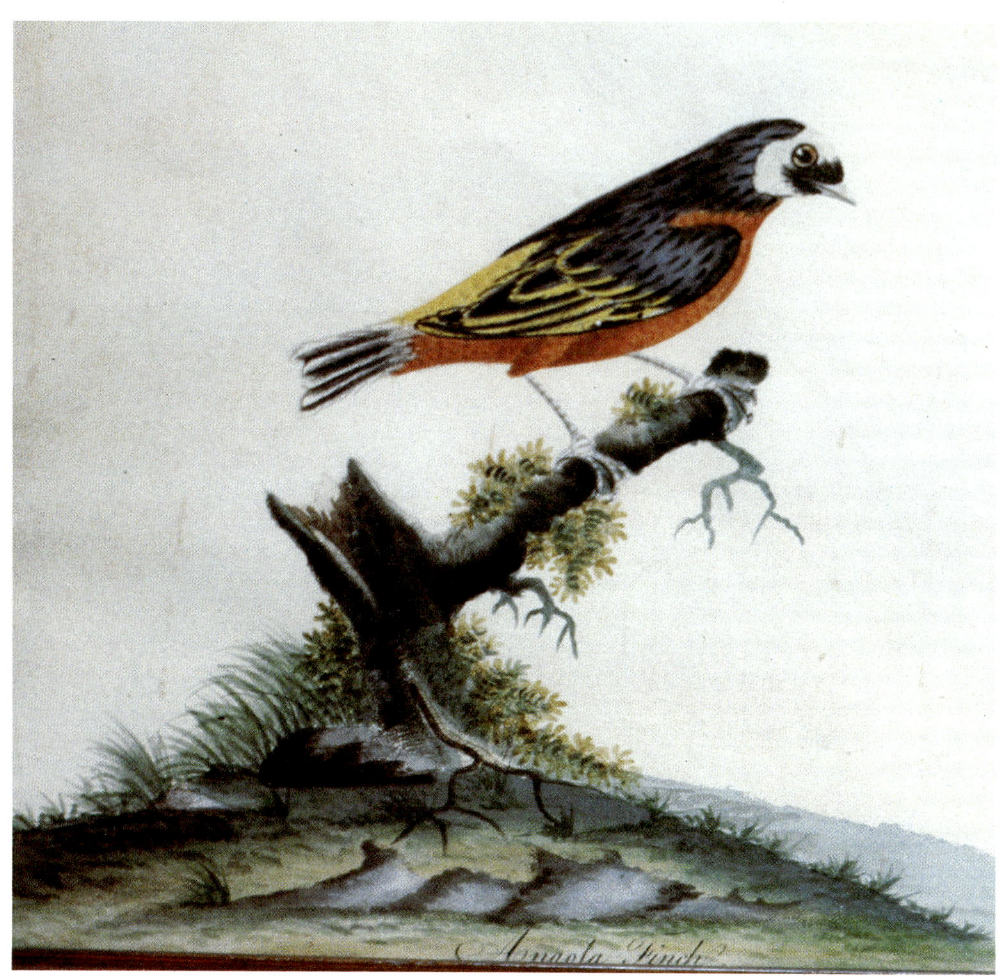

Lady Gwillim painted several small perching birds, adding their local names in pencil at the bottom of the sheet. Here she has depicted the colourful 'Angola finch'.

Opposite:
If vultures are the scavengers of the wilderness, then kites are the cosmopolitan refuse collectors. The pariah or black kite performs this useful service in India around villages and towns, while the brahminy kite forages by harbours and rivers. This immature brahminy kite can look forward to some easy pickings.

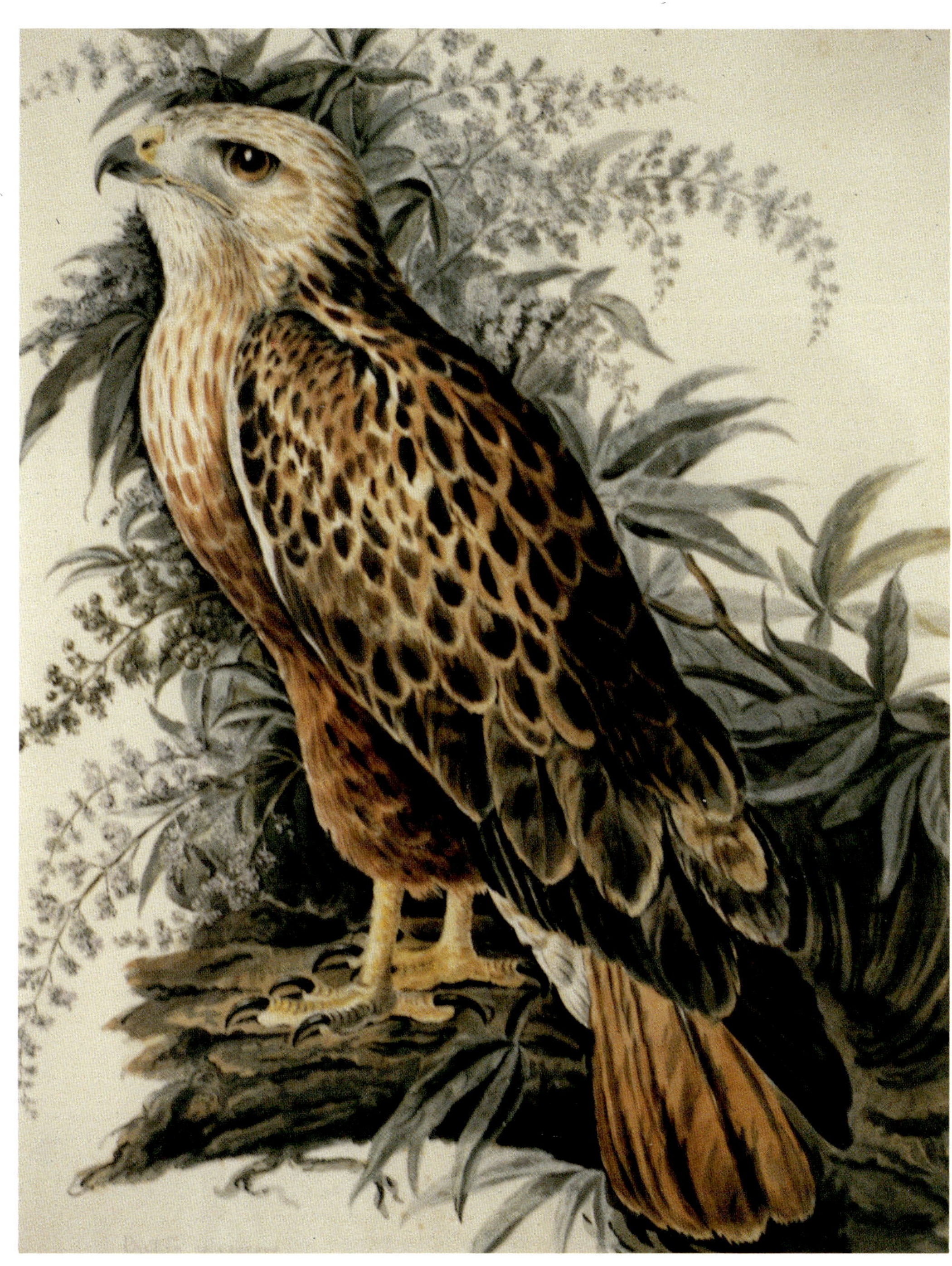

RICHALLET
flourishing 18th century

A PARROT IN A CIRCULAR GARLAND WITH MUSIC AND GOLDFINCHES
Oil on canvas, 64 x 54 cm
Courtesy of Rafael Valls, London

This painting is signed 'Richallet', but beyond that we know nothing more of this artist or his/her work.

Painting an object within a floral wreath was not a new idea. As with so many pictorial compositions, an idea, which often had roots far back in antiquity, was revived from time to time. Garlands were placed around the heads of heroes in ancient Greece and Rome, and before that in Egypt. When Howard Carter opened Tutankhamun's tomb he found many wreaths of flowers besides garlands of leaves and on the forehead of the young king there was a circlet of flowers. It was common pagan practice to garland sepulchres with flowers. At first the Christian church rejected this practice and it was not until the Reformation that garlands of flowers were used in churches to decorate walls and pillars. Later, even the clergy were decorated with garlands of roses on some feast days. So when artists first painted religious flower still life pictures it was quite natural that they should paint a religious motif, such as the Virgin and Child, surrounded by a garland of flowers. The first artist to develop this idea was the Flemish painter Daniel Seghers, born 1590, who was a pupil of the famous flower and animal painter Jan Brueghel. Seghers and those artists following him who painted this type of picture used specific flowers in their garlands for, like most other objects, each flower had its own symbolic meaning. A garland of roses inferred divine love, and the rose was the symbol of Mary. Similarly, we know that birds also were associated with religious meanings and it is no accident that the bird within the ring is a parrot – always held to be a Marian symbol in sixteenth to seventeenth century paintings. The goldfinch was a symbol of Christ's passion, and the dove embodied the meaning of the Holy Spirit.

The tight garland round the parrot was made with small flowers, using the bird's ring perch. At the top centre a jewelled brooch with drop pearl added a luxurious touch, but the whole careful composition suggests that it was placed there for a purpose other than mere ostentation. The structure, of flower covered perch within a larger garland, the music so placed that an observer could read it, the goldfinch, dove, and the deliberately arranged fruit, imply messages and symbolism which we can no longer read. While the use of a garland to surround a parrot, rather than a religious icon, makes this picture purely secular, nevertheless there are religious overtones. Richallet was probably working close in time to the period when it would have been more acceptable to place a painting of the Madonna and Child within a circlet of flowers.

Not only is the artist of this painting a mysterious person, but the picture also is a conundrum.

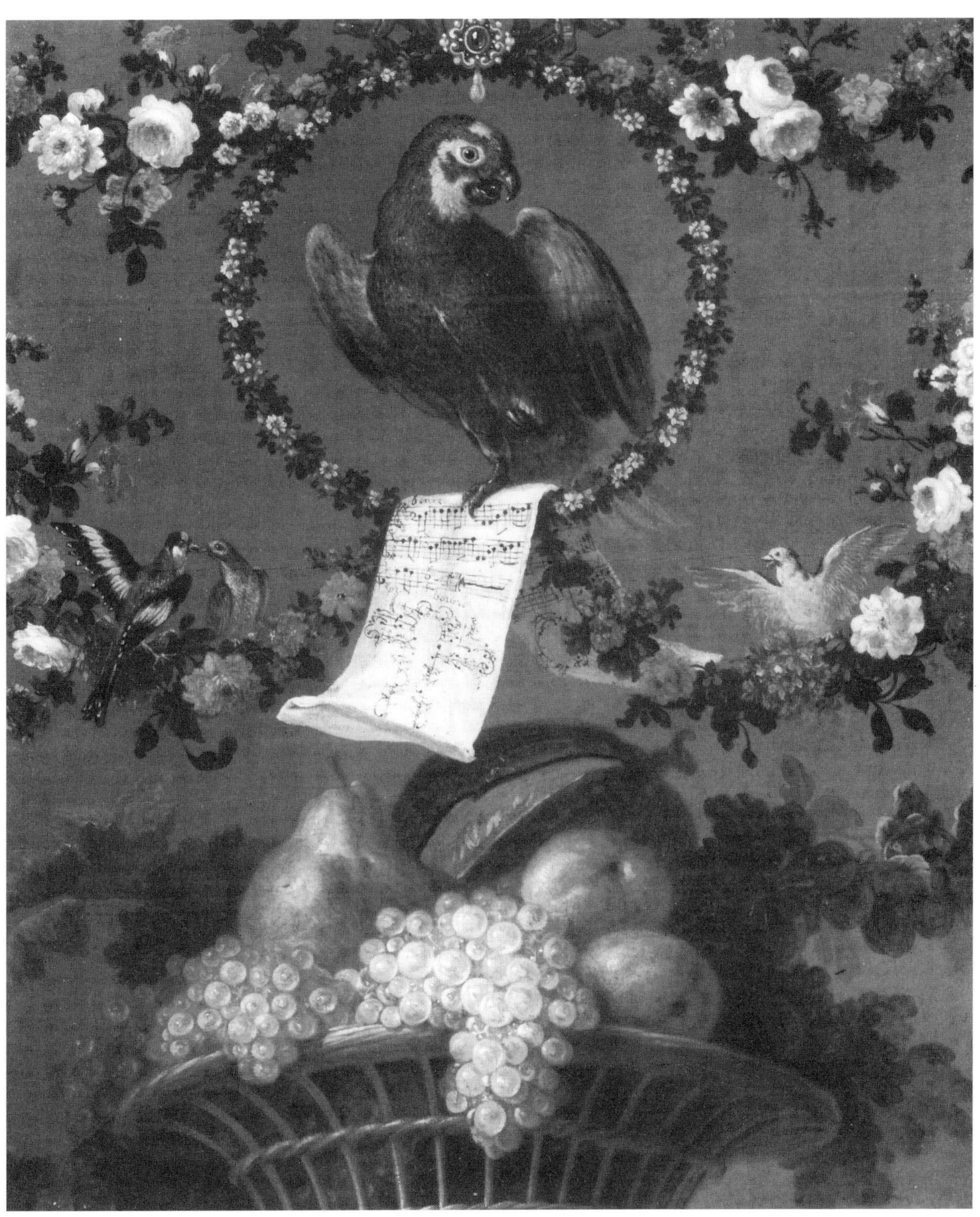

FERDINAND LUCAS BAUER
born 1760 Feldsberg, Austria, died 1826 Vienna

Ferdinand Bauer was the youngest son of Lucas, a court painter at the castle of the Prince of Liechtenstein which dominated the town of Feldsberg (now Valtice in Czechoslovakia). He copied paintings of plants and birds from his father's work but soon learned to go direct to nature and paint from life. He was trained to be a botanical artist, and moved to Vienna to work for Baron Nicolaus von Jacquin who was professor of botany at the university. He was set to work on making accurate drawings and could reproduce the minutest detail. Ferdinand's brother worked in England at Kew as botanical painter to George III, and Ferdinand's work was well known in England, so that when Sir Joseph Banks mounted an expedition to complete the detailed survey of the Australian coastline, under the command of Captain Matthew Flinders, Ferdinand was chosen to go as one of the scientific draughtsmen.

On l8 July 1801 the *Investigator* set sail from Southsea, with Robert Brown as chief director of the scientific operations, Ferdinand Bauer being his botanic draughtsman. They arrived on the west Australian coast on 6 December and sailed round the coast, heading north, calling at various bays and islands. At Shoalwater Bay, which they reached on 25 August 1801, despite the heat and humidity Bauer sketched a bandicoot and made several very detailed drawings of a kookaburra. His method was to draw in great detail and place numbers on the different areas of his drawing. These referred to a colour code, using up to four figures, which Bauer devised in order to paint a watercolour at his leisure, replicating every tint with astonishing accuracy.

Flinders continued to survey the coastline of Australia until 1803. The *Investigator* had always been a leaky ship, and when it was finally pronounced unseaworthy, Bauer was left in Sydney while it was repaired. He spent weeks there, collecting and sketching and then moved to Norfolk Island to find more subjects to paint. He returned to England in 1805 and proceeded to develop his botanical sketches in to fine watercolour studies of extraordinary beauty, and to work up his bird drawings too. These number 158 Australian species and twenty from Norfolk island in the Natural History Museum, London, collection. Ferdinand Bauer left England to return home to Vienna in 1814, and continued to paint from his sketches there.

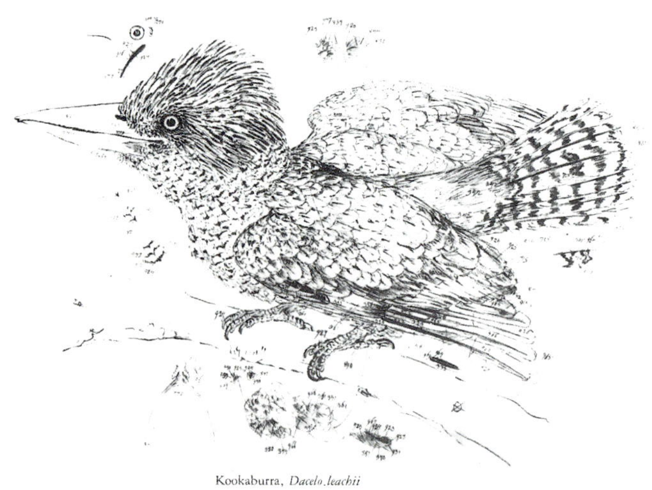

Kookaburra, *Dacelo leachii*

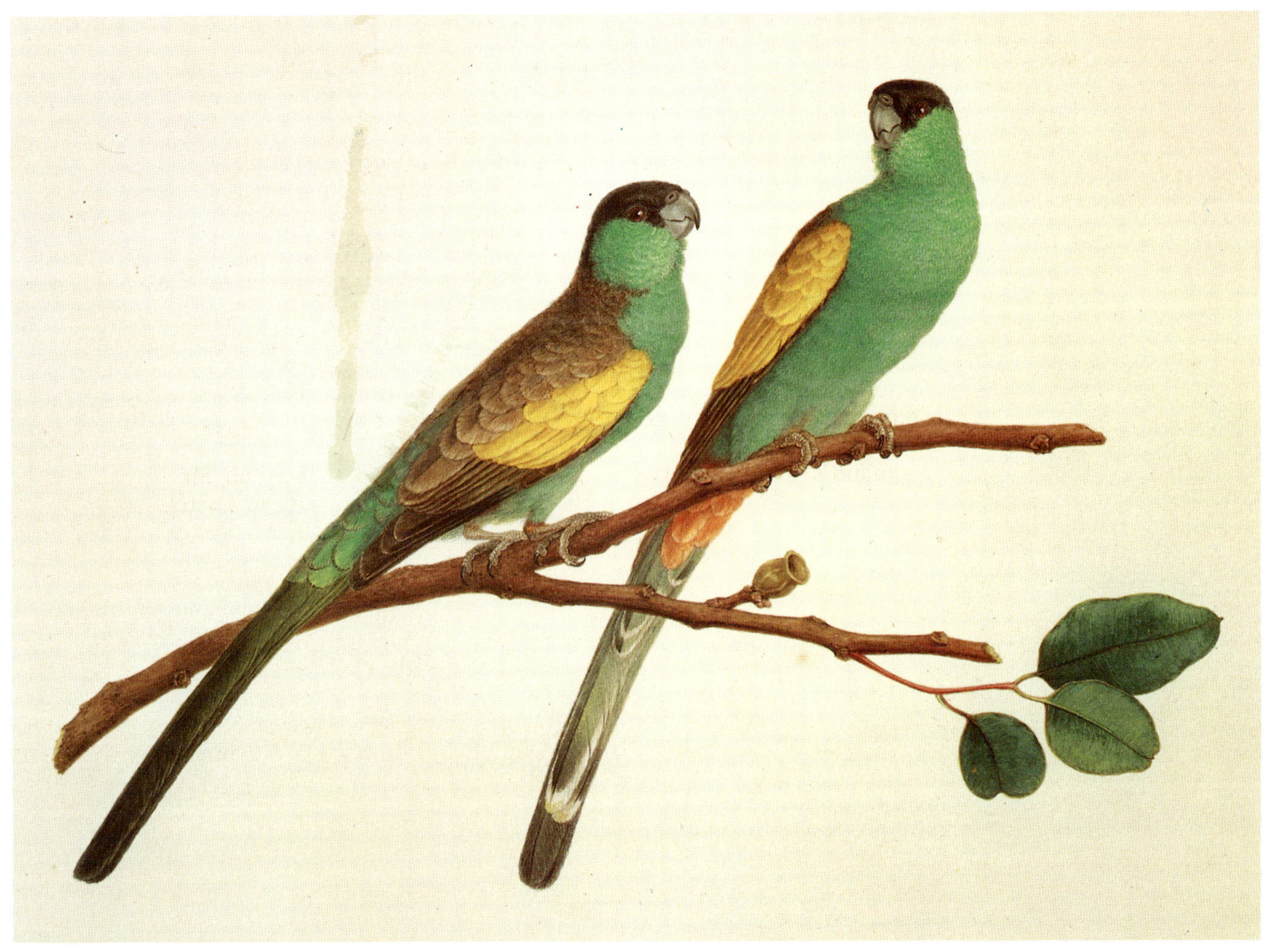

HOODED PARROT
Courtesy of Natural History Museum, London

The hooded parrot is now regarded as a subspecies of the golden-shouldered parrot. The distinctive black hood and golden patch on the wing identify this bird, which lives in north-eatern regions of the Northern Territory, Australia. These birds may be seen in eucalypts growing on rocky ridges near watercourses. They rest during the hottest part of the day perched in the branches, where their plumage blends, imperceptibly, with the foliage.

KOOKABURRA
pencil sketch.   Courtesy of Natural History Museum, Vienna

There are two species of kookaburra, one also known as the laughing jackass, whose voice and cries and wild crazy laughter are its most familiar characteristics. There is also the blue-winged kookaburra, which is the one painted by Bauer. It is a slightly smaller bird but has a voice as harsh which it uses in a cackling scream. *Dacelo leachii* has more blue in the wings, tail and rump. The two species only overlap in the north-eastern corner of Australia, the blue-winged species being present along the northern coast and in the islands to the north of the mainland. The kookaburras are regarded as useful birds when they catch snakes and lizards, but they are not so well regarded when they attack chickens and ducklings. Bauer's early sketch and painting of this remarkable species clearly demonstrate its colouring and characteristics and are eloquent testament to his very fine draughtsmanship and skill as an artist.

TOBIA VOOD
flourishing in Holland, c.1790

Signing and dating work is a sure way, one would think, to ensure future generations would know who had painted a particular picture, and when. Given a certain amount of good fortune coupled with integrity, that should be the situation for all time. However, several factors may intervene. Some canvases get cropped to fit into a smaller frame, and the signature and date are cut off. Signatures may be deliberately erased in order to attribute the work to an artist who is more highly regarded and whose work fetches a higher price. Dates may be altered so that an early, less mature and thus not so desirable example of an artist's output, is made to appear to be a later work. Added to this, signatures may be forged.

Such hazards can befall an artist who was meticulous in signing and dating his work. When an artist fails to sign and date his work clearly, then the problems in attribution increase tenfold. Lacking any signature, art historians and experts often disagree in attributions. Sometimes it is only possible to decide from the style, composition and use of certain pigments, to which century a picture belongs, and to which school – that is whether it is typically Germanic, French or Italian in character.

PEACOCK AND BIRDS IN A LANDSCAPE
signed and dated 1790, watercolour on vellum, 17 x 37 cm
Courtesy of Rafael Valls, London

This painting is thought to be by Tobia Vood, for that is the artist of this Dutch family name who was at work in 1790. Vood has both signed ('Vood P' for Vood pinxit) and dated this work. Even with this information it has not been possible to discover any further information about this very able but minor artist. Quite a large number of artists remain obscure and, however good their work, this tends to keep the price of their pictures in a lower bracket. Fortunately, none of this detracts from the enjoyment of the picture, which has been painted with as much care and thought for the pleasure of a future owner as a painting by one of the well-known and documented masters.

The very smooth effect of this painting is created by the use of vellum as the base. Vellum provides an artist with one of the finest grained surfaces of all materials. Using small brushes with few hairs, the artist can work in the kind of detail needed to reproduce feathers with extremely intricate patterns and range of tone on each single feather. Working on vellum demands the utmost precision and delicacy in the handling of the paint.

Parchment, made from the skins of sheep and goats, was used as a writing material by the ancient Greeks and Romans. The finest parchment, known as vellum, was made from the skins of young animals, lambs, kids and calves. The knowledge of paper-making was brought to Europe through the Crusades (undertaken eleventh to fourteenth centuries) and artists had few difficulties in procuring paper for drawing purposes from the beginning of the fourteenth century onwards. By the time that Vood was painting, parchment was used almost exclusively by the legal profession, and vellum only occasionally by artists who liked to work in fine detail.

Vood has used all the potential qualities of the medium, more particularly in the train of the peacock, the bird which attracts our attention and that of nearly all the other birds. These are mostly colourful European species, with a few parrots. Movement has been introduced by the egret raising its wings, the magpie looking down, the moorhen putting its beak in the water, the jay singing and three birds flying. Providing two trees for the birds, one further back, has given added depth to the picture which has a landscape that also has considerable detail, even in the distance.

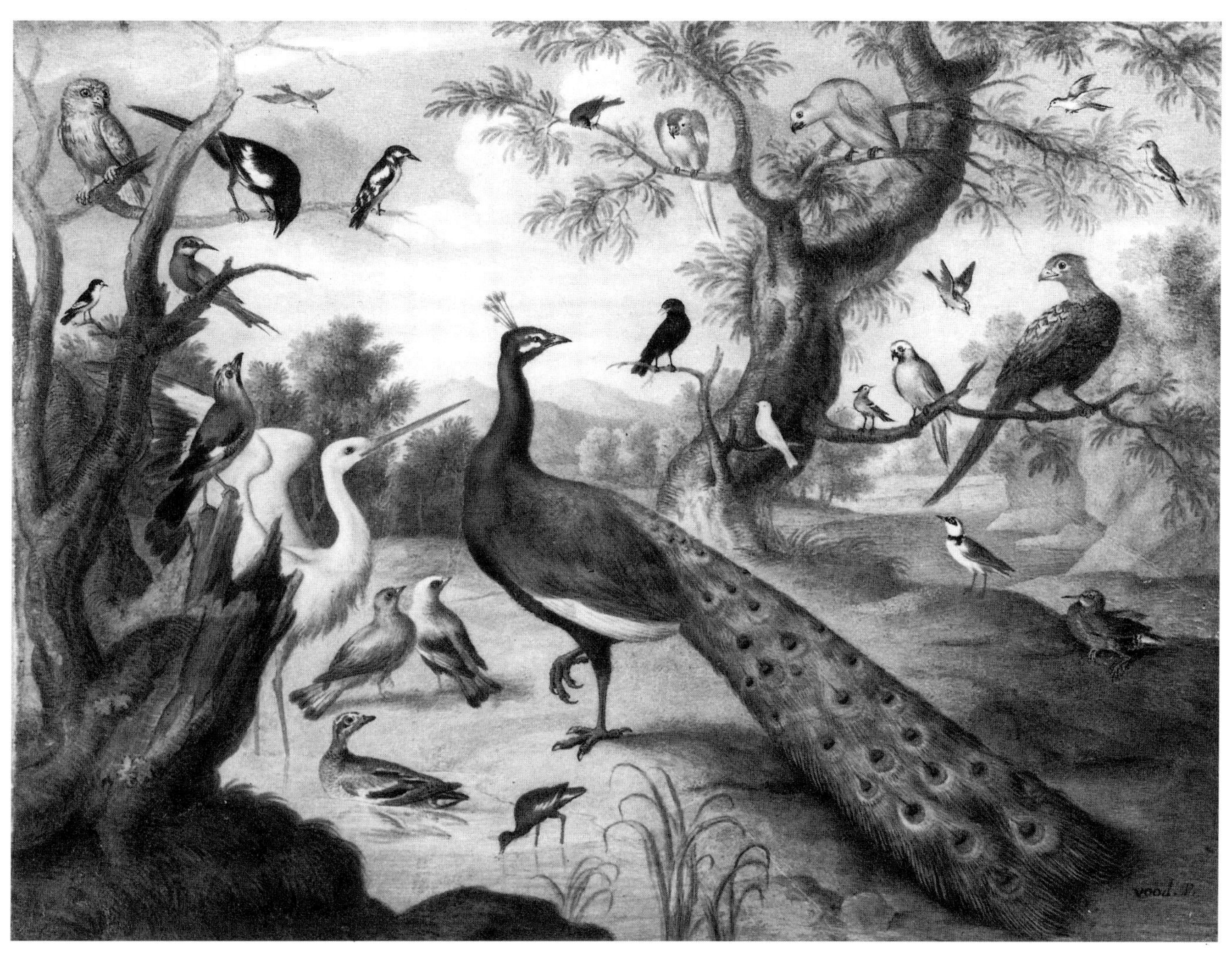

JOHAN WENZEL PETER
born Carlsbad 1745, died Rome 1829

Peter went to Rome at an early age, and later was appointed a professor of art at the Academy of St Luke in Rome. He painted and taught in a period when the calm simplicity and noble grandeur ideals of neo-classicism had displaced the baroque style of naturalism and verisimilitude and a deliberate involvement of the onlooker in the picture. Peter's exact, sharp and accurate drawing and painting of both fur and feathers is done in the spirit of cool and detached observation. His compositions are arrangements of a few birds, for example peacocks and doves in a farmyard or a peacock with a turkey and a rabbit by a classical column, with no interaction between the assembled birds and nothing to evoke an emotional response from the onlooker.

The Accademia di S. Luca in Rome, where Peter taught, had been set up in 1593, about thirty years after the first academy proper was inaugurated by Duke Cosimo de Medici in 1562 at Florence. These art schools had been established in order to emancipate artists from control by the old Middle Ages guilds. Tradesmen then had formed themselves into guilds for economic, religous and social purposes and often several trades had united to form a single guild. For example, in Florence, painters belonged to the doctors' and apothecaries' guild, St Luke being the patron saint of both artists and physicians. Painters, like druggists, were dependent for the materials of their art or craft on imported gums and pigments. To become a member of the guild it had been necessary to have been an apprentice and to produce a piece meeting the required high standards set by the guild, following which a man could call himself a master. Painters, including Leonardo, resented the tendency to uniformity this created and insisted on the freedom and originality of the individual and demanded that he be regarded as an inspired artist, or professional man, rather than an honest tradesman. This had led to the decline of the guild and the formation of the academies which took over the function of teaching young artists. In France the Paris Academy of Painting and Sculpture was founded by the king in 1648 and other art academies were formed in Germany, Spain and elsewhere between the middle and end of the seventeenth century. It was not until the middle of the eighteenth century, however, that academies flourished throughout Europe. By 1790 there were over one hundred art academies in Europe, including the lately founded Royal Academy in London, established in 1768. Peter was at the centre of Italian academic painting in the last quarter of the eighteenth century and in the early years of the nineteenth century. His work is preserved in the Galeria Borghese, Rome and also in the museum of his native Carlsbad. Since he held so prestigious a position, it is a little surprising that he chose to paint live birds in simple settings, but his picture of the *Turkeys with Young* shows the combination of realistic, natural painting with no embellishments or drama, that were the essence of neo-classical art.

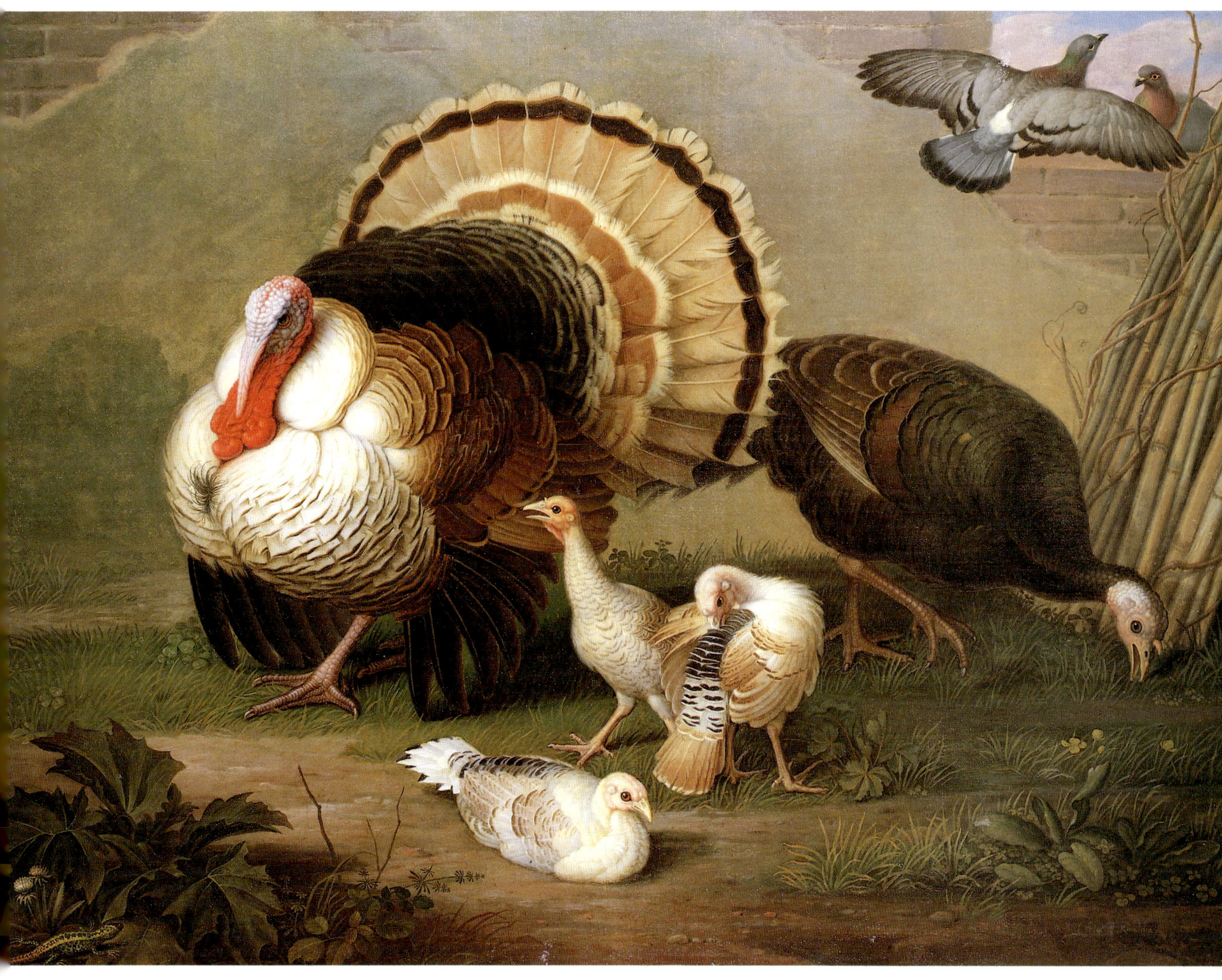

TURKEYS WITH YOUNG AND ROCK DOVES
signed and dated 'Rome 1823', oil on canvas, 112.4 x 143.5 cm
Courtesy of Rafael Valls, London

The manner in which the plants are painted is enough to delight any botanist, just as
the beautifully careful portraits of the male and female turkey with their three young,
and the pair of rock doves satisfy an ornithologist's demands for accuracy. Peter is more
interested in the beauty of these species than in the fact that they were both table birds,
kept in the homestead buildings for that purpose. All the birds are perfect specimens,
painted with immaculate precision.

INDEX OF BIRDS

INDEX

PHOTOGRAPHIC ACKNOWLEDGEMENTS

We would like to thank the following for kindly supplying photographs:

The Witt Picture Library, Courtauld Institute, pages 19 and 85; National Trust Photographic Library/John Hammond, pages 31, 52, 53, 63, 69, 90 and 91; The Bridgeman Art Library, London, pages 42 and 43; RBK, The Hague, Tim Koster, page 58; Christie's Images, pages 66 and 92; Sotheby's, Monte Carlo, page 77; Sotheby's, London, pages 100, 105, 108, 109 and 116; Newcastle upon Tyne City Libraries and Arts, pages 112 and 113; Agence Photographique de la Réunion des Musées Nationaux, page 127.

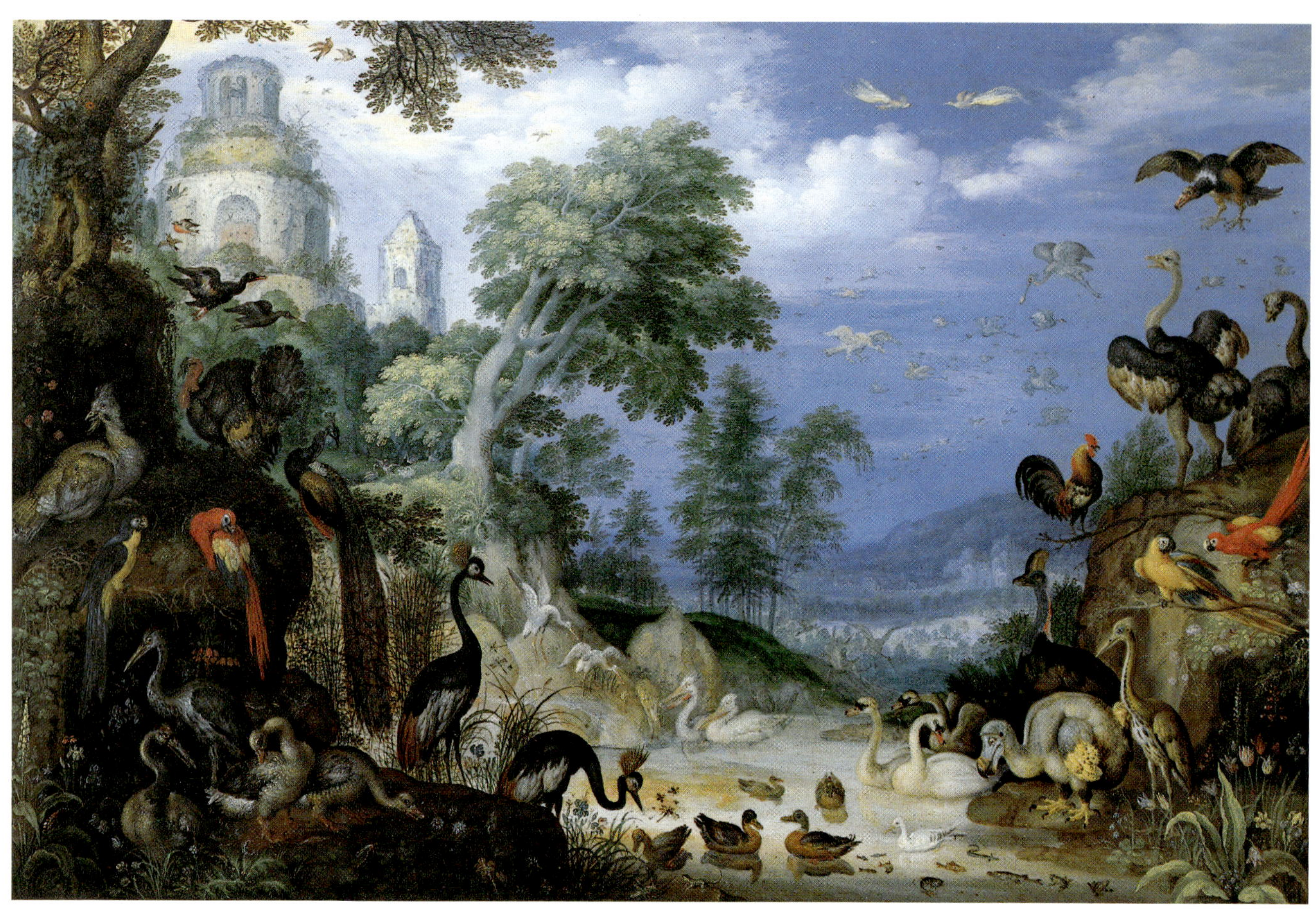

GREAT
BIRD PAINTINGS
OF THE WORLD

VOLUME I: The Old Masters

Christine E. Jackson

The first volume in this series includes pictures painted in oils or watercolours before 1699. For centuries, Western art was tied to the discipline of the Roman Catholic church so artists wishing to paint birds had to include them in religious scenes such as 'Noah's Ark' or 'The Garden of Eden'. As these restrictions were relaxed, the balance altered and birds began to feature in the foreground while the biblical context retreated into the distance. By the middle of the seventeenth century hundreds of marvellous canvases full of delightful birds were being produced. Painters could at last indulge their delight in painting beautiful birds in still life and landscape paintings.

Through her scholarly research Christine E. Jackson has traced the development of bird painting during this exciting period which produced artists such as Bosch, Dürer, Holbein, Brueghel, Rubens, Rembrandt and Leonardo. With her ornithological knowledge she describes the types of bird that were common, and the exotic birds being brought back to Europe by trading ships from newly colonised parts of America, Asia and South America which so inspired the Old Masters. Parrots and lovebirds now shared people's homes and larger unusual species, such as cassowaries and ostriches, could be seen in royal parks and menageries.

To help the reader with a fuller appreciation of the more detailed paintings, there are plans which identify the birds in them, often displayed in extraordinary combinations of indigenous birds such as mallards and owls with colourful exotics like macaws, toucans and peacocks.

PUBLISHED IN 1993 BY THE ANTIQUE COLLECTORS' CLUB

142

FORTHCOMING PUBLICATION

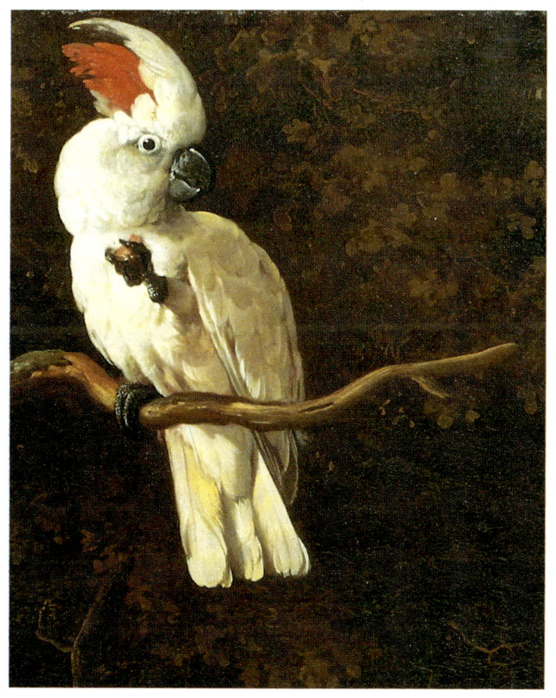

A DICTIONARY OF
BIRD PAINTERS
OF THE WORLD

Christine E. Jackson

This is the first dictionary of bird painters of the world to be published for almost fifty years. It contains more biographical information than has hitherto been available, with many more illustrations. Approximately 5000 artists, past and present, who have made two-dimensional portraits of birds as the main motif in their paintings are included in this Dictionary, with their biographical details.

Some painted large canvases filled with birds for an imaginary earthly paradise, while others made detailed studies of a single species. Many great masters painted a bird, and the specialist bird painters knew not only how to paint feathers, but also understood the birds' anatomical structure. These artists were given commissions to record newly-discovered species.

The variety of their approach is well illustrated in some 1000 colour and black and white plates. The introduction surveys varying aspects of bird portraiture by different cultures. The artists' biographies, arranged alphabetically, include comments on their individual style and achievements. A list of galleries where their work may be viewed is also included. An additional benefit of the Dictionary is that sales and auctions of bird paintings in both salerooms and galleries during the past ten years are listed, with the prices realised.

The Dictionary is a worthy addition to the long list of important art reference books published by the Antique Collectors' Club over the last twenty years.

TO BE PUBLISHED BY THE ANTIQUE COLLECTORS' CLUB LATE 1995

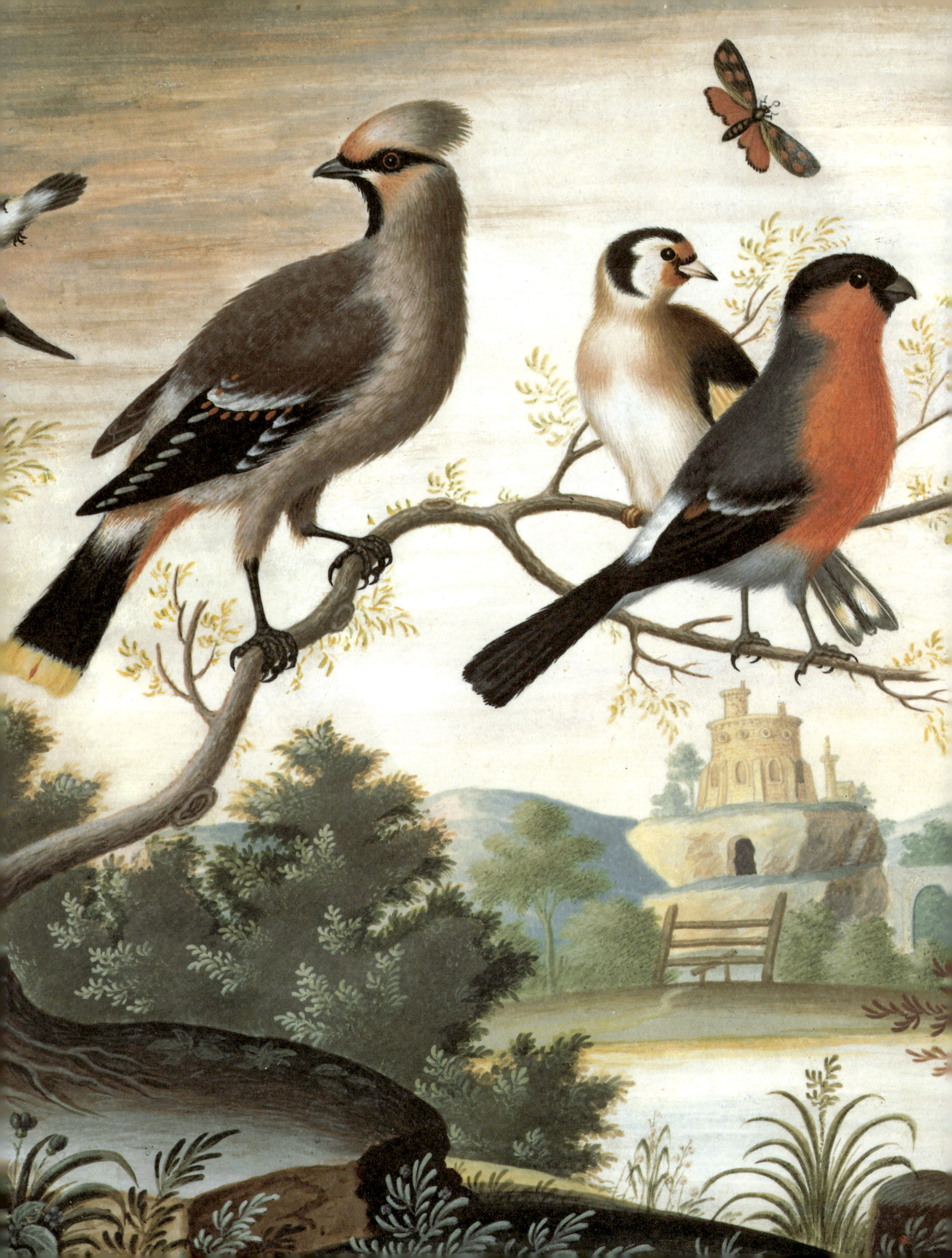